PATTERNS, MODELS, and APPLICATION DEVELOPMENT

a C++ programmer's reference

PATTERNS, MODELS, and APPLICATION DEVELOPMENT

a C++ programmer's reference

Julio Sanchez

Montana State University - Northern

Maria P. Canton

North Dakota State University

CRC Press

Boca Raton   New York

Library of Congress Cataloging-in-Publication Data

Sanchez, Julio, 1938–
      Patterns, models, and application development : a C++ programmer's
reference / Julio Sanchez, Maria P. Canton.
        p. cm.
      Includes bibliographical references and index.
      ISBN 0-8493-3102-1 (alk. paper)
      1. C++ (Computer program language) 2. Application software–
–Development. I. Canton, Maria P. II. Title.
QA76.73.C153S26 1997
005.13'3—dc21
for Library of Congress
                                                          97-26398
                                                            CIP

No claim to original U.S. Government works
International Standard Book Number 0-8493-3102-1
Library of Congress Card Number 97-26398
Printed in the United States of America 1 2 3 4 5 6 7 8 9 0
Printed on acid-free paper

Table of Contents

Introduction

About This Book

This book is about object-oriented programming in C++ on the Personal Computer. It is also about program development by a smaller sized programming team. The contents include topics related to software engineering, to object orientation, to systems analysis and design, to patterns and models, and to C++ programming. Although the material sometimes refers to implementation details, most of it is about application development. This activity is sometimes referred to as *programming in the large*, in contrast with the coding of routines or short programs, which are called *programming in the small*. For the most part, this book is about programming in the large.

Our notion of a smaller programming team is one that ranges from a single programmer to a programming group of no more than eight individuals. Our typical reader profile is a person with some programming skills in C++, perhaps equivalent to what results from having taken one or two undergraduate programming courses, or a comparable level of self-acquired skills. In other words, the book assumes some elementary knowledge of C++ programming and some level of familiarity with object orientation, but not a mastery of either topic.

Our principal goal in writing this book has been to collect, select, and interpret information from several fields of computer science (software engineering, system analysis and design, object-oriented methods, design patterns, and C++ programming) in order to provide a unified reference that allows taking a smaller development project from its initial conception to a successful completion. The keywords that describe our effort are *collect*, *select*, and *interpret*. Collecting implies putting together and interrelating elements that are usually dispersed. Selecting means choosing and picking the components that we think are more relevant and applicable. Interpreting implies that we have often tried to decipher and translate information into more understandable terms.

1

Technical Level

A reader usually wants to know if a book is elementary, intermediate, or advanced in its coverage of the subject matter, but this classification is not always easy to apply. The first problem in making a judgment about a book's technical level is that the terms elementary, intermediate, and advanced are relative ones. Material that may be considered advanced by someone struggling with the fundamentals may be quite elementary to a person who has already mastered the subject matter. In addition, books often do not sustain the same technical level throughout their contents. In reality, many tutorials are designed to start the discussion at the elementary level, proceed to an intermediate one, and conclude by considering advanced topics. Allowing for this uncertainty regarding technical levels, our opinion is that the book is mostly intermediate. It is not an elementary one since we assume some initial knowledge of C++ and object orientation, as well as a basic level of programming skills. It is certainly not an advanced book since we intentionally have stayed away from topics that are difficult to grasp and apply or that are mostly of a scholastic nature.

Target Audience

Programming in the large has a rather undefined extension. One project can be developed by dozens of specialists, including professional project managers; experts in analysis and design, in coding, and in evaluating and testing; all of which are supported by groups of experts in documentation, installation, maintenance, and other complementary activities. At the other extreme, a programming project could be the work of a single programmer, who takes on all tasks simultaneously and becomes project manager, designer, coder, tester, and documentation expert. On the other hand, a programming project can be a commercial venture intended for the mass market, another one can consist of the contractual development of a customized application, and a third one a research experiment. One programmer or programming team may be working for hire, a second one self-employed, and a third one may not pursue financial goals.

According to these varying contexts the task of programming in the large takes on different meanings. The problem-set of developing a commercial product using scores of specialists is not the same as that of an academic experiment, by a small group of programmers, with no intentions of financial gain or plans for commercial distribution.

In selecting the typical target project for this book we have been guided by the following practical consideration: companies that develop major software projects for commercial purposes will hardly need our assistance. They usually have on-staff experienced software engineers and project managers who are well versed in all the complications of bringing a programming project to a satisfactory conclusion. It is the smaller project that is often in trouble: the entrepreneur who puts together a small programming team to develop a promising application, or the college professor who must direct a research group in a software development project.

In view of this reality we have limited our target audience to a small group of programmers, with no significant expertise in managing software projects, and with no extensive knowledge of software engineering. We have committed to C++ as a development environment and to the Personal Computer as the host machine. The target project is a medium-size application, which we define as one that can be completed in 100 to 5,000 programmer hours.

About Coding and Programming

We are often deceived by the assumption that some individual or group capable of developing a routine or short program is equally capable of developing a full-size application. The fact that a program can be naively described as a collection of routines and code fragments apparently supports this supposition. In reality, there are different predicaments for coding than for programming. Coding requires a fundamental knowledge of the language, as well as skills in applying this knowledge to the solution of a particular problem of a more-or-less limited scope. Programming requires not only coding abilities, but organizational and task management skills beyond those typically needed to bring a coding project to a satisfactory conclusion. Programming is coding, plus organization, plus management, plus financial planning. The success of a program development endeavor is an accomplishment in thinking, in coding, in organization, in task and group management, and in applying economic principles such as division of labor and reusability of resources.

Several major fields of computer science are related to the development of efficient programming methodologies. The most comprehensive one is software engineering. The fields of systems analysis, project modeling, and program design are but disciplines of software engineering. Furthermore, researchers are currently attempting to structure much of our intuitive knowledge of systems design into a formal discipline called *software architecture*. This emerging field, which is also a part of software engineering, is an effort at defining software systems in terms of their computational components and of the interactions between them. Software architecture attempts to provide a product architecture approach to software engineering.

Many tools have been developed to facilitate programming in-the-large. These range from development environments such as object-oriented languages, to specific techniques such as object models and design patterns. Some of these tools have been in use for many years, while others are a recent creation or formalization. The result is that a working programmer or a programming team seeking direction and guidance in the development of a substantial programming project will find a smorgasbord of applicable fields and topics. The fields include the disciplines of software engineering, software architecture, and systems analysis and design. In addition, a host of related topics appear at the level of the development environment. In the case of object-oriented languages we find themes such as object-oriented analysis and design, object modeling, design patterns, and reusable coding techniques, all of which attempt to provide substantial support to developers.

Finally, at the level of the particular hardware and software platform it is likely that other useful tools are available. For instance, in a project that consists of a graphics application to be developed in C++ for the PC machine environment, the developers may find that selecting a particular commercial compiler, a specific operating system, and a suitable programming toolkit will save considerable development effort.

It is often accepted as fact that for any programming project that exceeds minimal complexity it is practically imperative to use organizational, task management, and software development tools. Without these tools the enterprise is likely to become the proverbial bowl of spaghetti, which no one will be capable of understanding, managing, interfacing, adding to, or maintaining.

Software development tools are often pigeonholed, somewhat arbitrarily, into three different categories:

1. *Project engineering tools* are those found in the disciplines of software

engineering, systems analysis and design, and in software architecture.

2. *Structural tools* are those that serve to organize a project and simplify its development. Some, such as modularization, are independent of the development environment. Others are provided by the environment itself. For example, C++ developers can resort to object-oriented analysis and design techniques, object models, and design patterns.

3. *Programming mechanics tools* are related to a specific hardware or software platform. They include the choice of machine architecture and operating systems, as well as commercial compilers and assemblers and their associated toolkits and application frameworks.

The program developer is thus confronted with an impressive list of fields, topics, and tools that are necessary for success in the conception, development, implementation, and maintenance of a software product.

In this book we attempt to present a pragmatic methodology for software development in-the-large. We must consider the use of tools from the project engineering, structural, and platform levels previously mentioned. Our main goals are to unify a somewhat disperse knowledge base to make its most important elements conveniently accessible to the software practitioner, and to assist in the practical endeavor of developing a computer program of substantial proportions. Our intention has been to produce a practical book, intended for programmers and project managers confronted with the real-world problem of reducing the complexity of developing a meaningful computer program, and of using and reusing the available tools to increase coding efficiency.

Scope and Application

We have already mentioned that the scope of the book is the development of smaller applications in C++ on a PC. These three restrictions are necessary in order to focus the contents so that the material can be covered to a sufficient depth. The first restriction excludes from the book's subject matter the development of major systems, such as operating systems and the large application projects typically undertaken by major software companies using scores of programmers. Our reason for this exclusion is that the development of operating systems programs and of large and complex applications is associated with a problem set different and more extensive from that of smaller ones. Considering the fact that proportionally few projects are in the field of operating systems development, or consist of large applications, we have felt justified in excluding these topics from the contents. The decision to exclude operating systems development also eliminates the need to discuss several of the more complicated software engineering techniques, such as Petri nets, which are of limited interest outside of this specialty field.

We have selected C++ as a programming language for two reasons: first, its popularity, and second, the fact that an object-oriented language provides an additional toolset with which to model the problem domain, achieve code reusability, and increase programming performance. However, like all high-level languages C++ is a convenient but limited tool. The fact that software products have proliferated during the past decade or so determines that the commercially successful program of today must offer a functionality or a performance level that exceeds that of its competitors. This places on program designers and programmers the responsibility of creating unique and powerful products that are well differentiated from other ones on the market. The task usually implies pushing the hardware and software resources to extremes, which, in turn, often requires simultaneously coding in several languages, a topic mentioned throughout the book and discussed specifically in Chapter 13.

A final limitation of the book's scope is the IBM and IBM-compatible Personal Computer. Here again, our main purpose in defining a hardware boundary is to allow the treatment of a host of important subjects to sufficient depth. Furthermore, applications programmers are usually specialists in a specific platform. This focusing of the book's contents should serve to increase the applicability of its contents for those readers within the targeted field of interest.

1. Part I briefly covers topics related to project engineering as found in the discipline of software engineering and the related fields of systems analysis and design and software architecture. The intention is to provide the reader with a very general background of software engineering and a survey of its most important ideas.

2. Part II covers topics related to object-oriented analysis and design in C++. We first discuss object orientation in general and then apply object-oriented methodologies to systems analysis and design.

3. Part III is about programming mechanics. In this part we discuss a host of topics that go from indirection, object orientation, reusability, inheritance and object composition, class and object constructs and patterns, and multifile programs.

Project Engineering Topics

Part I covers a selection of topics from software engineering and systems analysis and design. Our selection begins with a summary of the nature of software and the fundamental principles of software engineering, continues with the elements of software specification and design, and concludes with a description of the software production process. The material includes software engineering tools that are often used in application development, such as data flow and entity relationship diagrams. However, it does not cover many management issues that would be applicable at the administrative level of a software project.

Software architecture is an emerging discipline in the field of software engineering. It attempts to provide a formal specification for the functions and topology of a software system in order to show the correspondence between requirements and components. Its main purpose is to furnish a rationale for making design decisions, which are important in applications development. In this sense architectural styles provide useful patterns for systems organization. These ideas are not new; for many years software designers have been speaking of client-server systems, distributed processes, and layered design. However, the formalization of this concept into well-defined patterns, with their particular nomenclature and idioms, as well as the concept of computational components and connectors, provides a framework for the more detailed descriptions of architectural styles. The more formal notation replaces intuition and supplies a specialized vocabulary, as well as a set of constraints for combining the conceptual components. Thus far the practitioners of software architecture have been busy formalizing a rigorous theoretical base for their new discipline. They have had little time in which to develop pragmatic methodologies that could be used by the practical program designer. For this reason our discussion of topics related to software architecture is very limited.

Object-Oriented Topics

One of the difficulties of a software project is dealing with its inherent complexity. Reducing this complexity to manageable limits requires organizational tools at all stages of production. In this regard we identify two different but complementary approaches: modularization and object orientation.

Modularization is a conventional and quite useful mechanism for reducing complexity that transcends programming languages, environments, and even paradigms. In the software engineering literature this topic is often dealt with by means of a few comments or approached from a theoretical perspective that stresses the qualities of effective modular design with little discussion of how to modularize a project. However, modularization is not the trivial function of partitioning code into smaller segments. Nor should modules be equated with procedures, subroutines, or program files. A module is a logical unit of program division. It can be based on structural or functional considerations, or on both. In any case, two things are certain: bad modularization is little better than useless, and good modularization is achieved only after many modifications, reconsideration, and adjustments. In the book we stress program modularization and attempt to provide practical guidelines for modularizing the project.

It is often stated as fact that object orientation as a programming methodology is a direct result of the so-called *software crisis*. In other words, the low productivity of software developers and the inadequate reliability of their products spurred the creation of object-oriented methods as a more rational approach to programming. Whether this is historically true or not is inconsequential in view of the general acceptance of object-oriented programming techniques. Few will argue with the statement that object-oriented methods of analysis, design, and development improve programmer productivity, generate better quality products that are easier to maintain, and increase reuse of software components. On the other hand, we cannot conceal the fact that object-oriented programming is difficult to master.

Object-oriented methods and techniques apply at the analysis, design, and coding stages of application development. In Part II we are concerned with object-oriented analysis and design issues. Object-oriented programming is covered in Part III. All of these are topics well discussed in the literature. Most of our task in this regard consists of selecting a few core principles and techniques and applying them in practical program development. We have favored the Coad and Yourdon notation for object-oriented analysis because of its simplicity and general acceptance. However, we have followed some of our own ideas regarding the design stage.

Topics in Programming Mechanics

Application development also requires know-how. At some point the conception, planning, and engineering efforts must give way to the mundane and uneventful task of coding the specific functions that the code must perform. These *mechanics of programming* are considered in Part III.

The use of patterns and models can serve to simplify and facilitate program design in object-oriented environments and to sponsor reuse. Design patterns are software structures that are repeatedly used by expert designers and can therefore be applied under many different circumstances. For example, implementing a programmer's toolkit poses a similar problem set whether the toolkit is intended to facilitate string management operations, to provide a set of mathematical functions, or to expedite graphics application development. In any case the developer's intention is usually to furnish the simplest possible user interface and to maximize its power and flexibility. Once we have found a pattern of classes or objects that approximates these goals, this pattern can be reused under similar circumstances, thus saving us from the ungrateful task of "reinventing the wheel." Much of the material in Part III leads to design patterns and to object composition as applicable to C++ object-oriented programming.

Reusability is a pervasive topic in object orientation. It relates to class design, object modeling, inheritance, portability, efficiency, and many other issues. Writing reusable code is a mind-set, not a necessary conclusion or a fortuitous achievement. Just as a C++ programmer must learn to think "objects," he or she must also learn to think "reuse." There are coding styles that make reuse attractive and profitable and styles that make it unprofitable and difficult. At the same time, each programming language and development environment contains mechanisms for code reuse. Reuse in object-oriented environments takes advantage of the abstraction mechanism, of extensibility, of inheritance, and of object composition. Reuse of the code and design elements of a program is also discussed in Part III.

Because this book is about programming in-the-large, the discussion of programming mechanics does not extend to algorithm selection or development. The book leaves the subject of algorithms to the many excellent textbooks and monographs in this field. In Part III we address some technical details of PC application development in C++. Multifile programs are discussed in general, as well as some mixed-language programming specifics. We feel that multilanguage programming is a powerful tool. Multilanguage programming in C++ and x86 assembly language is a "killer" combination that every professional should master.

PART I

Project Engineering

Chapter 1

Fundamentals of Systems Engineering

1.0 Introduction

In this chapter we attempt to provide a technical overview of some topics from the field of software engineering, stressing those that would be most useful to the working developer. The contents are an arbitrary selection of the topics that would be most useful to the working analyst, designer, or programmer, operating in the context of a smaller software project. We have avoided speculative discussions on the respective merits of the various software engineering paradigms. The purpose of this chapter is to serve as an informational background and to set the mood for the more practical discussions that follow. The discussion excludes object orientation since Part II is devoted exclusively to this topic.

1.0.1 Characteristics of a New Discipline

Software engineering was first introduced in the 1960s in an effort to treat more rigorously the often frustrating task of designing and developing computer programs. It was around this time that the computer community became increasingly worried about the fact that software projects were typically over budget and behind schedule. The term *software crisis* came to signify that software development was the bottleneck in the advancement of computer technology.

During these initial years it became evident that we had introduced some grave fallacies by extending to software development some rules that were true for other fields of human endeavor, or that appeared to be common sense. The first such fallacy states that if a certain task takes a single programmer one year of coding, then four programmers would be able to accomplish it in approximately three months. The second fallacy is that if a single programmer was capable of producing a software product with a quality value of 25, then four programmers could create a product with a quality value considerably higher than 25, perhaps even approaching 100. A third fallacy states that if we have been capable of developing organizational tools, theories, and techniques for building bridges and airplanes, we should also be capable of straightforwardly developing a scientific methodology for engineering software.

The programmer productivity fallacy relates to the fact that computer programming, unlike ditch digging or apple harvesting, is not a task that is easily partitioned into isolated functions that can be performed independently. The different parts of a computer program interact, often in complicated and hard-to-predict ways. Considerable planning and forethought must precede the partitioning of a program into individually executable tasks. Furthermore, the individual programmers in a development team must frequently communicate to ensure that the separately developed elements will couple as expected and that the effects of individual adjustments and modifications are taken into account by all members of the group. All of which leads to the conclusion that team programming implies planning and structuring operations as well as interaction between the elements of the team.

The cumulative quality fallacy is related to some of the same interactions that limit programmer productivity. Suppose the extreme case of an operating system program that was developed by ten programmers. Nine of these programmers have performed excellently and implemented all the functions assigned to them in a flawless manner, while one programmer is incompetent and has written code that systematically crashes the system and damages the stored files. In this case it is likely that the good features of this hypothetical operating system will probably go unnoticed to a user who experiences a destructive crash. Notice that this situation is different from what typically happens with other engineered products. We can imagine a dishwasher that fails to dry correctly, but that its other functionalities continue to be useful. Or a car that does not corner well, but that otherwise performs as expected. Computer programs, on the other hand, often fail catastrophically. When this happens it is difficult for the user to appreciate any residual usefulness in the software product.

This leads to the conclusion that rather than a cumulative quality effect, software production is subject to a minimal quality rule, which determines that a relatively small defect in a software product can impair its usability, or, at best, reduce its appraised quality. The statement that "the ungrateful look at the sun and see its spots" justifiably applies to software users. Also notice that the minimal quality rule applies not only to defects that generate catastrophic failures, but even to those that do not affect program integrity. For example, a word processor performs perfectly except that it hyphenates words incorrectly. This program may execute much more difficult tasks extremely well; it may have excellent on-screen formatting, a high-quality spelling checker, an extensive dictionary of synonyms and antonyms, and many other important features. However, very few users will consider adopting this product since incorrectly hyphenated text is usually intolerable.

Finally, there is the unlikely assumption that we can engineer software programs in much the same way that we engineer bridges, buildings, and automobiles. The engineering methods fallacy is a consequence of the fact that software does not deal with tangible elements, subject to the laws of physics, but with purely intellectual creations. A program is more a *thought* than a *thing*. Things can be measured, tested, stretched, tempered, tuned, and transformed. A construction engineer can take a sample of concrete and measure its strength and resistance. A mechanical engineer can determine if a certain motor will be sufficiently powerful to operate a given machine. Regarding software components these determinations are not unequivocal. At the present stage-of-the-art a software engineer cannot look up a certain algorithm or data structure in a reference manual and determine rigorously if it is suitable for the problem at hand.

1.0.2 The Programmer as an Artist

Donald Knuth established in the title of his now classic work that programming is an art. He starts the preface by saying:

> *"The process of preparing programs for a digital computer is especially attractive, not only because it can be economically and scientifically rewarding, but also because it can be an aesthetic experience much like composing poetry or music."*

Therefore, it is reasonable to deduce that any effort to reduce the *art of programming* to the following of a strict and scientifically defined rule set is likely to fail. What results is like comparing the canvas by a talented artist with one produced by using a paint-by-the-numbers toy. Without talent the programmer's productions will consist of the dull rehashing of the same algorithms and routines that are printed in all the common textbooks. With genius and art the code comes alive with imaginative and resourceful creations that make the program a beautiful conception.

The fact that computer programming is an art and that talented programmers are more artists than technicians does not preclude the use of engineering and scientific principles in pursuing this art. Software engineering is not an attempt to reduce programming to a mechanical process, but a study of those elements of programming that can be approached technically and of the mechanisms that can be used to make programming less difficult. However, we must always keep in mind that technique, no matter how refined, can never make an artist out of an artisan.

1.1 Software Characteristics

From an engineering viewpoint a software system is a product that serves a function. However, one unique attribute makes a computer program much different from a bridge or an airplane: a program can be changed. This *malleability* of software is both an advantage and a danger. An advantage because it is often possible to correct an error in a program much easier than it would be to fix a defect in an airplane or automobile. A danger because a modification in a program can introduce unanticipated side effects that may impair the functionality of those components that were executing correctly before the change.

Another notable characteristic of programs relates to the type of resources necessary for their creation. A software product is basically an intellectual commodity. The principal resource necessary for producing it is human intelligence. The actual manufacturing of programs is simple and inexpensive compared to its design, coding, testing, and documenting. This contrasts with many other engineered products in which the resources used in producing it are a substantial part of the product's final cost. For example, a considerable portion of the price of a new automobile represents the cost of manufacturing it, wile a less significant part goes to pay for the engineering costs of design and development. In the case of a typical computer program the proportions are reversed. The most important element of the product cost is the human effort in design and development while the cost of manufacturing is proportionally insignificant.

1.1.1 Software Qualities

An engineered product is usually associated with a list of qualities that define its usability. For example, in performing its functions a bridge supports a predetermined weight and withstands a given wind force. An airplane is capable of transporting a specific load, at a certain speed and altitude. By the same token, a software product is associated with a given set of qualities that define its functionality. The principal goals of software engineering is to define, specify, and measure software qualities and to describe the principles that can be applied to achieve them.

The classification of software qualities can be based on the relation with the software product: we can speak of qualities desirable to the user, to the developer, or to the manager. Table 1.1 lists some qualities according to this classification.

Table 1.1 *Software Qualities*

USER	DEVELOPER	MANAGER
reliable	verifiable	productive
easy to use	maintainable	controllable
efficient	extensible	lucrative
		portable

In this sense we can also talk about software qualities internal and external to the product. The internal ones are visible to developers and managers, while the external ones are visible to the user. It is easy to see that reliability from the user's viewpoint implies verifiability from the developer's viewpoint. On the other hand, this distinction is often not well defined. The following are some of the most important qualities usually associated with software products.

Correctness

A term sometimes incorrectly used as a synonym for reliability or robustness relates to the fact that a program behaves as expected. More technically we can say that a program is correct if it behaves according to its functional specifications (described later in this chapter). Correctness can be verified experimentally (by testing) or analytically. Certain programming tools and practices tend to improve correctness while others tend to diminish it.

Reliability

Relates to a program's trustworthiness or dependability. More formally, reliability can be defined as the statistical probability that a program will continue to perform as expected over a period of time. We can say that reliability is a relative measure of correctness.

The immaturity of software engineering as a technical discipline is made evident by the fact that we expect defects in software products. Without much embarrassment, developers often release programs accompanied by lists of *known bugs*. Who would purchase a car that came with a lists of known defects? What is more, programs are often sold with disclaimers that attempt to void any responsibility on the part of the producer for program defects. Warnings state that breaking the shrink-wrap cancels any accountability on the part of the producer. Not until we are willing to assume accountability for our products will software engineering become a technical field. We must be liable for the correctness of products that we claim have been technically engineered.

Robustness

This software quality attempts to measure program behavior in circumstances that exceed those of the formal requirements. In other words, it is a measure of the program's reaction to unexpected circumstances. For example, a mathematical program assumes that input values are within the legal ranges defined for the operations. A user should not input a negative value to the square root function since this operation is undefined. A more robust program will recover from this error by posting an error message and requesting a new input, while a less robust one may crash.

Although robustness and correctness are related qualities they are often quite distinct. Since correctness is a measure of compliance with the formal specifications, the mathematical program that crashes on an invalid input value may still be correct; however, it will not be robust. Obviously, robustness is a quality difficult to measure and specify. Reliability is also related to robustness since robustness usually increases reliability.

Efficiency

This quality is a measure of how economically a system uses available resources. An efficient system is one that makes good use of these resources. In software engineering efficiency is equated with performance, so the terms are considered equivalent. A slow application or one that uses too much disk space reduces user productivity and increases operational cost.

Often software efficiency is difficult and costly to evaluate. The conventional methods rely on measurement, analysis, and simulation. Measurement consists of timing execution of a program or a part thereof. The stopwatch is sometimes used, but a more sensible approach consists of three timing routines: one starts an internal timer, another one stops it, and a third one displays the time elapsed between the timer start and stop calls. In this case we let the computer measure the execution time between two points in the code, an operation that is quite complicated when using an external timing device. Notice that this method requires access to the source code.

A favorable outgrowth of execution time measurements is locating possible processing bottlenecks. In this case the execution times of different program sections are measured separately, using a progressively finer grid, until the code section that takes longest to execute is isolated. One problem with measurements of execution time as a way of determining efficiency is that the values are often meaningless without a point of reference. However, when comparing two or more processing routines no other method is as simple and effective.

The analytical method consists of determining efficiency by analyzing the complexity of the algorithms used by the code. The field of algorithm analysis defines theories that determine the worst, best, and average case behaviors in terms of the use of critical resources such as time and space. But algorithm analysis is often too costly to be used in the smaller application development project.

The simulation method of determining efficiency is based on developing models that emulate the product so that we can analyze and quantify its behavior. Although this method may occasionally be useful in determining the efficiency of medium-size applications, more typically its cost would be prohibitive.

Verifiability

A software product is verifiable if its properties can be easily ascertained by analytical methods or by testing. Often verifiability is an internal quality of interest mainly to the developers. At other times the user needs to determine that the software performs as expected, as is the case regarding program security. Some programming practices foster verifiability while other ones do not, as will be shown often in this book.

Maintainability

Programmers discover rather early in their careers that a software product is never finished: a finished program is an oxymoron. Programs evolve throughout their life span due to changes that correct newly detected defects or modifications that implement new functionalities as they become necessary. In this sense we refer to software maintenance as a program upkeep operation. The easier that a program is to upkeep, the greater its maintainability. If the modification refers to correcting a program defect, we speak of *repairability*. If it refers to implementing a new function, we speak of *evolvability*.

User Friendliness

This is perhaps the least tangible software property since it refers to a measurement of human usability. The main problem is that different users may consider the same program feature as having various degrees of friendliness. In this sense, a user accustomed to a mouse device may consider a program that uses this interface as friendly, while one unaccustomed to the mouse may consider the program unfriendly.

The user interface is often considered the most important element in a program's user friendliness. But here again user preference often varies according to previous level of expertise. Also notice that several other attributes affect a program's user friendliness. For example, a program with low levels of correctness and reliability and that performs poorly could hardly be considered as user friendly. We revisit the topic of user friendliness in a later discussion of human engineering topics.

Reusability

The maturity of an engineering field is characterized by the degree of reusability. In this sense the same electric motor used in powering a washing machine may also be used in a furnace fan and a reciprocating wood saw. However, notice that in the case of the electric motor reusability is possible due to a high degree of standardization. For instance, different types of belts and pulleys are available off-the-shelf for adapting the motor to various devices. Also, the electric power is standardized so that the motor generates the same power and revolutions per minute in the various applications.

Perhaps the most important reason for promoting software reusability is that it reduces the cost of production. On the other hand, reusability of software components is often difficult to achieve because of lack of standardization. For example, the search engine developed for a word processor may not be directly usable in another one due to variations in the data structures used for storing and formatting the text file. Or a mathematical routine that calculates the square root may not be reusable in another program due to variations in required precision or in numeric data formats.

Another interesting feature of reusability is that it is usually introduced at design time. Reusable software components must be designed as such, since reusability as an afterthought is rarely effective. Another consideration is that certain programming methodologies, such as object orientation, foster and promote reusability through specific mechanisms and techniques. Throughout this book we discuss reusability as it relates to many aspects of software production.

Portability

The term is related to the word *port*, which is a computer connection to the outside world. Software is said to be *portable* if it can be transmitted through a *port*, usually to another machine. More generally, a program or part thereof is portable if it can execute in different hardware and software environments. Portability is often an important economic issue since programs often need to be transferred to other machines and software environments.

One of the great advantages of developing applications in high-level languages is their greater portability. A program that uses no machine-specific features, written entirely in C++, on the PC, can probably be converted to run on a Macintosh computer with no great effort. On the other hand, program developers often need to use low-level machine features, related to either specific hardware or software properties, to achieve a particular functionality for their products. This decision often implies a substantial sacrifice in portability.

Other Properties

Many other properties of software are often mentioned in software engineering textbooks, among them are timeliness, visibility, productivity, interoperability, and understandability. In special circumstances these and other properties may take on special importance. Nevertheless, in general application development, those specifically listed appear to be the most significant ones.

1.1.2 Quality Metrics

One of the greatest challenges of software engineering is the measurement of the software attributes. It is relatively easy to state that a program must be robust and reliable and another matter to measure its robustness and reliability in some predetermined units. If we have no reliable way of measuring a particular quality it will be difficult to determine if it is achieved in a particular case, or to what degree it is present. Furthermore, in order to measure a quality precisely we must first be capable of accurately defining it, which is not always an easy task.

Most engineering fields have developed standard metrics for measuring product quality. For example, we can compare the quality of two car batteries by means of the cold cranking amps which they are capable of delivering. On the other hand, nonengineered products are typically lacking quality measurements. In this sense we cannot determine from the label on a videocassette what the entertainment value of the movie is that it contains, nor are units of information speified in the jacket of a technical book. Software is also a field in which there are no universally accepted quality metrics, although substantial work in this direction is in progress. The verification of program correctness, discussed later in the book, directly relates to software quality metrics.

1.2 Principles of Software Engineering

We started this chapter on the assumption that software development is a creative activity and that programming is not an exact science. From this point of view even the term *software engineering* may be considered unsuitable since we could preferably speak of *software development technique*, which term does not imply the rigor of a formal engineering approach. In our opinion it is a mistake to assume that programs can be mechanically generated by some mechanical methodology, no matter how sophisticated. When software engineering falls short of producing the expected results it is because we overstressed the scientific and technical aspects of program development over those that are artistic or aesthetic in nature or that depend on talent, personal endowments, or know-how. Nevertheless, as there is technique in art, there is technique in program development. Software engineering is the conventional name that groups the technical and scientific aspects of program development.

Smaller software projects usually take place within the constraints of a limited budget. Often financial resources do not extend to hiring trained software project managers or specialists in the field of software engineering. The person in charge of the project usually wears many hats, including those of project manager and software engineer. In fact, it is not unusual that the project manager/engineer is also part-time designer, programmer, tester, and documentation specialist. What this all means is that the formality and rigor used in engineering a major project may not apply to one of lesser proportions. In other words, the strictness and rigidity of software engineering principles may have to be scaled down to accommodate the smaller projects.

In this sense we must distinguish between principles, techniques, and tools of software engineering. Principles are general guidelines that are applicable at any stage of the program production process. They are the abstract statements that describe desirable properties, but that are of little use in practical software development. For example, the principle that encourages high program reliability does not tell us how to make a program reliable. Techniques or methods refer to a particular approach to solving a problem and help ensure that a product will have the desirable properties. Tools are specific resources that are used in implementing a particular technique. In this case we may state as a principle that floating-point numbers are a desirable format for representing decimals in a digital machine. Also that the floating-point techniques described in the ANSI standard 754 are suitable for our application and should be followed. Finally, that a particular library of floating-point routines, which complies with ANSI 754, would be an adequate tool for implementing the mathematical functions required in our application. Figure 1.1 graphically shows the relationship between these three elements.

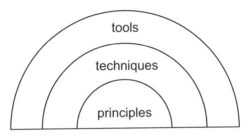

Figure 1.1 *Relation between Principles, Techniques, and Tools*

1.2.1 Rigor

One of the drawbacks of considering a program as an art form is that it places the emphasis on inspiration rather than on accuracy and preciseness. But programming is an applied rather than a pure art. We may find it charming that Michelangelo planned his statue of David rather carelessly and ended up with insufficient marble for sculpturing the feet. But a client may not be willing to forgive an artistically-minded programmer who did not find inspiration to implement hyphenation in developing a word processor program. We must conclude that the fact that programming is often a creative activity does not excuse us from pursuing program design and development with the necessary rigor.

Some authors distinguish between degrees of rigor. The highest degree, called *formality*, requires that development be made strictly according to laws of mathematics and logic. In this sense formality is a high degree of rigor. One field in which the issue of rigor and formality gains particular importance is in software specifications. A logical formalism has been developed which allows the precise specification of software. The mathematical expressions, usually based on the predicate calculus, allow the representation of complete programs, or of program fragments, in symbolic expressions that can be manipulated according to mathematical laws. Some of the advantages of this methodology claimed by it advocates are the following:

1. Formal methods allow the software engineer to specify, develop, and verify a software system using a *formal specification language* so that its correctness can be assessed systematically.

2. They provide a mechanism for the elimination of program ambiguity and inconsistency through mathematical analysis, thereby discovering errors that could otherwise go undetected.

3. They allow a software problem to be expressed in terms of an algebraic derivation, thus forcing the specifier to think in more rigorous terms.

4. These methods will eventually make possible the mechanization of programming, thereby revolutionizing software development.

On the other hand, the detractors of formal methods of specification also have their own counter arguments:

1. Formal specifications are difficult to learn. Nothing short of a graduate course is required to obtain even a cursory understanding of this subject.

2. So far these methods have not been used successfully in practical program development.

3. Most programmers, even most software engineers working today, are unfamiliar with formal specifications.

At this point we could declare that because the scope of our book is the development of smaller size programs we will be satisfied with rigor and exclude formal methodologies from its contents. But the fact is that some smaller programs that deal with a particular subject matter can (perhaps should) be specified formally. Therefore, we exclude the consideration of formal methods of specification based purely on expediency. Our excuse is that this is a rather intricate subject, and that most program development done today still takes place without the use of formal methods of specifications.

Therefore we settle for the lowest level of rigor, which we define as the methodology for program development based on following a sequence of well-defined and precisely stated steps. In the programming stage of development rigor is unavoidable. In fact, programming is performed in a formal context of well-defined syntax and semantics. But rigor should also apply in every stage of the program development process, including program design, specification, and verification. A program developed according to a rigorous methodology should contain the desirable attributes previously mentioned. In other words, the results should be reliable, understandable, verifiable, maintainable, and reusable.

1.2.2 Separation of Concerns

It is common sense that when dealing with complex issues we must look separately at its various facets. Since software development is an inherently complex activity, separation of concerns becomes a practical necessity. A coarse-grain observation of any construction project immediately reveals three concerns or levels of activity: technical, managerial, and financial. Technical concerns deal with the technological and scientific part of the project. The managerial concerns refer to project administration. The financial concerns relate to the monetary and fiscal activities.

An example shows this notion of separation of concerns into technical, managerial, and financial. Suppose homeowners are considering the possibility of building a new garage. The project can be analyzed by looking at the three separate activities required for its completion. Technically, the homeowners must determine the size, type, and specifications of the garage to be built and its location within the property. A finer level of technical details could include defining the preparatory groundwork, the concrete work necessary for the foundation, the number and type of doors and windows, the siding, the electrical installation, roofing, as well as other construction parameters. The managerial aspects of the project may include supervising of the various subcontractors, purchasing materials, obtaining necessary building permits, and the timely disbursing of funds. Financial activities include evaluating how much the project would add to the value of the property, selecting the most desirable bids, and procuring a construction loan.

It is important to realize that separation of concerns is a convenience for viewing the different aspects of a project. It is an analytical tool which does not necessarily imply a division in the decision authority. In the previous example, the homeowners may decide to perform the financial activities themselves, while they delegate the managerial activities to a general contractor, who, in turn, leaves the technical building details to the subcontractors. Nevertheless, it is a basic rule of capitalism that whoever pays the bills gives the orders. Therefore the homeowners would retain the highest level of authority. They would have the right to request managerial or even technical information from the general contractor, who they may override as they see fit, or even fire if they deem it necessary.

By the same token, the participants of a software development project should always be aware of the fact that separation of concerns does not imply any permanent delegation of authority. The fact that a software designer is assigned the task of defining and specifying the program does not mean that whoever is in charge cannot step in at any point in the project's development and override the designer. In this respect two extremes should be avoided. In one case the participants in the project lose sight of where the final authority resides and are misled by the assumption that it has been totally and permanently delegated in their favor. This misconception often generates a take-it-or-leave-it attitude on the part of the project's technical staff who seem to state: "this is what is best, and disagreement only proves your technical ignorance." The other extreme occurs when authority is held so closely that the participants are afraid of showing their knowledge or expertise for fear of being ridiculed or overridden.

It is the task of those in charge of a project to make their subordinates aware of where final authority resides and of the fact that this authority will be used if necessary, perhaps even in a form that may seem arbitrary. Also, what are the delegated levels of decision and the boundaries within which each participant can be freely creative? This initial definition of the various levels of concern, responsibility, and authority is a most important element in the success of a software development project.

We have seen that the notion of separation of concerns is related to separation of responsibilities; furthermore, it is related to specialization of labor. At the coarser level this determines the separation of activities into financial, managerial, and technical. Each of the groups can be further subdivided. For example, the technical staff can be divided into specialists in program design, coding, and testing. The coding personnel can be further specialized in low- and high-level languages, and the high-level language ones into C++, Pascal, and Cobol programmers. By the same token, the program designers can be specialists in various fields, and so can the managers and financial experts.

1.2.3 Modularization

Modularization is a general-purpose mechanism for reducing complexity which transcends programming languages or environments. Modules should be conceptualized as units of program division, but not necessarily equated to subroutines, subprograms, or disk files. For smaller software development projects modularization is a most effective organizational tool.

Two modularization methods are usually identified: one called *top down* decomposes a problem into subproblems that can be tackled independently; another one, called *bottom up,* builds up a system starting with elementary components. In this same context it is often stated that the main advantage of modularization is that it makes the system understandable. However, this understandability is usually achieved in stages during program development. Modularization typically takes place progressively. Since it is often impractical to wait until a system is fully understood to start its development, the most practical approach is to define an initial modular division and progressively refine it as the project progresses and the participants become more acquainted with its features.

The term *modular cohesion* refers to the relationship between the elements of a module. For example, a module in which the processing routines, procedures, and data structures are strongly related is said to have high cohesion. Plugging into a module some unrelated function just because we can find no better place for it reduces the module's cohesion. It is usually preferable to allocate a catch-all module, which we can somewhat euphemistically call the *general-support module,* in which we can temporarily place those functions or data structures for which no ideal location is immediately apparent. Later in the development we may rethink the program's modularization and move elements from the catch-all into other modules.

The term *modular coupling* refers to the relationship between modules in the same program. For example, if one module is heavily dependent on the procedures or data in another module, then the modules are said to be tightly coupled. Modules that have tight coupling are difficult to understand, analyze, and reuse separately; therefore, tight coupling is usually considered an undesirable property. On the other hand, all the modules in a program must be coupled in some way since they must interact in producing a common functionality. It is difficult to imagine a module that is entirely uncoupled from the system and still performs some related function.

It is often stated, as a general principle, that a good modular structure should have high cohesion and loose coupling. The elements must be closely related within the module and there should be a minimum of intermodular dependency.

1.2.4 Abstraction and Information Hiding

It is a unique property of the human mind that it can reduce a problem's complexity by concentrating on a certain subset of its features while disregarding some of the details. For example, we can depict an automobile by its component parts: motor, transmission, chassis, body, and wheels. This functional abstraction, which is based on the tasks performed by each component, ignores the details of certain parts that are included in the abstraction. For example, the abstraction may assume that the trunk lid need not be mentioned specifically since it is part of the body, or the starter, since it is part of the motor.

Since an abstraction is a particular representation of reality, there can be many abstractions of the same object. The previous automobile abstraction into motor, transmission, chassis, body, and wheels may be useful for a general description. However, a car-wash operation may not be interested in the components with which it does not have to deal. Therefore a car-wash project may define that an automobile abstraction composed of hood, trunk, fenders, roof, windshield, and windows is more useful to its purpose. Regarding software we often find that the abstraction that could be useful in describing a system to a user may not be the most suitable one for the developers. By the same token, those charged with the task of testing a software system may prefer an abstraction that is different from the one adopted by the users, designers, or programmers.

Since abstraction helps define the entities that comprise a software product it is a modularization tool. We modularize by abstraction.

Information hiding and *encapsulation* are terms that appeared during the 1970s in relation to object-oriented design and programming. The notion was proposed by David Parnas who states that each program component should encapsulate or hide a design decision in such a way that it will reveal as little as possible about its inner workings. In other words, information hiding is one of the most desirable properties of abstraction. Its main usefulness, according to Coad and Yourdon, is that it localizes volatility thus facilitating changes that are less likely to have side effects. The notions of encapsulation and information hiding will be revisited in the chapters related to object-oriented analysis and design.

1.2.5 Malleability and Anticipation of Change

A program should not be envisioned as a finished product but as a stage or phase in a never-ending development process. We can speak of a program as satisfying a certain set of requirements, as being suitable for a given purpose, or a certain version being ready for market, but to a software developer the notion of a "finished program" is an oxymoron. For a program to be finished we must assume that it has no remaining defects, that all present or future user requirements are perfectly satisfied, and that no improvements or modifications will ever be necessary. Since none of these conditions can ever be proved, a program can never be considered finished.

It is all a matter of semantics, but the ever-changing nature of software makes it preferable that we consider a program as a category more than as a product. In this sense we can say that the program WordMaster consists of the various implementations named WordMaster 1.0, WordMaster 2.1, and WordMaster Deluxe. In this same sense we speak of the automobile category named Chevrolet which includes the models '56 Corvette, '78 Station Wagon, and '94 Pickup.

The fact that software products are fundamentally fragile encourages the previous view. Knowing this, we must design software so it is malleable, which means that we must anticipate change. The reason for change comes from two possible causes: program repair and evolution. It is indeed a naive software developer who does not know that defects will be detected after a program's release, or who cannot anticipate that new requirements will be identified and old ones will change. It is perhaps this inherent fragility that distinguishes software from many other industrial products.

The two desirable features of program maintainability and evolvability, previously mentioned, are closely related to program malleability and anticipation of change, as well as reusability, since a software component is reusable if it can be easily adapted to perform a different function or to execute in a new context. This usually requires that the component be malleable, which in turn implies that the original designers anticipated change.

1.2.6 Maximum Generalization

The more generalized a software product, the larger the audience to which it appeals. The more generalized a program routine or procedure, the greater its possibilities for reusability. This implies the convenience of maximum generalization at the level of the application's design and of the individual routines, procedures, or modules. In these cases the maximum generalization approach is based on trying to discover a more general problem that is equivalent to the one presented, or a more general solution.

At the product development level the principle of maximum generalization advises that we search for more general problems hidden behind the one at hand. For example, a DOS image processing application is required to execute in a true-color graphics mode. The initial approach may be to incorporate into the application low-level drivers for a VESA true-color mode. However, a careful analysis of the problem shows that a more general approach would be to develop a library of support functions for several true-color VESA modes. The library could be used by the application under development and also furnished as a commercial toolkit. In this case the greater development effort required for creating the library may prove to be well justified.

1.2.7 Incremental Development

Sculpturing is a creative activity that resembles programming. How would a sculptor approach building a realistic marble statue of Franklin D. Roosevelt? One conceivable method would be to start at the top and attempt to carve out and finish the hat, then the head, then the torso, then the arms, and so forth until reaching the shoes, at which point the statue would be finished. But this method is not very reasonable since it assumes that each part of the anatomy of FDR would be finished to its finest details before the next one is started. An actual sculptor would probably approach the problem by progressive approximations. He or she would start by making a drawing of what the final statue is to look like. Then the basic traces of the drawing would be transferred to the marble block in order to determine which parts of the block could be roughly chipped away. The process of chipping away the unnecessary material would continue progressively on the whole figure, which would begin to approximate the final result by stages, rather than by parts.

An inexperienced sculptor could possibly err in two ways: he or she may be tempted to skip the drawing stage (program design) and proceed directly into the carving (coding), or may devote too much time to the details of the drawing and delay the carving unnecessarily. On the other hand, the experienced artist knows that the drawing is a basic guide but that the finer details of the statue come during the creative process. If the drawing shows FDR with his hands in his pockets, later the sculptor will not be able to change his or her mind and show the president waving at the crowd, since the necessary material would no longer be available. Therefore, FDR's general form and pose must be decided before the carving starts. However, the exact dimension of the cigarette holder, his facial expression, or the texture of his coat are details that can be decided at a later stage.

Regarding software, incremental development sometimes consists of the creation of product subsets that can be delivered to the customer for early evaluation and feedback. In reality, very few software projects can be exactly defined at the starting point. Therefore it is often reasonable to divide the program specifications into progressive stages, perhaps associating each stage with a test version of the final product. One advantage of this method is that the customer gets to examine and evaluate several prototypes.

However, the iterative development method introduces new management and organizational problems due to the fact that the project itself is defined "on the fly." One issue that must be specifically addressed is the management of the documentation for each of the various development stages as well as for the corresponding prototypes. A badly managed incremental development project can easily turn into disorder and anarchy.

1.3 Software Engineering Paradigms

Some software engineering authors, including Pressman, speak of a series of steps in program development that encompass the use of specific methods, tools, and policies. In software engineering the term *methods* refers to technical procedures used in the development of a project. It includes project planning, systems and requirements analysis, data structure design, algorithm selection and evaluation, coding, estimation of program correctness, and maintenance procedures.

Software engineering tools are software aides to program development. These tools, usually called *computer-aided software engineering*, or CASE tools, create a development environment that tends to automate development and provides support for the methods.

The policies (sometimes called procedures) bind together the methods and tools into a practical methodology of program development. For example, the policies adopted for a particular project define the methods that will be applied, the deliverables that will be generated during the development process, the controls that will help assure the quality of the final product, and the various control points in the development schedule.

A particular series of steps (methods, tools, and policies) gives rise to specific paradigms. Three of these paradigms have been extensively discussed in the literature: the waterfall model, the prototype methods, and the spiral development model. A fourth one, sometimes called a *fourth-generation technique*, is based on the use of nonprocedural languages and specialized software tools. Because of its unconventionality we will not discuss fourth-generation techniques, although the reader should note that many authors envision a promising future for this development methodology.

1.3.1 The Waterfall Model

This classical model of a software engineering project is based on the notion of a system life-cycle. Although the name *waterfall model* is rather recent, and so is the notion of a life-cycle paradigm, the notion of a flow of development activities can be found in the early software engineering literature. Tausworthe talks about a flow of activities in top-down development and provides a graph in which one activity follows another one in a waterfall-like fashion. Figure 1.2 is a representation of the classic waterfall model for a software project.

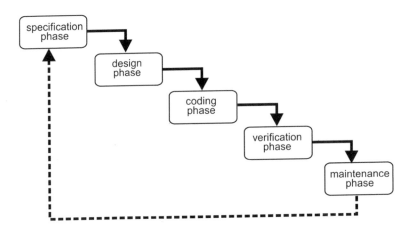

Figure 1.2 *The Waterfall Model*

The *specification phase* of the system life-cycle consists of a requirements gathering process through analysis and systems engineering. Whenever the project must interface with existing software or hardware elements the specification phase must include a systems requirements definition. During this phase customer and developer work very closely: the customer provides the requirements and the developer reflects these requirements in a formal specification that is, in turn, reviewed by the customer. The requirements/specification cycles continue until both parties agree that the project has been clearly and unambiguously defined.

The *design phase* of the software life-cycle focuses on four elements: data structures, program architecture, procedures, and interfaces. This phase concludes with a representation of the software that can be evaluated and assessed on its own. The maxim that states that *engineering is design* is also applicable to software engineering, since the design stage is often the most critical and difficult one.

During the *coding phase* we convert the design into a machine-executable product.

In the life cycle paradigm it is conventionally accepted that the *verification phase* starts at the conclusion of the coding phase. Once the code executes in a machine it must be evaluated for correctness. This means that we must ascertain that it meets the requirements developed during the specifications phase and that it is free from defects. Although this phase is sometimes associated with debugging, it should also include all formal and experimental verifications of program correctness.

Although the *maintenance phase* was not included in the original model, today it is generally accepted that programs will undoubtedly undergo change and that these changes are part of the software life-cycle. The reason for changes includes errors detected, modifications in the program's hardware or software environment, or the implementation of new functional requirements identified by the customer. Maintenance procedures require revisiting all the stages of the software life-cycle, as depicted by the dotted arrow in Figure 1.2.

Although the waterfall model has been used successfully in many software engineering projects and is still considered an effective method for program development, several shortcomings have been pointed out. The most notable one is that software development projects can rarely be specified and defined in one sitting. A more typical scenario is a series of iterative development cycles such as those mentioned in regards to the incremental development principle. Another difficulty in applying this model is that projects do not often follow the sequential flow described in the paradigm. For example, program verification is often done concurrently with the coding phase, as are the design and specification phases. Another criticism is that maintenance operations often require a repetition of the program life-cycle. For instance, developing a new version of an existing program in order to correct known defects and to incorporate recently defined features requires revisiting all the life-cycle stages, starting with the specification phase. Therefore it is difficult to consider program maintenance as a typical development phase since it has unique effects that are not evident in the other phases of the model.

In spite of these and other weaknesses of the waterfall model, this paradigm is the one most widely used in software engineering practice. Although other more complicated models are usually judged to be more rigorous and accurate, the waterfall model remains the most popular and simplest methodology for software development.

1.3.2 Prototyping

Many software development projects are of an experimental or speculative nature. Consider the following examples:

1. A research group wishes to determine if it is possible to develop an expert system that uses data obtained by remote-sensing satellites in order to determine pollution levels in the lakes and streams of the United States.

2. An entrepreneur wishes to determine if it is feasible to develop a word processing program in which the user is equipped with foot pedals that activate some of the program functions.

In either of these cases we can see that the software development project can hardly be stated *a priori*. The objectives are described so generally that it is difficult to define specific program requirements that could serve as a base for a detailed design. In both cases, as well as in many others in which an initial detailed design is not possible or practical, a prototyping approach could be a feasible alternative.

In prototyping the developer is able to create a model of the software. This model can later be used to better define the final product or to ascertain its feasibility. The prototype can be a simple paper model of the software, which can be produced with little or no coding, a working prototype that implements a subset of the program functions, or a complete program in which some functions are not implemented.

The purpose of the prototype is to allow both customer and developer to make decisions regarding the feasibility and practicality of the project, and, if judged feasible and practical, to better define the final product. Prototyping is often depicted as a development cycle with the sequence of steps shown in Figure 1.3.

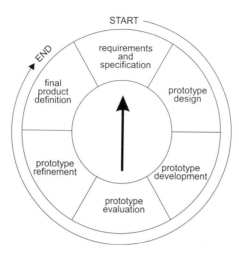

Figure 1.3 *The Prototyping Model*

Prototype development begins by collecting requirements and specifications. Then the prototype is designed, usually by following an abbreviated process which produces results quicker than conventional program design procedures. The prototype is built, also shortening the development processes by skipping all processing steps that are not strictly necessary for the purpose at hand. The prototype is finally evaluated, first by the developer and later by the customer. If necessary, it is further refined and tuned in an iterative cycle. The finished prototype is used to further define the final software product.

One major risk of prototype development relates to customers that misunderstand its purposes. This misconception can give rise to the following:

1. A customer not aware that the prototype is an unfinished product, usually with less functionality and lower performance than can be achieved in the final version, may make wrong decisions regarding the suitability of the final product. In extreme cases a promising project may be cancelled by the customer due to misconceptions that originated in the prototype.

2. The customer, in a rush to get a product to market or to put a product to practical use, decides that the prototype itself is sufficiently adequate. The customer then requests that the developer perform some final adjustments and modifications and deliver the prototype as a fi-

nal product. One incentive this customer could have is the antici-pated lower cost of using the prototype itself rather than following the development process as originally planned.

In most cases the possibility of a misunderstanding regarding the prototype phase can be eliminated by clearly explaining these risks to the customer. Alternatively, it may be advisable to exchange a memo-randum of agreement between developer and customer regarding the reduced functionality of the prototype or the fact that it will not be suitable as a finished product. Unfortunately, in some cases, the risks of the prototype being misinterpreted by the client have made devel-opers decide against adopting this paradigm.

1.3.3 The Spiral Model

This model, first suggested by Boehm in 1988, proposes to merge the best features of the life-cycle and the prototyping paradigm with the principle of incremental development. Figure 1.4 (based on Press-man) shows a spiral progression through four different stages.

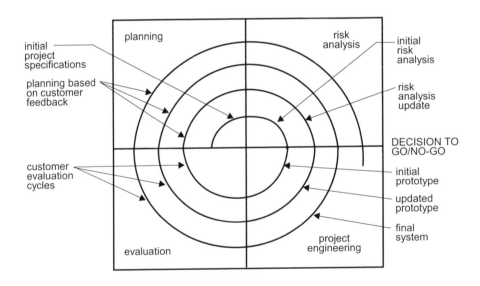

Figure 1.4 *The Spiral Model*

Notice that the drawing in Figure 1.4 is meant as a general illustration of the method and is not to be interpreted literally. For example, the number of cycles around the spiral will vary from project to project.

A unique feature of the spiral model is the introduction of a risk analysis stage, which culminates in a go or no-go decision at the conclusion of each development cycle. However, this phase is also its most controversial feature. In the first place, risk analysis requires a particular expertise, and is trivialized when performed by untrained personnel. In fact, the risk analysis phase is undesirable if it can lead to invalid interpretation of results. In addition, customers often believe that they performed a risk analysis of the project before deciding to undertake it, and that further consideration of this matter is unnecessary. Furthermore, the possibility that at the conclusion of each development cycle the entire project could be scrapped by a no-go decision may lead to apprehensions on the part of the customer.

On the other hand, if the difficulties and perils associated with the risk analysis phase can be conjured, then the spiral model constitutes the most satisfactory paradigm for the development of large software systems. The incremental development approach proposed by this model, with its repeated prototyping and risk evaluation phases, provides a realistic framework for program development. Both customer and developer have repeated opportunities in which to identify possible defects and shortcomings and make the necessary adjustments. Note that this model is relatively new and that not much experience regarding its application has been collected yet.

1.3.4 A Pragmatic Approach

The practicing software developer must decide, in each case, which model or combinations of models are most suitable to the project at hand. The decision is often based on practical risks and limitations rather than on theoretical applicability. For example, a developer may consider that the most adequate paradigm is the prototyping model, but a substantial risk that the customer will misinterpret the results advises against its use. In another case a project may fit quite well within the spiral model but the fact that personnel trained in risk analysis will not be available suggests a modification of the paradigm or the adoption of the more conventional waterfall model.

A wise man once said: "All systems and no system: behold the best system." This maxim is quite applicable to the various software engineering paradigms mentioned in the preceding sections, in particular when they concern smaller projects in which development time and resources are limited. The most common scenario is a combination of paradigms. Often the most useful one is a spiral model in which the risk evaluation function is scaled down to accommodate two factors. The first one is customer nervousness that results from the possibility of a project cancellation. The second one is the short supply of experts in the risk analysis field. Since the spiral model is in itself a combination of the waterfall and the prototyping model, all of the mentioned paradigms will actually be used. A possible scaling of the risk analysis phase could consist of limiting it to the first or the first and second cycles around the model. Thereafter it will be assumed that a go decision is permanently on. This modification certainly compromises one of the best features of the spiral model, but in many cases practical considerations will make the adjustment necessary.

Other circumstances may also require modifications of the theoretical models. For instance, most software engineering and system analysis textbooks assume that the roles of customer and developer are undertaken by separate individuals or entities. In real life many software development projects take place in circumstances where customer and developer are the same person or commercial firm. This is the case when a software company develops a project that will be marketed directly, or when a scientific research group develops its own project. In either case one possible remedy is to artificially emulate the customer function.

For example, the marketing department of the software company can play the customer role, or the head of the research project can pretend to be the client for which the product is being developed. The dual roles of developers and customer are so important in the software development process that any solution that will preserve it, even fictitiously, is an attractive option. However, we should always keep in mind that a virtual customer is a fictional creation, which may be overridden by higher authority at any time. When this happens, the integrity of the paradigm is seriously compromised, since the division between judgment and authority ceases to exist. The project then becomes like a democracy in which the executive branch takes on the power of firing the members of the judicial branch. In either case, although appearances may be preserved, the actual check-and-balances mechanism ceases to exist.

1.4 Concurrent Documentation

One of the most important lessons of software engineering refers to the need for adequate and rigorous project documentation. By the same token, the most notable difference between a correctly engineered development project and a haphazard effort is the documentation. Too often the tendency has been to consider program documentation as a secondary problem, one that can be addressed once the project is finished. This tendency is probably traceable to the same human fallacy that makes some programmers believe that comments can be inserted into the code after the programming has concluded. As writing comments is part of the chore of programming, documentation is part of the task of program development. Either one cannot be approached as an afterthought, at risk of writing spaghetti code or of developing undecipherable projects.

Tausworthe, who is responsible for the notion of concurrent documentation, states:

> *"The second principle guiding this work is that the definition, design, coding, and verification phases of development cannot be regarded as complete until the documentation is complete and certified by some form of correctness audit... good documentation is inextricably bound up in each facet of the project, from conception, to design, to coding, testing, etc., and because the formalization enforces a discipline, creating a program methodology."*

It has been the information systems community that has stressed the importance of documenting the software development project. Often a book on software engineering will devote little space to this topic; on the other hand, one on system analysis and design is more likely to contain a detailed discussion of the topic. Capron's *System Analysis and Design* contains a thorough treatment of documentation. Perhaps the awareness of the importance of documentation is more natural to the business community than to programmers and program designers, who often show distaste for paperwork.

In regards to software project development the following types of documentation can be clearly identified:

1. Written reports that mark the conclusion of a phase of the development cycle. These documents are sometimes called the *deliverables*,

since they are often presented to the client as each development phase concludes. Typical deliverables are the feasibility study, the analysis and requirements document, and the detailed design document.

2. User manuals and training guides, which can be printed or used on-line.

3. Operations documents, more often found in large computer environments, include run-time schedules, input and output forms and media, delivery, routing, and distribution charts, data file specifications, update schedules, recovery procedures, and security controls.

4. The project scrapbook is used to collect memos, schedules, meeting minutes, and other communications generated during the project.

1.4.1 Objections and Excuses

Software projects are developed by programmers who often resent having to spend time in what some consider useless paperwork. Even when the project managers are aware of the importance of documentation, they often have to overcome considerable resistance on the part of their technical staff. The following are excuses used to rationalize the documentation aversion:

1. Our time is better spent in programming and other technical matters than in useless paperwork.

2. If we attempt to document this activity now, the results will shortly be outdated. Therefore it is preferable to wait until the project is closer to its completion before we start on the documentation.

3. People do not read manuals, so why bother writing them.

4. We are programmers and designers, not writers. We should hire technical writers to do the manuals and paperwork.

1.4.2 Advantages of Good Documentation

The reasons why the excuses mentioned in the previous section are effective is that they have some truth value. It is only by realizing that documentation is one of the fundamental results of a development project, and that it should never be an afterthought at project conclusion time, that we can invalidate these arguments. The project manager must be conscious of the fact that program documentation is at least as important as any other technical phase of development. The following are undeniable advantages of concurrently documenting the development project:

1. A well-documented project is better able to resist personnel changes since new programmers can catch up by studying the project documents.

2. Documentation can serve as a management tool by requiring that each development stage conclude in a document, which must be approved before the next stage can proceed.

3. Concurrent documentation establishes a project history and can serve, among other things, as a progress report. Documents can be used as scheduling landmarks and therefore serve to measure and evaluate project progress.

The most important principle of project documentation is that of concurrency. Documentation must be a substantial part of the development effort and must take place simultaneously with each development phase. At the same time, documentation is often the development activity most easily postponed or even sacrificed. When time is running short it is tempting to defer documentation. At this point the project manager must be aware that when documentation loses its concurrency it also loses a great portion of its usefulness.

Chapter 2

System Description and Specification

2.0 System Analysis Phase

The engineer's first task is understanding the system, the second one is specifying it, and the third one is building it. Analysis must precede specification since it is impossible to define or describe what is unknown. Specification must precede construction, since we cannot build what has not been defined. The first two tasks (understanding and defining the system) can be quite challenging in the software development field, particularly regarding small- to medium-size projects.

The system analysis phase refers to the evaluation of an existing system. Therefore it may be arguable that this phase can be skipped when implementing a system which has no predecessor. In any case, we should not assume that the analysis phase can be circumvented simply because a system has been judged obsolete or because a decision has already been reached regarding its replacement. Outdated, obsolete, and even totally unsuitable systems may contain information that is necessary or convenient for designing and implementing a new one. Very rarely would it be advisable to completely discard an existing system without analyzing its operation, performance, and implementation characteristics. At the same time, the feasibility of a new system must often be determined independently of the one being replaced. In fact, a system's feasibility should be evaluated even when it has no predecessor.

2.0.1 The System Analyst

In the information systems world the specialist attempting to understand and define a software system is usually called the *system analyst*. In computer science-oriented environments this person is often referred to as a *systems engineer*. Other terms used to describe this computer professional are programmer analyst, systems designer, systems consultant, information system analyst, and information system engineer.

Under whatever name, the systems analyst's job description is usually quite different from that of a programmer. While the responsibility of a programmer ends with the computer program, the analyst's duties extend into management and administration. Typically the analyst is responsible for equipment, procedures, and databases. Furthermore, the system analyst is usually in charge of the software development team. Therefore, the analyst's job requires management skills in addition to technical competence. Oral and written communications skills are often necessary since the analyst usually has to perform presentations to clients, lead specifications discussions, and oversee the generation of multiple documents and reports.

Programming and system-building projects are usually directed by a lead or principal analyst, who may take on the responsibility of managing and overseeing the activities of a team of analysts, programmers, program designers, software testers, and documentation specialists. The ideal profile for the principal system analyst is that of an experienced programmer and program designer (preferably holding a graduate degree in computer science or information systems) who has experience and training in business. In addition, the lead analyst should be a person who has successfully directed the analysis and development of software or systems projects of comparable complexity. The job description includes gathering and analyzing data, executing feasibility studies of development projects, designing, developing, installing, and operating computer systems, and performing presentations, recommendations, and technical specifications.

However, the smaller software project can rarely count on the services of an ideally-qualified lead analyst. Quite often a person with less-than-optimal skills is appointed to the task. In this respect it is important for the project directors to realize that it is the lead system analyst, or project manager, who should be the most highly qualified member of the development team. One common mistake is to think of the principal analyst as a chore that can be undertaken by a professional administrator with little or no technical knowledge. Another is to judge that the personnel with higher technical qualifications are best employed as programmers or program designers. Experience shows that appointing someone who is not the most highly qualified and technically competent member of the development team to the task of lead system analyst is an invitation to disaster.

Although the lead system analyst often wears many hats, the most necessary skills for this job are technical ones. A competent programmer and designer can be coached or supported in administrative and business functions and helped regarding communication skills. But it would be indeed astonishing that a person without the necessary technical skills could analyze, specify, and direct a systems development project.

2.0.2 Analysis and Project Context

The conventional treatment of systems analysis, as found in most current text and reference books, assumes that a typical project consists of developing a commercial system to be implemented in a particular business enterprise. In this context the systems analysis phase consists of evaluating and describing the existing system and its *bottom line* is determining whether the new system will be a realistic and profitable venture. This business system orientation is typical of computer information systems and management information systems programs as taught in many of our universities. On the other hand, the software engineering textbooks (sometimes considered as the counterpart of systems analysis in a computer science curricula) view the analysis phase more from a systems modeling point and usually stress the requirements analysis element in this development phase.

In other words, the term systems analysis has different connotations when seen from the information systems viewpoint than when seen from a computer science perspective. Furthermore, sometimes neither perspective exactly suits the problem at hand. For example, to assume that a typical systems development project consists of replacing an outdated business payroll program (information systems viewpoint) or designing a new, more efficient operating system (computer science viewpoint) leaves out many other real-life scenarios. For example, a development project could be an experimental, scientific, or research enterprise for which there is no precedent and in which profit is not a factor. Or it may consist of creating a software product that will be marketed to the public, such as a word processor application, a computer game, or a toolkit for performing engineering calculations. In either case, many of the systems analysis operations and details, as described in books on systems analysis and design or on software engineering, are not pertinent.

Another conceptualization that can vary with project context relates to the components of a computer system. Normally we think of a computer system as an integration of hardware and software elements. Therefore systems engineering consists both of hardware systems and software systems engineering. Therefore, the systems analysis phase embodies an investigation and specification of the hardware and the software subsystems. In reality it often happens that either the hardware or the software elements of a computer system take on a disproportionate importance in a particular project. For instance, in a project consisting of developing a computer program to be marketed as a product to the user community, the hardware engineering element becomes much less important than the software engineering ingredient. Under different circumstances the relative importance of hardware and software elements could be reversed.

Consequently, the details of the systems analysis phase often depend on project context. What is applicable and pertinent in a typical business development scenario, or in a technical development setting, may have to be modified to suit a particular case. Two elements of this phase are generally crucial to project success: the feasibility study and the project requirements analysis. Each of these activities is discussed in the following sections.

2.1 The Feasibility Study

Often a software development project starts with a sketchy and tentative idea whose practicality has not been yet determined. Other projects are initially well defined and enjoy the presumption of being suitable and justified. In the first case the systems analyst must begin work by performing a technical study that will determine if the project is feasible or not. According to Pressman, given unlimited time and resources, all projects are feasible. But in the real world resources are limited and often a project's feasibility is equated with the economic benefits that can be expected from its completion. This excludes systems for national defense, investigative and research projects, or any development endeavor in which financial returns are not a critical consideration.

In most cases the first project activity is called the feasibility or preliminary study. It can be broken down into the following categories:

1. Technical feasibility is an evaluation that determines if the proposed system is technologically possible. Intended functions, performance, and operational constraints determine the project's technical feasibility.

2. Economic feasibility is an evaluation of the monetary cost in terms of human and material resources that must be invested in its development, compared with the possible financial benefits and other advantages which can be realistically anticipated from the project's completion.

3. Legal feasibility is an evaluation of the legal violations and liabilities that could result from the system's development.

Before the feasibility study phase begins, intermediate and high-level management (often in consultation with the lead analyst) must determine if the effort will be advantageous and how much time and resources will be invested in this phase. It is difficult to define arbitrary rules in this respect since the convenience of a feasibility study as well as the time and human resources devoted to it are frequently determined by financial and practical considerations. It is reasonable to expect that a minor development project, anticipated to generate large revenues and requiring a relatively small investment, will often be undertaken with a less rigorous feasibility study than a major project involving greater complexity and uncertainty.

Two business management techniques are often used in the feasibility study phase of a system analysis: risk analysis and cost-benefits analysis. By means of risk analysis we attempt to establish the dangers associated with the project and to define the points at which it is preferable to cancel the project than to continue it. By means of cost-benefit analysis we attempt to measure the gains that will result from developing the system and the expenses associated with it. A feasible project is one in which the risks and costs are acceptable in consideration of its expected benefits.

Some books on systems analysis and design propose that risk analysis and cost-benefits analysis are activities that precede the main system analysis effort. Therefore, they should be considered as parts of a phase sometimes called the preliminary analysis. The rationale for this approach is that if a project is judged to be not feasible or financially not justifiable, then no further analysis or design effort is necessary. This is consistent with the accepted definition of risk analysis as a technique that serves to ascertain a project's technical feasibility, and cost-benefits analysis as a method to determine the project's economic feasibility. In reality, the technical and economic feasibility of many projects are taken for granted. In these cases risk analysis and cost-benefit analysis become either a formality, or as a justification of the original assumptions. The analyst should keep in mind that loss of objectivity in risk analysis or cost-benefit analysis renders these activities virtually useless.

A unique problem-set of the smaller-size software project is that technically qualified personnel for performing feasibility studies and cost-benefit analysis are often not available. Therefore, linking the feasibility study to risk analysis and cost-benefit analysis techniques may result in no feasibility study being performed. Since in most system development projects it is important that some form of feasibility study be executed, to the highest degree of rigor that circumstances permit, then it is preferable to consider risk analysis and cost-benefit analysis as alternative phases. The project feasibility flowchart in Figure 2.1 illustrates this view.

A word of caution regarding the feasibility study relates to the fact that those performing it may have a vested interest in the results. For example, we may suspect that the feasibility study could turn into a self-fulfilling prophesy if it is performed by a software company that is likely to be the eventual project developer. In such cases it may be advisable to contract an independent consultant to either perform or evaluate the feasibility study, thus assuring the objectivity of the results.

2.1.1 Risk Analysis

One of the factors considered in the feasibility study is the project's risk. For example, a large project, with a great potential for financial gain, could be a big risk if it could lead to a costly lawsuit. In this case a detailed analysis of this risk factor is indicated. By the same token, a small project, with questionable technical and economic feasibility,

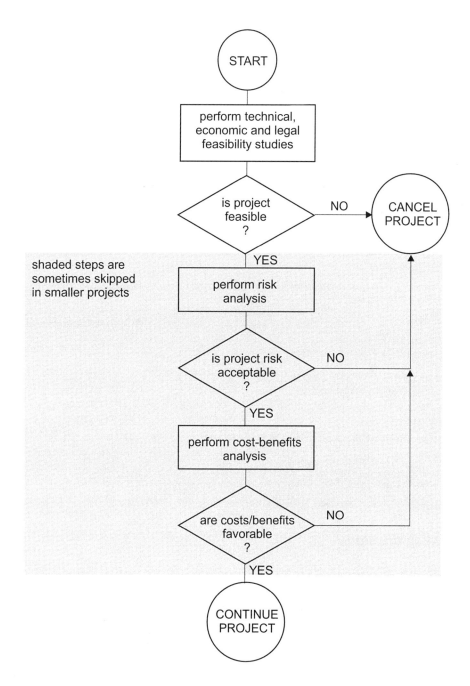

Figure 2.1 *Project Feasibility Flowchart*

could be a desirable risk if its successful completion represents a substantial gain. In this case the potential for gain may make it acceptable to undertake the project even if the feasibility study has determined that the possibilities for its completion are doubtful. In other words, the project is judged to be a good gamble.

Risk analysis is usually associated with the following activities:

1. risk identification

2. risk estimation

3. risk assessment

4. risk management

We discuss each of these risk-related operations separately.

Risk Identification

Consists of categorizing risk into particular fields. In this sense *project risk* relates to budget, schedule, and staffing problems that may impact development. In this sense project type and complexity may pose additional risk factors. *Technical risk* is related to the possibility of encountering difficulties that were not initially anticipated. For example, an unexpected development in the field may make a project technically obsolete. *Business risk*, perhaps the most deluding one, relates to market changes, company strategy changes, sale difficulties, loss of management support, and loss of budgetary support.

Risk Estimation

In this phase of risk analysis we attempt to rate the likelihood and consequences of each risk. The first step is to establish the risk probability, the second one to describe the consequences of the risk, the third one to estimate the risk's impact on the project, and finally to determine the accuracy of the risk estimate itself. These four items can be quantified with a "yes" or "no" answer, but a better approach is to establish a probability rating for risk likelihood, consequence, impact, and projection accuracy. Historical data collected by the developers can often serve to quantify some of the project risks. As a general rule we can assume that the higher the probability of occurrence and impact of a risk the more concern that it should generate.

Risk Assessment

Is based on the aforementioned impact and probability of occurrence of a risk, as determined during the risk estimation phase. The accuracy of the risk estimate is also a factor that must be taken into account. The first task at this stage is the establishment of acceptable risk levels for the project's critical activities. For system development projects three typical critical activities are cost, schedule, and performance. A degradation of one or more of these factors will determine the project's termination. Risk analysts talk about a *referent point* (or break point) at which the decision to terminate or continue a project is equally acceptable. Since risk analysis is not an exact science, the break point can better be visualized as a *break area*.

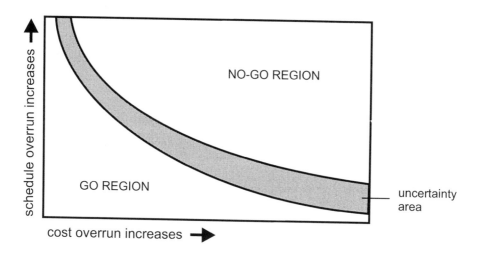

Figure 2.2 *Referent Level in Risk Assessment*

Figure 2.2 shows the effects of cost and schedule overruns on a software project. The dark region bound by the curves (the uncertainty or break area) represents the region in which the decisions to stop or continue the project are approximately of equal weight. Below this area is the go region, in which the project continues without question.

The area above the curve (no-go region) represents conditions that determine the cancellation of the project. Note that in Figure 2.2 we have considered only two project risks; often there are others that can influence the decision to terminate. The reader should not assign any meaning to the particular shape of the curve in Figure 2.2. The fact that it is not uniform simply indicates that the uncertainty factor in risk assessment may not be a smooth function.

The following steps are usually followed during the risk assessment process:

1. The referent level is defined for each significant risk in the project.

2. The relationship between the risk, its likelihood, and its impact on the project is established for each referent level.

3. The termination region and the uncertainty area are defined.

4. An attempt is made to anticipate how a compound risk will affect the referent level for each participating risk.

Risk Management

Once the elements of risk description, likelihood, and impact have been established for each project risk, they can be used to minimize the particular risk or its effects. For example, assume that the analysis of historical data and the risk estimation process determine that for the particular project there is a substantial risk of schedule overruns due to low programmer productivity. Knowing this, management can attempt to locate alternative manpower sources which could be tapped if the identified risk is realized. Or perhaps steps can be taken to improve productivity by identifying the causes of low programmer output.

Risk management, in itself, can become costly and time-consuming. Scores of risks can be identified in a large development project. Each risk may be associated with several risk management measures. Keeping track of risks and remedies can become a major project in itself. Therefore, managers and directors must sometimes perform cost-benefit analysis of the risk management activities to determine how it will impact project cost. The Pareto principle, sometimes called the 80/20 rule, states that 80 percent of project failures are related to 20 percent of identified risks. The risk analysis phase should help recognize this critical 20 percent, and eliminate the less significant risks from the risk management plan.

2.1.2 Risk Analysis in a Smaller Project

Risk analysis is a specialty field on which numerous monographs and textbooks have been published. A frivolous or careless attempt at risk analysis and management is often counterproductive. In the smaller software project it is common that specialized personnel are unavailable to perform accurate risk analysis. Furthermore, even if technically qualified personnel could be found, it is doubtful that a formal risk investigation would be economically justified. Consequently, most smaller projects take place with no real risk analysis and without a risk management plan. In this case the feasibility study or other project documents should clearly state that risk analysis and risk management efforts have not been performed, the reasons why this step was skipped, and the dangers that can result from the omission.

Perhaps a greater danger than the total omission of a formal risk analysis is its trivialization. When risk analysis has been performed superficially, with little rigor, and by untrained personnel, the most likely results are the identification of unreal risks, or, worse, a false feeling of confidence resulting from a plan that has failed to identify the real perils associated with the project. If the risk analysis and management have been performed with less-than-adequate resources then the resulting low accuracy of the risk projection should be clearly noted in the project documentation. Occasionally, it may be considered valid to attempt some form of perfunctory risk analysis for the purpose of gaining experience in this field or for experimenting with a specific methodology. This should also be clearly noted so that management does not place undue confidence in the resulting plan.

Table 2.1 is a variation of the risk management and monitoring plan as presented by Charette. We have simplified the plan to include only those elements that, in our judgment, should never be omitted.

Most computer systems development projects demand a tangible economic benefit. This does not mean that every system must generate a profit, but rather that the expected benefits must justify the cost. Exceptions to this rule are systems that are legally mandated or those whose purpose is beyond economic analysis, as could be the case with a project for national defense, or a scientific or academic experiment. Under normal circumstances the system's economic justification is the most important result of the feasibility study since it is a critical factor in deciding project support.

Table 2.1 *Simplification of a Risk Management Outline*

I. Introduction

II. Risk Analysis

  1. Risk Identification

    a. Risk Survey

    b. Risk Item Checklist

  2. Risk Estimation

    a. Probability of Risk

    b. Consequence of Risk

    c. Estimation Error

  3. Risk Evaluation

    a. Evaluation of Risk Analysis Methods

    b. Evaluation of Risk Referents

    c. Evaluation of Results

III. Risk Management

  1. Recommendations

  2. Options for Risk Aversion

  3. Risk Monitoring Procedures

2.1.3 Cost-Benefit Analysis

Cost-benefit analysis is a standard business evaluation instrument, but not all project results can be exactly measured in dollars and cents. Some systems bring about less tangible benefits that relate to factors such as the company's long-term plans, a higher quality of product or services, or increased employee morale. It could be a taxing task to attempt to attach a dollar value to some of the less concrete project benefits. It is often preferable to include a category of intangible benefits in the cost-benefit analysis document rather than to attempt to quantify these gains.

The reference point for evaluating the benefits of a new system is usually the existing system. For example, a manufacturer called Acme Corporation plans to upgrade its present inventory management system with a new one based on the use of bar codes to identify products in stock. The new system requires an investment of $500,000 in software and computer equipment but has the following advantages:

1. The number of employees used in inventory management functions will be reduced by 4. This will bring about a saving of $90,000 per year.

2. The flow of materials and supplies to the assembly line will be improved, with an estimated reduction in lost time of 200 work hours per month. Since an hour of lost time at the assembly line costs the company $12, this will bring about a saving of $2400 per month.

3. The better control of stocks will allow the company to reduce the size of its inventory. The smaller investment and the reduction in warehousing costs is estimated to bring the company a saving of $20,000 per year.

In this case the cost-benefit analysis could appear as follows:

```
Acme Corporation
Cost-benefit analysis for new inventory management system
over a 5-year period

1. COST
     a. Computer and peripherals .......................... $300,000
     b. Software .........................................   110,000
     c. Installation and technical support ...............    90,000
                                                            =========
                                total investment ..........$500,000
2. BENEFITS
     a. Personnel reductions .......... $450,000
     b. Reductions in down time .......  144,000
     c. Savings in inventory costs ....  100,000
                                        ========
            total savings .............. $694,000
            Balance ....................$194,000
```

In the case of Acme Corporation the benefits over a five-year period are relatively modest. Therefore it is likely that Acme's higher management would like to see a more detailed and accurate analysis before committing to a major overhaul of the company's existing system. On the other hand, some systems can be economically justified clearly and definitively. Under different circumstances the development and implementation of a computerized inventory control would bring about savings that leave no doubt regarding the project's benefits, even without considering less tangible factors such as improvements in distribution operations.

2.2 Requirements Analysis and Specification

Once the feasibility of a proposed system has been established, the next task that the analyst must undertake is defining the system's requirements. Requirements analysis, or requirements engineering as it is sometimes called, has been considered a critical phase of computer systems development since the original conception of an engineering methodology for software development. The fundamental notion consists of generating an unambiguous and consistent specification that describes the essential functions of the proposed system. In other words, the specifications phase of the system development process must describe *what* the system is to do. *How* it is to do it is addressed during the design phase.

2.2.1 The Requirements Analysis Phase

Before the systems requirements can be specified, the interface between the system and the real world must be analyzed. Based on this interface, a set of specifications of the software requirements is developed. The documents containing the program specification play a decisive role during the entire development process. For example, the development of a software system to control the operation of a probe vehicle via remote to operate on the surface of the planet Mars should be based on a detailed analysis of the interface requirements. In this case the following elements may be considered critical:

1. What information is returned by the sensors on the Mars probe.

2. What vehicle operation controls installed on the probe are governed by the software.

3. What is the time lapse between perception by the probe's sensors and reception by the earth system.

4. What is the time lapse between a command issued by the earth system and its execution by the probe.

The analysis of this data helps determine the operational specification of the system. In this case the delay in receiving information and transmitting commands may require that upon sensing certain types of obstacles, the vehicle come to a stop until a command signal is received. In this case the requirements analysis phase serves to define the system specifications.

Concrete system specification guidelines result from the requirements analysis phase. In particular this could refer to difficulties, tradeoffs, and conflicting constraints; also from the functional and nonfunctional requirements. Functional requirements are those which are absolutely essential while the nonfunctional ones are merely desirable features. In this sense a functional requirement of the Martian probe could be that the vehicle not be damaged by obstacles in its path. A nonfunctional requirement could be that given several possible safe paths to a destination point, the software selects the one that can be traversed in the shortest time.

Customer/User Participation

An ideal scenario is that the customer, client, or eventual user of a system provides the detailed specification. In this "neat" world all the developer has to do is implement a system according to these specifications thus ensuring that the client's needs are thoroughly satisfied. In reality the customer/user often has little more than a sketchy idea of the intended system; its specification must be developed through a series of interviews, proposals, models, and revisions. Communications skills and systems analysis experience are important factors in the success of this difficult and critical phase.

The developer of systems specifications must not assume that a customer does not really know what he or she wants. It is the client's system, not the developer's. New systems often encounter considerable resistance from employees who must devote time and effort to learning its operation, often with little or no compensation. Furthermore, employees may feel threatened by a new system which could make their jobs unnecessary. The more participation that clients and users have in the systems specifications and definition the less resistance that they will present to its implementation.

If there is a single secret to being a successful analyst it is to maximize the client's participation in the specification, design, development, and implementation phases, thus making sure that the participants include those who will be the effective users of the new system. A regrettable situation is that the developer initially deals with an administrative elite, while the actual systems operators, administrators, and users do not become visible until much later in the development process.

The Virtual Customer

While in many development projects there is a clearly identifiable customer, in others the client role is not quite visible. For example, a software company developing a program that is to be marketed to the public may not have a visible client who can participate in the system's specification, design, and development phases. Another example: a research group at a university or a private firm is often confronted with the task of developing a program for which no user or client is immediately at hand.

The customer/user element plays such an important role in the development process that in these cases it may be advisable to *invent* some sort of a virtual participant to play this role. In the context of research and development, the team's director sometimes takes on this function. Or perhaps a higher level of management will play the devil's advocate for the duration. As separation of powers ensures the operation of a democracy, separation of interests between clients and developers promotes the creation of better systems. When this duality does not naturally exist, creating it fictitiously may be an option.

2.2.2 The Specifications Phase

Once the systems requirements have been determined the analyst creates a list of program specifications. These specifications serve to design, code, and test the proposed program and, eventually, validate the entire development effort; their importance can hardly be overstressed.

Since specifications are derived directly from the requirement

analysis documents, a preliminary step to composing a list of specifications is to validate the requirements analysis phase. Whatever
method or notation is used in requirements analysis, the following
goals should be achieved:

1. Information contents and flow are determined.

2. Processes are defined.

3. Systems interfaces are established.

4. Layers of abstraction are drawn and processing tasks are partitioned
   into functions.

5. A diagram of the system essentials and its implementation is made.

We can adopt varying degrees of formality and rigor in composing
the actual specifications. Many difficulties in system design and coding can be traced to imprecise specifications. The English language (in
fact, any natural language) contains terms and expressions that require interpretation. For example: the statement that a routine to calculate mathematical functions must do so with the "highest possible
degree of precision" may seem a strict specification. However, at system design and coding time the expression "the highest possible degree of precision" has to be interpreted to mean one of the following:

1. The precision of the most accurate computer in the world.

2. The precision of the most accurate machine of a certain type.

3. The highest precision that can be achieved in any high-level language.

4. The highest precision that can be achieved in a particular programming language.

5. The highest precision that can be achieved in a certain machine.

6. The highest precision that will be required by the most demanding
   user or application.

7. The highest degree of precision that will be required by the average
   user or application.

This list could be easily expanded to include many other alternatives. On the other hand, the specifications could have stated that mathematical functions will be calculated "so that the resulting error will not exceed 20 units of machine Epsilon." In this case very little interpretation is possible at design or coding time. Furthermore, the specification could later be used to validate the resulting product by performing tests that ascertain that the numerical error of the mathematical calculations is within the allowed error range.

In recent years the software engineering and programming communities have moved towards stricter and more formal methods of specification, some of which are discussed later in this section. The analyst should be wary of imprecise terms and expressions in the specification documents and should aim at describing the problems and tasks at hand in the least unambiguous terms possible.

The Software Specifications Document

The Software Specifications Document (SSD), also called the Software Requirements Specification, is the culmination and the conclusion of the system analysis. The elements always present in the SSD include the following:

1 An information description

2. A functional description

3. A list of performance requirements

4. A list of design constraints

5. A system testing parameters and a criterion for validation

The National Bureau of Standards, the IEEE, and others have proposed formats for the SSD. Table 2.2 is a simplified outline of the fundamental topics that must be visited in this document.

Headington and Riley propose a six-step program specifications plan consisting of the following parts:

1. Problem title

2. Description

Table 2.2 *Outline of the Software Specifications Document*

I.   Introduction
   1. Purpose and Scope
   2. System Overview
   3. General Description and Constraints
II. Standards and Conventions
III. Environment Elements
   1. Hardware Environment
   2. Software Environment
   3. Interfaces
IV. Software Specifications
   1. Information Flow
   2. Information Contents
   3. Functional Organization
   4. Description of Operations
   5. Description of Control Functions
   6. Description of System Behavior
   7. Database and Data Structures
V.   Testing and Validation
   1. Performance Parameters
   2. Tests and Expected Response
   3. Validation Protocol
VI. Appendices
   1. Glossary
   2. References

3. Input specifications

4. Output specifications

5. Error handling

6. Sample program execution (test suite)

Although this simplification is intended for the specification of small projects within the context of an undergraduate course in C++ programming, it does cover the fundamental elements. Even if it is not used as a model, it may be a good idea to check the actual specification against this plan.

2.3.4 Formal and Semiformal Specifications

The proposers of formal specifications methods postulate that software development will be revolutionized by describing and modeling programs using strict syntax and semantics based on a mathematical notation. The fundamentals of formal specification are in set theory and the predicate calculus. The main advantages of formal specifications are their lack of ambiguity and their consistency and completeness, thus eliminating the many possible interpretations that often result from problem descriptions in a natural language. Of these attributes, lack of ambiguity results from the use of mathematical notation and logical symbolism. Consistency can be ensured by proving mathematically that the statements in the specification can be derived from the initial facts. However, completeness is difficult to ensure even when using formal methods of specification, since program elements can be purposefully or accidentally omitted from the specification.

The original notion of applying the methods of the predicate calculus to problems in computing, and, in particular to the formal development of programs, is usually attributed to Professor Edsger W. Dijkstra (University of Texas, Austin TX, USA) who achieved considerable fame in the field of structured programming, first expressed his ideas in a book titled *A Discipline of Programming*. Professor David Gries (Cornell Univeristy, Ithaca NY, USA) and Edward Cohen have also made major contributions to this field.

One of the most interesting postulates made by the advocates of formal specifications is that once a program is mathematically described it can be coded automatically. In this manner it is claimed that formal specifications will eventually lead into automated programming, and thus, to the final solution of the software crisis.

In this book we have opted not to discuss the details of formal specifications for the following reasons:

1. So far, the viability of this method has been proven only for rather small programs dealing with problems of a specific and limited nature.

2. The use of this method assumes mathematical maturity and training in formal logic. It is considered difficult to learn and use.

3. Although formal specifications, program proving, and automated coding have gained considerable ground in recent years, these methods are not yet established in the systems analysis and programming mainstream. Many still consider them more an academic refinement than a practical procedure.

2.2.4 Assertions Notation

Although formal specification methods have not yet achieved the status of a practical methodology applicable in general systems analysis and programming, there is little doubt that reducing the ambiguity and inconsistency of natural languages is a desirable achievement in the software specifications stage. Some current authors of programming textbooks (including Headington and Riley) have adopted a method of program documentation which can also serve as a model for semiformal specifications. This technique, sometimes referred to as an *assertion* notation, consists of a specific style of comments that are inserted into the code so as to define the state of computation. Although assertions were originally proposed as a code documentation technique, the notation can also be used as a semiformal method of specification during the analysis phase. The following types of assertion are described:

ASSERT

This comment header describes the state of computation at a particular point in the code. Before this notation was suggested, some programmers inserted comments in their code with headers such as **AT THIS POINT:** that performed a functionally equivalent purpose. The idea of the **ASSERT:** header is to state what is certainly known about variables and other program objects so that this information can be used in designing and testing the code that follows.

Consider the following C++ example: a function called **Power()** is implemented so that it returns a float, the result of raising a float-type base to an integer power. The resulting code could be documented as follows:

```
Power(base, index);
// ASSERT:
//        Power() == base raised to index
//        (variables base and index are unchanged by call)
```

Certain symbols and terms are often used in the context of assertions. For example, the term **Assigned** is used to represent variables and constants initialized to a value. This excludes the possibility of these elements containing "garbage." In C++ assertions the symbols **&&** are often used to represent logical AND, while the symbol **||** represents logical OR regarding the terms of the assertion. The symbol **==** is used to document a specific value and the symbol **??** indicates that the value is unknown or undeterminable at the time. Finally, the symbol —, or the word **Implies**, is sometimes used to represent logical implication. The programmer should also feel free to use other symbols and terms from mathematics, logic, or from the project's specific context, as long as they are clear, unambiguous, and consistent.

INV

This comment header represents a loop invariant. It is an assertion which is used to describe a state of computation at a certain point within a loop. The intention of the loop invariant is to document the fundamental tasks to be performed by the loop. Since the invariant is inserted inside the loop body, its assertion must be true before the body executes, during every loop iteration, and immediately after the loop body has executed for the last time. The following example in C++ is a loop to initialize to zero all the elements of an array of integers.

```
// ASSERT:
//        All set1[0 .. sizeof (Set1)/ sizeof (int)] == ??
for (int i = 0, i <= (sizeof (Set1) / sizeof (int)), i++)
                        // INV:
                        //   0 <=i <= elements in array
Set1[]
     set1(i) = 0;
// ASSERT:
//        All set1[0 .. sizeof (Set1) / sizeof *int)] == 0
```

In this example the number of elements in an array is determined at compile time using the C++ **sizeof** operator. The expression:

sizeof Set1

returns the number of bytes in array **Set1**. This value is divided by the number of bytes in the array data type to determine the number of elements. Although this way of determining the number of elements in an array is generally valid in C++, it should be used with caution since the calculation is only permissible if the array is visible to **sizeof** at the particular location in the code where it is used. The loop invariant states that at this point in the loop body the index to the array (variable **i**) is in the range 0 to number of array elements, which can be deduced from the loop statement.

PRE and POST

These comment headers are assertions associated with subroutines. In C++ they are used to establish the conditions that are expected at the entry and exit points of a function. Before the assertion notation was proposed some programmers used the terms **ON ENTRY:** and **ON EXIT:**.

The **PRE:** assertion describes the elements (usually variables and constants) that must be supplied by the caller and the **POST:** assertion describes the state of computation at the moment the function concludes its execution. Thus, the **PRE:** and **POST:** conditions represent the terms of a contract between caller and function, stating that if the caller ensures that the **PRE:** assertion is true at call time, the function guarantees that the **POST:** assertion is satisfied at return time. For example, the following function named **Swap()** exchanges the values in two integer variables.

```
void Swap( int& var1, int& var2)
// PRE:    Assigned var1 && var2
// POST:   var1 == var2 && var2 == var1
{
  int temp = var1;
  var1 = var2;
  var 2 = temp;
  return;

}
```

FCTVAL

This assertion is also used in the context of subroutines to indicate the returned value. In C++ **FCTVAL** represents the value returned by a function and associated with the function name. Therefore it should not be used to represent variables modified by the function. For example, the following trivial function returns the average of three real numbers passed by the caller.

```
float Avrg( float num1, float num2, float num3)
// PRE:    Assigned num1 && num2 && num3
//                   num1 + num2 + num3
// POST:   FCTVAL == ----------
//                          3
{
   return ((num1 + num2 + num3) / 3));

}
```

2.3 Tools for Process and Data Modeling

Technical methodologies for system development propose that the documents that result from the analysis phase serve as a base for the design phase. Therefore the more detailed, articulate, and clear the analysis documents, the more useful they will be in program design. One way to accomplish this is through the use of modeling tools that allow representing the essence of a system, usually in graphical terms. Many such tools have been proposed over the years and two have achieved widespread acceptance, namely, data flow diagrams and entity-relationship diagrams.

Data flow diagrams originated in, and are often associated with, structured analysis. Entity-relationship diagrams are linked with data base systems and with object-oriented methods. Nevertheless, we believe that either method is useful independently of the context or analysis school in which it originated. In fact, data flow diagrams and entity-relationship diagrams have been used in modeling processes and data flow in both the structured analysis and the object-oriented paradigms.

System modeling can be undertaken using varying degrees of abstraction. One type of model, sometimes called a physical or implementation model, addresses the technical details as well as the system's essence. Program flowcharts are often considered as an implementation modeling tool since a flowchart defines *how* a particular process can be actually coded. Essential or conceptual models, on the other hand, are implementation independent. Their purpose is to depict *what* a system must do without addressing the issue of *how* it must do it.

Although implementation models are useful in documenting and explaining existing systems, it is a general consensus among system analysis that conceptual models are to be preferred in the analysis phase. The following arguments are often listed in favor of conceptual models:

1. Some incorrect solutions that result from implementation-dependent models can be attributed to bias or ignorance on the part of the designers. A conceptual model, on the other hand, fosters creativity and promotes an independent and fresh approach to the problem's solution.

2. Excessive concern with implementation details at system specification and analysis time takes our attention away from the fundamentals. This often leads to missing basic requirements in the specification.

3. Implementation-dependent models require a technical jargon that often constitutes a communications barrier between clients and developers.

The target of this modeling effort can be either an existing or a proposed system. In this respect we should keep in mind that the fundamental purpose of modeling an existing system is to learn from it. The learning experience can be boiled down to avoiding defects and taking advantage of desirable features.

2.3.1 Data Flow Diagrams

In his work on structured analysis DeMarco suggests that one of the additions required for the analysis phase is a graphical notation to model information flow. He then proceeds to create some of the essential graphical symbols and suggests a heuristic to be used with these symbols. A few years later Gane and Sarson refined this notation calling it a *data flow diagram* or DDF.

A data flow diagram is a process modeling tool that graphically depicts the course of data thorough a system and the processing operations performed on this data. Figure 2.3 shows the basic symbols and notation used in data flow diagrams.

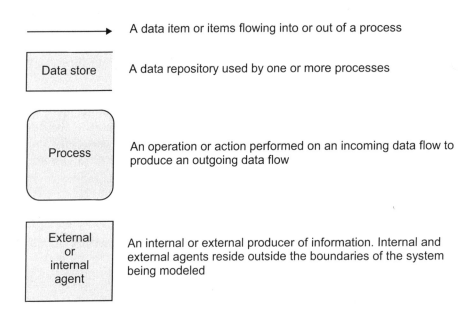

A data item or items flowing into or out of a process

A data repository used by one or more processes

An operation or action performed on an incoming data flow to produce an outgoing data flow

An internal or external producer of information. Internal and external agents reside outside the boundaries of the system being modeled

Figure 2.3 *Gane and Sarson Symbols for Data Flow Diagrams*

One variation often used in the Gane and Sarson notation is to represent processes by means of circles (sometimes called bubbles). A valid justification of this alternative is that circles are easier to draw than rounded rectangles.

Processes are the core operation depicted in data flow diagrams. A process is often described as an action performed on incoming data in order to transform it. In this sense a process can be performed by a person, by a robot, or by software. Processes are usually labeled with action verbs, such as Pay, Deposit, or Transform, followed by a clause that describes the nature of the work performed. However, on higher level DFDs we sometimes see a general process described by a noun or noun phrase, such as accounting system, or image enhancement process. Routing processes that perform no operation on the data are usually omitted in essential DFDs. The operations performed by processes can be summarized as follows:

1. Perform computations or calculations

2. Make a decision

3. Modify a data flow by splitting, combining, filtering, or summarizing its original components

Internal or external agents or entities reside outside the system's boundaries. They provide input and output into the system. In this sense they are often viewed as either sources or destinations. An agent is external if it is physically outside the system, for example, a customer or a supplier. Internal agents are located within the organization, but are logically outside of the system's scope. For example, another department within the company can be considered as an internal agent.

It is possible to vary the level of abstraction and magnification of details in a DFD. Some authors propose the designation of specific abstraction levels. In this sense a level 0 DFD, called a *fundamental system model*, consists of a single process bubble which represents the entire software system. A level I DFD could depict five or six processes which are included in the single process represented in the level 0 bubble. Although the notion that several DFDs can be used to represent different levels of abstraction is useful, the requirement that a specific number of processes be associated with each level could be too restrictive. Figure 2.4 shows an initial level of detail for representing a satellite imaging system.

Notice that in Figure 2.4 the process bubble has been refined with a header label that adds information regarding the process. In this case the header refers to *who* is to perform the process. Also notice that the processes are represented by noun phrases, which is consistent with the general nature of the diagram. Although this initial model provides some fundamental information about the system, it is missing many important details. For example, one satellite may be equipped with several sensing devices that generate different types of image data, each one requiring unique processing operations. Or a particular satellite may produce images that are secret; therefore, they should be tagged as such so that the delivery system does not make

them available to unqualified customers. Figure 2.5 shows a second
level refinement of the image processing system

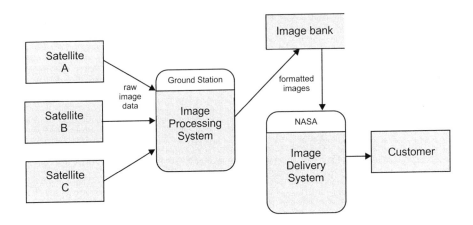

Figure 2.4 *Initial Model of a Satellite Imaging System*

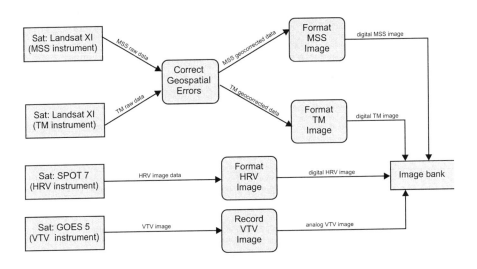

Figure 2.5 *Refined Model of the Satellite Image Processing System*

The level of detail shown by the DDF in Figure 2.5 is much greater than that in Figure 2.4. From the refined model we can actually identify the various instruments on board the satellites and the operations that are performed on the image data produced by each instrument. However, the actual processing details are still omitted from the diagram, which are best postponed until the system design and implementation phases. Note that in Figure 2.5 the process names **correct**, **format**, and **record** are used as verbs, consistent with the greater level of detail shown by this model. Note that the names of satellites, instruments, and image formats do not exactly correspond to real ones.

Event Modeling

Many types of systems can be accurately represented by modeling data flow, but some cannot. For example, a burglar alarm system is event driven, as is the case with many real-time systems. First, Ward and Mellor, and later Hatley and Pribhai, introduced variations of the data flow diagram which are suitable for representing real-time systems or for the event-driven elements of conventional systems. The Ward and Mellor extensions to DFD symbols are shown in Figure 2.6.

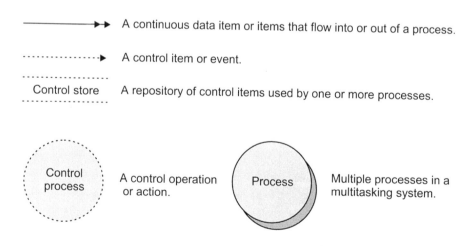

Figure 2.6 *Ward and Mellor Extensions to Data Flow Diagrams*

The resulting model, called a *control flow diagram* or CFD, includes the symbols and functions of a conventional DFD plus others that allow the representation of control processes and continuous data flows required for modeling real-time systems. Equipped with this tool we are now able to model systems in which there is a combination of data and control elements. For example, a burglar alarm system as installed in a home or business includes a conventional data flow component as well as a control flow element. In this case the conventional data flow consists of user operations, such as activating and deactivating the system and installing or changing the password. The control flow elements are the signals emitted by sensors in windows and doors and the alarm mechanism that is triggered by these sensors. Figure 2.7 represents a CFD of a burglar alarm system.

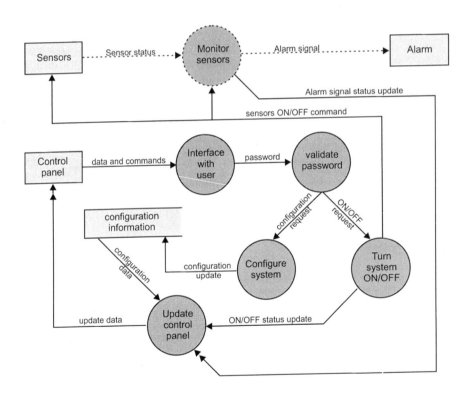

Figure 2.7 *Control Flow Diagram of a Burglar Alarm System*

In depicting the burglar alarm scheme of Figure 2.7 we have merged the Gane and Sarson symbol set of conventional DFDs with the extensions proposed by Ward and Mellor. By combining both symbol sets in a control flow diagram we are able to model a system that contains both conventional data flow and real-time elements. Notice that the sensors and the alarm mechanism are a real-time component, since the status of the sensing devices must be monitored continuously. The control panel and user interface, on the other hand, are activated by a user request and do not require continuous data flow. However, the on-demand and real-time elements sometimes interact. For example, when the system is turned on or off the corresponding signals must be sent to the control panel as well as to the sensors and sensor control logic. Another interaction between subsystems results from the fact that the sensor status is displayed on the control panel. Therefore the sensor monitoring logic sends a continuous signal (double-headed arrow) to the update control panel process so that the sensor status is displayed in real time.

2.3.2 Entity-Relationship Diagrams

Currently the most used tool in data modeling is the entity-relationship (E-R) diagram. This notation, first described in the early 1980s by Martin and later modified by Chen and Ross, is closely related to the entity-relationship model used in database design. E-R diagram symbols have been progressively refined and extended so that the method can be used to represent even the most minute details of the schema of a relational database. However, in the context of general system analysis we will restrict our discussion to the fundamental elements of the model.

Since one of the fundamental operations of most computer systems is to manipulate and store data, data modeling is often a required step in the system analysis phase. E-R diagrams are often associated with database design; however, their fundamental purpose is the general representation of data objects and their relationship. Therefore the technique is quite suitable to data analysis and modeling in any context. Furthermore, E-R notation can be readily used to represent objects and object-type hierarchies, which makes this technique useful in object-oriented analysis.

The entity-relationship model is quite easy to understand. An entity, or entity type, is a "thing" in the real world. It may be a person or a real or a conceptual object. For example, an individual, a house, an automobile, a department of a company, and a college course are all entity types. Each entity type is associated with attributes that describe it and apply to it. For example, the entity type *company employee* has the attribute's name, address, job title, salary, and social security number; while the entity type *college course* has attribute's name, number, credits, and class times. Notice that the entity *employee* is physical, while the entity *college course* is abstract or conceptual.

The entity-relationship model also includes relationships. A relationship is defined as an association between entities. In this sense we can say that the entity types *employee* and *department* are associated by the relationship *works for* since in the database schema every employee works for a department. By the same token we can say that the *works on* relationship associates an employee with a project, thus associating the entity types *employee* and *project*. Figure 2.8 shows the elementary symbols used in E-R diagrams.

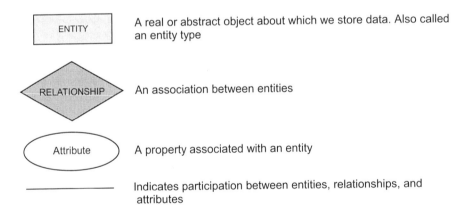

Figure 2.8 *Symbols Used in Entity-Relationship Diagrams*

As shown in Figure 2.8, it is conventional practice to type entity and relationships in uppercase letters while attribute names have initial caps. Singular nouns are usually selected for entity types, and verbs for relationships. Attributes are also nouns that describe the characteristics of an entity type. An entity type usually has a *key attribute* which is unique and distinct for the entity. For example, the social security number would be a key attribute of the entity type employee, since no two employees can have the same social security number. By the same token, job title and salary would not be key attributes since several employees could share this characteristic. Notice that while some entities can have more than one key attribute, others have none. An entity type with no key attribute is sometimes called a *weak entity*. Key attributes are usually underlined in the E-R diagram.

In regards to relationships we can distinguish two degrees of participation: total and partial. For example, if the schema requires that every employee work for a department, then the *works for* relationship has a total participation. Otherwise, the degree of participation is a partial one. *Cardinality constraints* refer to the number of instances in which an entity can participate. In this sense we can say that the *works for* relationship for the types DEPARTMENT:EMPLOYEE has a cardinality ratio of 1:N; in this case an employee works for only one department but a department can have more than one employee. Figure 2.9 shows an entity-relationship diagram for a small company schema.

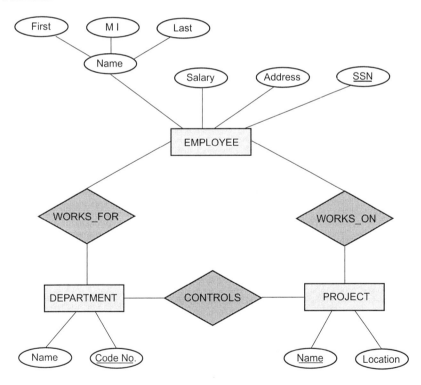

Figure 2.9 *Entity-Relationship Diagram for a Company*

The diagrams are read left to right or top to bottom. This convention is important: for example, when the diagram in Figure 2.9 is read left to right it is the department that controls the project, not vice versa.

PART II

Object Orientation

Chapter 3

Foundations of Object-Oriented Systems

3.0 History and Chronology

Although the object-oriented approach appeared in the computing mainstream during the early 1980s, its origin dates back to the 1960s. Three concepts are associated with object-oriented systems: data abstraction, inheritance, and dynamic binding.

The first notions of data abstraction are due to Kristen Nygaard and Ole-Johan Dahl working at the Norwegian Computing Center. Nygaard and Dahl developed a computer language named SIMULA I, intended for use in simulations and operations research. A few years later SIMULA I was followed by SIMULA 67, which was actually an extension of ALGOL 60. Although SIMULA 67 had little impact on programming, its historical importance was the introduction of the *class construct*.

The basic idea of a class is a form or template that packages together data and processing routines. Note that this definition of class as a template implies that a class is a formal construct, rather than a concrete entity. The programmer creates instances of a class as they become necessary. In modern-day terminology the instances of a class are called *objects*. It is interesting to note that although SIMULA 67 actually implemented data abstraction by classes it was not until 1972 that this connection was formally recognized.

But although data abstraction is clearly an ingredient of SIMULA 67, inheritance is implemented in a limited way, and dynamic binding is altogether missing. It was Alan Kay who first described a fully operational object-oriented language. Kay's vision was that desktop computers would become very powerful machines, with megabytes of memory and execute millions of instructions per second; since these machines would be used mostly by nonprogrammers, a powerful graphical interface would have to be developed to replace the awkward teletype terminals and batch processing methods of the time. It actually took over ten years for these machines to become available.

Kay's original solution to a friendly and easy-to-use interface was an information processing system named Dynabook. Dynabook was based on the visualization of a desk in which some documents were visible and others were partially covered. By means of the keyboard a user would select documents. A touch-sensitive screen allowed moving the documents on the desk. The result was very similar to some of our present day windowing environments. Processing was to be performed by the Flex programming language which Kay had helped design and which was based on SIMULA 67. Kay eventually went to work at the Xerox Palo Alto Research Center where these ideas evolved into a mouse-controlled windowing interface and the Smalltalk programming language. Both of these notions, windows and object-oriented systems, were destined to become major forces in computing technology.

The first fully operational object-oriented programming language to become available was Smalltalk 80. The Smalltalk 80 design team at Xerox PARC was led by Adele Goldberg and the language soon became the *de facto* description of object-oriented programming. Several object-oriented languages have since been developed. Perhaps the most notable ones are Eiffel, CLOS, ADA 95, and C++. Smalltalk 80 adopted a dynamically typed approach in which there is no typing system outside the class structure. Eiffel is also a pure implementation but with static typing. The other ones are hybrid languages that use a mixture of static and dynamic typing and have type systems that extend beyond the class structures.

3.1 Object-Oriented Fundamentals

Different object-oriented languages implement the paradigm differently and to varying degrees of conceptual purity. In recent years the development and marketing of object-oriented products has become a major commercial venture. Thus, to the natural uncertainties of an elaborate and sophisticated concept, we must add the hype of commercial entrepreneurs and promoters. The resulting panorama for object-oriented methods is a confusing mixture of valid claims and unjustified praise, some of it originating in the real virtues of a new and useful model, some of it in pure mercantilism.

In the following sections we will attempt to provide the reader with a description of the fundamentals of the object-oriented approach and to point out what, in our opinion, are the strengths of this model. Because object-oriented programming languages vary in the purity of their treatment of the underlying paradigm, we have focused our description on a particular one: C++. This does not imply a judgment on the suitability of the C++ approach, but is determined by the fact that C++ programming is the central topic of this book.

3.1.1 Problem-Set and Solution-Set

A computer program, whether it be a major operating system or a small application, is a machine-code solution to a real-world problem. Therefore, at the beginning of any programming project is a problem-set that defines it and at its conclusion there is a solution-set in the form of a group of instructions that can be executed by a digital computing machine. The art and science of programming are a transit from the real-world problem-set to the machine-code solution-set. In this wide conceptualization, programming includes the phases of analysis, design, coding, and testing of a software product. Figure 3.1 graphically represents this concept.

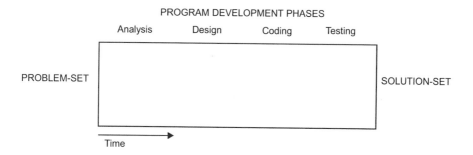

Figure 3.1 *Evolution of a Programming Project*

The smooth, white-to-black gradation in Figure 3.1 indicates that the various program development phases (analysis, design, coding, and testing) have no discrete boundaries. It is difficult to determine exactly where one phase ends and the next one begins. Furthermore, in a particular project some of the phases (except for the coding phase) could be missing altogether. In one extreme case a program is developed by coding alone, with no analysis, design, or testing. In fact, some programs are developed in this manner, sometimes successfully but more often unsuccessfully.

Many methodologies have been developed to facilitate the transition from a real world problem to a digital solution in machine instructions. Assemblers, high-level programming languages, CASE tools, analysis and design methodologies, formal specifications, and scientific methods of program testing are all efforts in this direction. Perhaps the most significant simplifications are those based on generalized abstractions. In this sense structured programming can be considered as an abstraction that focuses on the solution-set, while the object-oriented approach focuses on the problem-set. Therefore, a project engineered in terms of structured programming is based on a model of the solution set, while a project analyzed and designed using object-oriented methods closely focuses on the problem set.

There is an additional factor to be considered in this comparison of object-oriented versus structured techniques. The development of high-level, object-oriented programming languages serves to close the gap between the problem-set and the solution-set. It is the simultaneous use of object-oriented analysis, object-oriented design, and object-oriented programming that makes a smooth transition possible. In reality, although the use of a uniform model can be a considerable advantage, there is also a price to pay in terms of program performance and code size, and very much so in programming complications. In order to use a real-world model we are forced to introduce several additional levels of complexity to the coding phase.

3.1.2 Rationale of Object Orientation

The result of object-oriented methods can be summarized by stating that we have complicated the coding phase in order to simplify the analysis and design phases of program development. The defenders of the object-oriented approach make the following reasonable claims:

1. Object-oriented analysis and design methods facilitate communications with clients and users since the model does not require technical knowledge of programming.

2. Many real-world problems are easier to model in object-oriented terms than when using structured analysis and design techniques.

3. Object-oriented programming languages promote and facilitate code reuse, which eventually increases programmer productivity.

4. Object-oriented programs have internal mechanisms that make them resilient to change; therefore, they are better able to accommodate the natural volatility of the problem-domain.

A question often raised is not whether these claims are valid but whether they are worth the complications. One answer can be found in the fact that the programming community appears to be leaning in favor of the object-oriented approach.

3.2 Classes and Objects

In the context of object orientation an *object* is a conceptual entity related to the problem domain. It is an abstraction, not a thing in the real world. A fallacy found in some books is the claim that a conceptual object, in the context of the paradigm, can be considered equivalent to an object in the conventional sense. This misconception can turn into a major stumbling block to understanding object orientation. In reality the OO object is a hybrid that shares some characteristics of common objects with features of a computer construct. Instead of giving a formal definition for an object, we start with a rather simplified, and stereotyped, listing of its properties:

1. Every object belongs to an *object class*. An object cannot exist without a class that defines it. In this sense we say that an object is an instance of a class. To understand the difference between a class and an object we can visualize the class as a cookie cutter and the object as the cookie. In programming terms a class relates to a type definition and an object to variable declaration.

2. An object (and the class that contains it) is an *encapsulation* that includes data and its related processing operations. The object's data elements are called its *attributes*, and the processing operations are

called its *methods*. Attributes and methods are the class members: the attributes are the data members and the methods are the member functions.

3. The object's attributes serve to store and preserve the object's state. An object's methods are the only way of accessing its data or modifying its state. This is accomplished by sending a *message* to the object.

3.2.1 Classes and Data Abstraction

In conventional programming we often think of a data type as mere grouping. In object-oriented terms we should think in terms of both the data type and its associated operations. For example, in a certain hardware environment the type *integer* includes the whole numbers in the range +32,767 to -32,768, as well as the operations that can be performed on integers, such as addition, subtraction, multiplication, division, remainder, and comparison. In this same context we can say that a variable is an instance of a type. For example, the variables **num1** and **num2** could be regarded as instances (objects) of the integer type. In C++ we declare and initialize these variables with the statements:

```
int num1 = 12;
int num2 = 6;
```

We can now perform any of the allowed operations on the instances (declared variables) of type **int**. For example:

```
int num3 = (num1 / num2) + num2;
```

which would result in assigning the value 8 ((12/6)+6) to the newly declared variable **num3**.

What happens if we need to operate on an entity that is not defined as a data type in our language? For example, suppose we needed to manipulate several integer values so that the last value stored is the first one retrieved. This mechanism corresponds to a data structure known as a stack, but C++ does not support the stack data type.

To solve this limitation, object-oriented languages have facilities for implementing programmer-defined data types, also called *abstract data types* or *ADTs*. In some languages (such as C++) an abstract data type is implemented in terms of one or more built-in data types plus a set of allowable operations. In the case of the stack the built-in data type could be an array of integers and the operations could be called **Initialize()**, **Push()**, and **Pop()**.

In C++ the program structures used for implementing abstract data types are classes and objects. In the previous example we could define a class *stack*, with the attribute **array of int**, and the methods **Initialize()**, **Push()**, and **Pop()**. This class would serve as a template for creating as many stacks as necessary. Each instantiation of the class would be an object of type stack. This is consistent with the notion of a class being equivalent to a type, and an object to a variable.

3.2.2 Classes and Encapsulation

In object-oriented terms *encapsulation* is related to information hiding, which is a fundamental notion of the paradigm. Instead of basing a programming language on subprograms that share global data or that receive data passed by the caller, the object-oriented approach adopts the notion that data and functions (attributes and methods) are packaged together by means of the class construct. The methods that are visible to the user are called the object's interface. The fundamental mechanism of encapsulation consists of hiding the implementation details while stressing the interface. The goal is to create an abstraction that forces the programmer to think conceptually. The first golden rule of object-oriented programming, as stated by Gamma et al. is:

> *program to an interface, not to an implementation.*

In a typical class the data members are invisible to the user. In C++ this is achieved by means of the keyword **private** (called an *access specifier*). In general, class members are either **private**, **public**, or **protected**. *Public members* are visible to the client and constitute the class interface. *Private members* are visible only to the other members of the class. *Protected members* are related to inheritance, which is discussed later in this chapter. If a data member must be made accessible to the client, then it is customary to provide a function that inspects it and returns its value. In C++ the **const** keyword can also be used to preclude the possibility of an unauthorized change in the value of the variable.

3.2.3 Message Passing

In structured programming, subroutines or subprograms are accessed in various manners: by means of a jump, a call, a trap, an interrupt, or, in distributed systems, an interprocess communication. Object-oriented systems make the actual access procedure invisible by means of a mechanism called *message passing*.

One of the advantages of message passing is that it eliminates hard-coded program structures such as jump tables, cascaded **if** statements, or *case* constructs. One disadvantage of hard-coded components is that they must be updated with every program modification or change. For example, suppose a conventional graphics package with functions to draw lines, rectangles and circles. In a non-object-oriented language these operations would be executed by individual subprograms. Typically, there would be a procedure named **DrawLine()**, another one named **DrawRectangle()**, and a third one named **DrawCircle()**. Somewhere in the program a selection logic would direct execution to the corresponding procedure. In C this logic may consist of cascaded **ifs** or a **case** construct. If we wanted to extend the functionality of the graphics package by providing a new function to draw an ellipse, we would not only need to code the ellipse-drawing routine, but also to modify the selection logic so that execution would be directed to this new function as necessary, which implies changing the existing code.

The message-passing mechanism used in object-oriented systems automatically directs execution to the corresponding member function. The object-oriented approach for an equivalent graphics package would be to create classes named **Rectangle**, **Line**, and **Circle**, each with a member function named **Draw()**. When we wish to display a rectangle we send a draw message to an object of the class rectangle, and so forth. If we now want to extend the functionality to draw an ellipse, we can create an Ellipse class, which has a **Draw()** function. Then we can draw an ellipse by passing a draw message to an object of type **Ellipse**. By using preprocessor services and run-time libraries we can add the new functionality without modifying existing code.

Evidently this method of adding functionality brings about two major advantages: first, we can avoid introducing new defects into code that has already been tested and debugged; second, systems can be expanded by supplying relatively small modules that contain the new functions.

3.2.4 Inheritance

The notion of *inheritance*, which originated in the field of knowledge representation, actually refers to the inheritance of properties. Knowledge is usually organized into hierarchies based on class relationships. (Note that now we are using the word *class* in its more common connotation.) Thus, we say that an individual inherits the properties of the class to which it belongs. For example, animals breathe, move, and reproduce. If fish belong to the animal class, then we can infer that fish breathe, move, and reproduce since these properties are inherited from the base class. Figure 3.2 is an inheritance diagram for some animal classes.

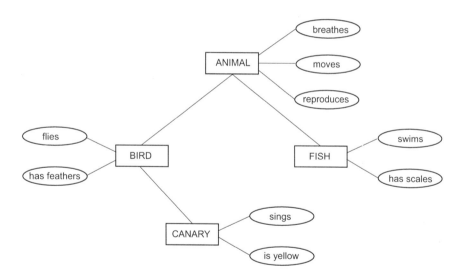

Figure 3.2 *Inheritance Diagram*

Inheritance systems are used in knowledge bases to ensure the highest levels of abstraction. For example, a knowledge base about birds first defines the traits that are common to all birds (fly and have feathers) and then the traits of the particular species (canary sings and is yellow). In this manner the species canary inherits the properties of its parent class, bird, which in turn inherits the properties of its parent class, animal. This reduces the size of the knowledge base by requiring that common properties be asserted only once. Inheritance also serves to maintain the consistency of the knowledge base and to simplify programming.

In object-oriented systems inheritance refers to the possibility of one class acquiring the public members of its parent class. As in knowledge bases, class inheritance promotes the highest level of abstraction, reduces code size, and simplifies programming. This allows the building of a class hierarchy, from the most general to the most specific. In the diagram of Figure 3.2 we could say that animal is a base class, and that bird, fish, and canary are derived classes. The derived class usually incorporates all the features of its parent classes and adds some unique ones of its own. Also, a derived class has access to all the public members of its base class. The terms *parent*, *child*, and *sibling* are sometimes used to express degrees of inheritance between classes. As in biological systems, sibling classes do not inherit from each other. Therefore the properties of fish (in Figure 3.2) are not inherited by its sibling class, bird.

3.2.5 Polymorphism

Etymologically the word polymorphism means "many forms." In object-oriented terms *polymorphism* relates to several methods that share the same name. One way to implement polymorphism is by overloading conventional functions or operators. For example, the standard C library contains three functions that return the absolute value of the operand: **abs()** refers to the absolute value of an integer, **labs()** to the absolute value of a long, and **fabs()** the absolute value of a float. The programmer must take into consideration the data type when calculating the absolute value. In object-oriented systems it is possible to overload the function **abs()** in order to use the same name for three different calculating routines. The compiler examines the data type of the operand to determine which of the **abs()** functions is pertinent to the call. Thus, the programmer need not remember three different names, nor be concerned with the operand's data type. Standard operators, such as the arithmetic symbols, can also be overloaded in C++.

Abstract Classes

Polymorphism is more than just overloading functions or operators. When combined with inheritance, polymorphism provides a mechanism for achieving the following desirable properties:

1. Allows the creation of extensible programs

2. Helps localize changes and hence prevents the propagation of bugs

3. Provides a common interface to a group of related functions

4. Allows the creation of libraries that are easy to extend and reuse, even when the source code is not available to the programmer

All of this is made possible through the use of a special type of functions called *virtual functions* and a construct called an *abstract class*. An abstract class is one in which a method's interface is defined but it is not implemented. This empty method serves as a template for the interface of a family of functions that share the same name. The concept of abstract classes requires that the polymorphic functions in the base and the derived classes be virtual functions and that they have the same name and identical interfaces. This makes abstract classes different from function overloading, which requires that either the number or the type of the parameters be different. In the context of virtual functions the word *overriding* is used to designate the redefinition of a virtual function by a derived class.

In C++ there are two types of virtual functions: regular and pure virtual functions. Both regular and pure virtual functions support polymorphism as well as early and late binding. For example, a graphics package has a base class called **GeometricalFigure** and three derived classes called **Rectangle**, **Line**, and **Circle**, all of which have a member function named **Draw()**. When we wish to display a rectangle we send a **Draw()** message to an object of type **rectangle**. Because each object knows the class to which it belongs, there is no doubt where the **Draw()** message will be directed, even though there are other classes with equally-named methods. Since the destination method is determined according to the object type, known at compile time, this type of polymorphism is said to use *early binding*.

However, when a virtual function is accessed by means of a pointer, the binding is deferred until run time. This type of late binding, or *run-time polymorphism*, is one of the most powerful mechanisms of object-oriented systems. A discussion of the details of implementation of polymorphism and virtual functions in C++ is postponed until Chapter 7.

3.3 A Notation for Classes and Objects

It seems that every author of a book on object-oriented topics feels the need to develop a new notation or to introduce a modification to an existing one. In this manner we have the Coad and Yourdon notation, the Booch notation, the Rumbaugh notation, as well as half a dozen refinements and modifications. These variations are not always due to simple matters of form or style. Each notation is designed to model a particular view of the problem and to do it with the desired degree of detail. Furthermore, each of the various notations is often associated with a particular phase of the development process or with a design methodology. For example, the Coad and Yourdon notation is often linked with the analysis phase, the Booch notation is associated with the design phase, and Rumbaugh's with models and design patterns. There is no easy way out of this notational labyrinth.

We will start by using the object and class notation proposed by Coad and Yourdon because we will be closely following these authors in our treatment of object-oriented analysis. Later on we will add refinements consistent with Rumbaugh's symbology as they become necessary for the discussion of models and patterns. Unable to resist the aforementioned tendency to modify, we will also introduce some minor variations to the Coad and Yourdon symbols. Our main objection to the Coad and Yourdon notation is that it requires shades of gray, which is difficult to achieve with pencil and paper. Since the class and object diagrams are often necessary during brainstorming sessions and informal meetings, it is better if the components can be easily drawn by longhand. Figure 3.3 shows the symbols for classes and objects.

In Figure 3.3 we notice that a normal class can be instantiated while an abstract class cannot. In their book on object-oriented analysis Coad and Yourdon refer to classes that can be instantiated as a Class-&-Object element in the diagram. Therefore, their class designation always refers to an abstract class. The methods in an abstract class constitute an interface with no implementation, as will be shown in the example in the following section.

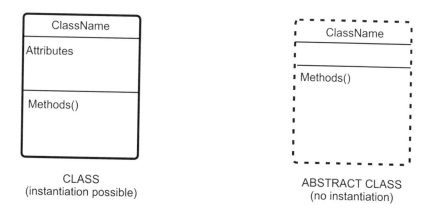

CLASS
(instantiation possible)

ABSTRACT CLASS
(no instantiation)

Figure 3.3 *Notation for Classes and Objects*

Figure 3.4 shows the Coad and Yourdon notation to represent inheritance and types of associations between classes. These types of associations are called *structures*. The Generalization-Specification structure (**Gen-Spec**) corresponds to the "is-a-kind-of" relation. For example, in a classification in which *vehicle* is the base class, *automobile* and *airplane* are specializations of the base class, since automobile "is a kind of" vehicle and so is airplane. On the other hand, classification may be based on the Whole-Part association, depicted with a triangle symbol in Figure 3.4. In this case the *chassis* is a part of an *automobile* and so is the *engine*.

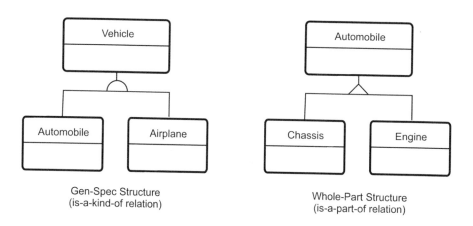

Gen-Spec Structure
(is-a-kind-of relation)

Whole-Part Structure
(is-a-part-of relation)

Figure 3.4 *Notation for Inheritance and Class Relations*

3.4 Example Classification

The concepts and notation covered in this chapter can be illustrated with an example. Suppose the following project:

We are to design and code a graphics toolkit that can display geometrical figures at any screen position. The figures are straight lines, rectangles, circles, ellipses, and parabolas.

A first reading of the problem description shows that the program is to draw geometrical figures of four different types: line, rectangle, circle, ellipse, and parabola. We also notice that circle, ellipse, and parabola belong to a family of curves called the conic sections. These are obtained by sectioning a right-circular cone, as shown in Figure 3.5.

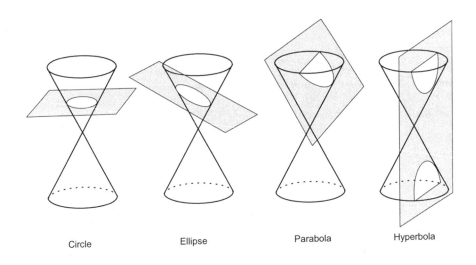

Circle   Ellipse   Parabola   Hyperbola

Figure 3.5 *Visualization of the Conic Sections*

A rough and instinctive classification can be based on using a class for each of the figure elements to be displayed. The notion of a geometrical figure could serve as a base class as shown in Figure 3.6.

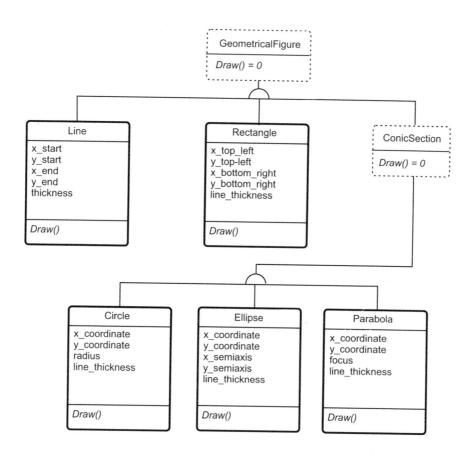

Figure 3.6 *Classification of a Graphics Toolkit*

Since **GeometricalFigure** is an abstraction, it is represented by an abstract class, with no attributes and no possible instantiation. Line and **Rectangle** are concrete classes since it is possible to draw a line or a rectangle, therefore they have attributes and can be instantiated. **Circle**, **Ellipse**, and **Parabola** are concrete classes of the abstract class **ConicSection**, which is also a subclass of **GeometricalFigure**. Observe that the interface, which is the **Draw()** method, is defined in the abstract classes (**GeometricalFigure** and **ConicSection**) and implemented in the concrete classes. We have used the C++ convention of equating the function to zero to indicate that the methods in the abstract classes are pure virtual functions and that no implementation is provided. Also note that virtual functions in the abstract and concrete classes are in italics.

Since the concrete classes can be instantiated, we can create objects of **Line**, **Rectangle**, **Circle**, **Ellipse**, and **Parabola**. There can clearly be no object of the abstract classes **ConicSection** or **GeometricalFigure** since there can be no possible instantiation of these concepts. For these reasons abstract classes have no attributes. We can now proceed to draw on the video display using objects. For example:

```
Object:             Attributes
Line_A              x_start = 10
                    y_start = 5
                    x_end = 40
                    y_end = 20
                    thickness = 0.005
Rectangle_A         x_top_left = 5
                    y_top_left = 20
                    x_bottom_right = 25
                    y_bottom_right = 30
                    line_thickness = 0.010
Rectangle_B         x_top_left = 30
                    y_top_left = 5
                    x_bottom_right = 45
                    y_bottom_right = 10
                    line_thickness = 0.030
Circle_A            x_coordinate = 40
                    y_coordinate = 30
                    radius = 5
                    line_thickness = 20
```

Figure 3.7 represents these objects on the video display. Note that each object is identified by its name and preserved by its attributes. Also that there are two objects of the class Rectangle, one is designated as Rectangle_A and the other one as Rectangle_B. The fact that there are no objects of the class Ellipse or Parabola means only that these classes have not been instantiated.

In Figure 3.5 we notice that there is a type of conic curve, the hyperbola, that is not defined in the toolkit. The class structure in the object-oriented paradigm allows later implementation of this subclass without introducing modifications to the existing code. The mechanics of how a library can be dynamically extended are discussed later in the book.

3.6 When to Use Object Orientation

The fact that this book's title includes C++ as a programming language does not mean that we assume that every programming project will benefit from an object-oriented approach. One advantage of hybrid languages, such as C++, is that they make object orientation optional. Furthermore, in a hybrid language environment we have the possibility of adopting some features of an object-oriented system while not others. For instance, we can design a program that uses classes and objects without inheritance, or one that uses inheritance but not run-time polymorphism. Or we may use some forms of inheritance and not others. In other words, the systems designer is free to decide how much object orientation, if any, is suitable for a particular project. This is often a crucial and significant decision which may determine a project's success or failure.

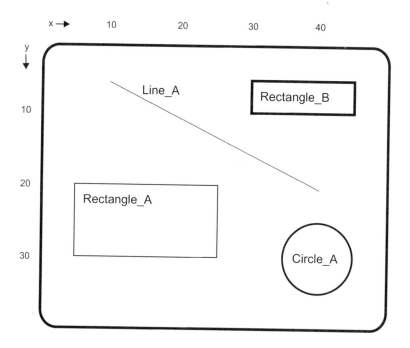

Figure 3.7 *Objects Displayed Using the Graphics Toolkit*

3.5.1 Operational Guidelines

Object-oriented methods have permeated programming activities to such depth that sometimes we forget that its fundamental objective is to provide a model of the problem domain. In Figure 3.1 we showed programming as a bridge from a real-world problem-set to a machine-coded solution-set. In this representation of programming we see that the object-oriented paradigm emphasizes modeling the problem domain while structured programming models the solution domain. Modeling the solution domain facilitates the coding phase (which it approximates). Modeling the problem domain facilitates analysis. In one case we concentrate on the tail end of the process and in the other one we concentrate on its start.

By emphasizing the problem domain in the analysis phase we are able to achieve two undisputable benefits: first, we are able to analyze more complicated problems; second, the analyst can communicate better with the domain experts since many technical elements are removed from the model. However, these benefits are considerably diminished if the object-oriented model that results from the analysis has to be translated into the code of a non-object-oriented programming language. In spite of the claims made by some hard-core defenders of object-orientation, this approach is of doubtful advantage when it does not permeate the entire development process. Therefore, it is usually undesirable to perform object-oriented analysis and design of a project to be coded in a non-object-oriented language. Mixing models and development tools is usually a bad idea.

Although in recent years the programming community appears to be favoring object-oriented methods, it is sometimes difficult to clearly ascertain the advantages of object-orientation over conventional structured programming for a particular project. In order to make a valid judgment we would have to follow through a host of major software projects developed using both methods, measure and keep track of the development effort, and critically evaluate the results. Even then, many subjective considerations would muddle our conclusions. In any case, we must not forget that the advantages of object orientation come at a high price in programming complications. Few will argue that object-oriented languages are more difficult to master and use, and that object-oriented analysis and design techniques are elaborate and complicated.

The decision whether to use or not to use an object-oriented approach should be given careful consideration by the analyst. The following elements favor the use of object-oriented methods:

1. Projects in which modeling the problem domain is a major issue

2. Projects in which communication with domain experts can be expected to be a difficult and critical part of the development activity

3. Volatile projects in which changes can be anticipated or in which frequent updates will be required

4. Projects with many elements with potential for reuse

5. Toolkits and frameworks are often good candidates for the object-oriented approach

On the other hand there are elements that often advise against object-orientation:

1. If the data structures and processing operations resulting from object orientation are not compatible with existing data bases. In other words, it may be a bad idea to develop an object-oriented database management system if the new system forces the redesign or restructuring of the existing data bases.

2. If the project, or a substantial part thereof, must be developed in a non-object-oriented programming language. Thus, object-oriented methods may be of doubtful use in developing a short, low-level device driver for a hardware accessory.

3. If the problem domain model is already well defined in non-object-oriented terms.

4. If the problem-domain is better expressed using a conventional, non-object-oriented model. Projects in which software elements are the subjects to be modeled sometimes fall into this category.

In general, major business and industrial applications are suitable for object orientation, while small, technical, or support utilities are not.

Chapter 4

Object-Oriented Analysis

4.0 Elements of Object-Oriented Analysis

It has been observed by several authors that both major software engineering paradigms (structured programming and object orientation) started with programming languages, were later extended to software design, and finally to analysis. This implies that the advent of a system analysis methodology marks the maturity of a particular paradigm. Regarding object-oriented systems we have seen that full-featured programming languages were already available in the late seventies and early eighties. System design discussions started at about that time, while the object-oriented analysis methodologies are a product of the late eighties and early nineties.

Observe that the object-oriented approach to analysis does not attempt to replace every technique and tool of conventional system analysis. The feasibility study, risk analysis, and cost-benefit analysis can be performed independently of whether the project is modeled using structured programming or an object-oriented approach. Object-oriented analysis provides a practical methodology for project modeling during the analysis phase. Its purpose is to complement, not to replace.

We mentioned in Section 3.5 that the analyst should critically evaluate if a project will gain from using an object-oriented approach and also that the greatest benefits of the object-oriented paradigm result when the methodology permeates the entire development process. In most cases, our decision to use object-oriented analysis implies that we will also follow object orientation in the design phase and that the program will be coded in an object-oriented programming language. Paradigm mixing is theoretically possible, and sometimes recommended by hard-core defenders of object orientation. However, regarding the smaller project, the complications brought about by simultaneously using more than one model far outweigh the uncertain advantages. In particular regarding the smaller development project, it is our opinion that the decision to proceed with object-oriented analysis should presuppose that object orientation will also be used during the design and coding phases of development.

In this chapter we follow Coad and Yourdon, although not very strictly. These authors are a principal force in the field of object-oriented analysis. In addition, their approach is elegant and simple. The Coad and Yourdon notation was described in Section 3.3.

4.0.1 Modeling the Problem-Domain

One of object orientation's principal characteristics, as well as its main justification, is that it provides a reasonable way of modeling the problem-domain. Other advantages often mentioned are that it makes modeling complex systems possible, facilitates building systems that are more flexible and adaptable, and promotes reusability.

Object-oriented analysis is most useful in problem-set modeling. One of the predicaments of software development is that the programmer must become an expert in the domain field. Thus, someone contracted to develop an air-traffic control system has to learn about radar, about air-to-ground communications, about emergency response systems, about flight scheduling, and about a multitude of other technical and business topics related to the activity at hand. How much knowledge must the analyst acquire, and to what technical level must this knowledge extend, is difficult to determine beforehand. Many projects have failed because the developers did not grasp important details of the problem set. The urge to "get on with the coding" often works against us during this stage.

Because the analyst needs to quickly understand the problem-domain, any tool that facilitates this stage of the process is indeed valuable. Once the analyst has grasped the necessary knowledge, then this information has to be transmitted to other members of the development team. Here again, any tool that assists in communicating the knowledge is greatly appreciated. Finally, the model of the proposed solution-set must be presented to the clients or users for their validation, and to obtain feedback. A model that facilitates this communication between clients and developers is an additional asset.

4.0.2 Defining System Responsibilities

In addition to providing a model of the problem-domain, object-oriented analysis must define the system's responsibilities. For example, the analysis of an air-traffic control system includes determining what functions and operations are within the system's burden. Does the air-traffic control system have the obligation of informing commercial airlines of delays in arrivals or departures of aircraft? How does the air-traffic control system interface with the emergency response system at the airport? At what point does the tracking of an aircraft become the responsibility of a particular air-traffic control system and when does this responsibility cease? A system's responsibilities refer to *what* a system should do. Answering this question is one of the fundamental tasks of object-oriented analysis. Questions related to *how* a system operates are left for the design and coding phases.

4.0.3 Managing Complexity

Analysis is necessary because natural systems are often so elaborate and complicated that they are difficult to understand or manage. Object-oriented analysis provides a toolset for managing complexity. This toolset is based on abstraction, encapsulation, inheritance, and message passing.

Abstraction

Abstraction consists of eliminating what is superfluous or trivial and concentrating on what is fundamental. Any definition is an exercise in abstraction. We can state that a fountain pen is a hand-held writing instrument that uses liquid ink, an ink discharge mechanism, and a fine tracing point. This description attempts to gather the fundamental attributes of a fountain pen that distinguish it from a typewriter, a ballpoint pen, and a pencil. However, it ignores the less important features such as the pen's color, the color of the ink, the instrument's exact dimensions, and its design or style.

In the context of object-oriented analysis, abstraction refers to the class mechanism which simultaneously provides procedural and data abstraction. In other words, the object-oriented notion of a class is an abstraction that represents both processing and data elements of the problem set.

Encapsulation

Encapsulation is one of the fundamental notions of object orientation. In the object-oriented approach encapsulation is related to the notion of data and functions (attributes and methods) being packaged together by means of the class construct. Those methods visible outside the class are its interface. The principal purpose of encapsulation is hiding the implementation details while stressing the interface.

Inheritance

In the object-oriented paradigm inheritance refers to the possibility of one class accessing the public and protected members of its parent class. Class inheritance promotes the highest level of abstraction, reduces code size, and simplifies programming. The result is a class hierarchy that goes from the most general to the most specific. Typically, a derived class incorporates all the features of its parent classes and adds some unique ones of its own.

Message passing

Object-oriented systems access processing functions by means of a mechanism called *message passing*. One of the disadvantages of hard-coded program structures such as jump tables, cascaded **if** statements, or **case** constructs is that they must be updated with every program modification or change. The message passing mechanism, on the other hand, automatically directs execution to the appropriate member function. This functionality brings about two major advantages: first, we avoid introducing new defects into code that has already been tested and debugged. Second, a system can be expanded by supplying relatively small modules that contain the new functions.

4.1 Class and Object Decomposition

The first discipline of object-oriented analysis is learning to think in terms of classes and objects. At this stage we must free our minds of concerns regarding algorithms, programming structures, or any other implementation issues. Our task during analysis is to model the problem-domain and to define the system's responsibilities. Both of these purposes are accomplished by means of class and object decomposition.

In this sense an object can be considered an abstraction of a discrete element in the problem domain. The object-oriented encapsulation is a matter of defining attributes and methods. An object is characterized by the possibility of its identity being preserved by the system. Therefore each object must have a uniqueness that allows its identification.

Every object belongs to a class of objects. A class is a description of a set of unique attributes and methods associated with an object type. An object is an instance of a class. An abstract class is a description of an interface which lacks implementation. Its fundamental purpose is to define an inheritance path. It is not possible to instantiate objects from an abstract class.

Do we start modeling by thinking of objects or of classes? It is a matter of semantics, but, strictly speaking, an object is a run-time construct while a class is an abstraction that groups common attributes and methods for an object type. Therefore it appears that we should think of object types or classes, rather than of possible instantiations. On the other hand, the mental concept of a class of objects requires that we visualize a typical object. For example, suppose we are attempting to model a system which uses a viewport window to display a text message. In order to define the text message window type we must first imagine what the object would look like. Figure 4.1 shows what may be our initial visualization of a text window object.

From the object's visualization we can deduce the attributes and methods of the object itself and the class that represents it. For example, the screen location and the object size are defined by the start and end coordinates. The object also has a border thickness and a color. Its text attributes are the window's title and its text. A control button on the top left corner of the object allows the user to erase the text message window.

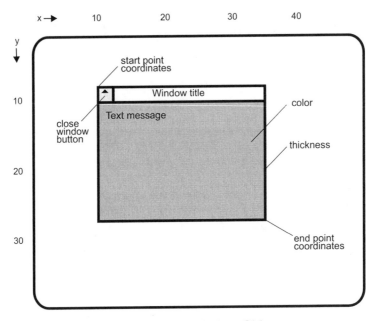

Figure 4.1 *Visualization of a Text Window Object*

There are three methods associated with this object: one to display the window, one to report its current status, and one to erase it. Using class diagrams we can now represent the object type **TextWindow** to any desired degree of detail. The left-hand diagram in Figure 4.2 merely states that there is an object class named **TextWindow**, while its attributes and methods are yet undefined. The diagram on the right shows the specific attributes and methods.

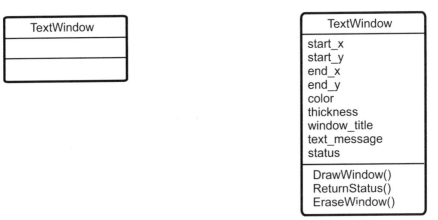

Figure 4.2 *Class Diagrams for a Text Window Object*

During classification it is common practice to make the class name a singular noun or an adjective followed by a noun. It is also a good idea to use the client's standard vocabulary when naming classes. Suppose we are modeling a home alarm system with a rather elaborate video display and command control. For historical reasons the client calls the video display and command control a "push-button panel." During analysis we may be tempted to rename this element so that its designation describes its actual functionality more exactly. Clearly the term "command console" would be more forceful and descriptive than "push-button panel." However, this new name would serve only to confuse clients, who would have to mentally translate "command console" for "push-button panel" every time they encounter the new term.

During the analysis phase the class name could be entered using any reasonable style of spacing and capitalization. However, if our class names are not compatible with the syntax to be used in the design and coding phases, then these names would have to be modified at a later date. Since any modification could be a source of errors, name classes, attributes, and methods use a style that is consistent with the later phases of the development environment. In the context of this book decisions regarding style are facilitated by the fact that we have committed to C++ as a programming language. Therefore, to improve readability, and in conformance with one popular C++ programming style, we capitalize the first letter of every word in class names and methods. Methods are followed by parenthesis to indicate processing. Attributes, which later become variables, are typed in lowercase, and the underscore symbol is used as a separator. Note that any other style is equally satisfactory as long as it can be consistently maintained throughout the development process.

While methods are depicted by verbs and verb phrases, attributes are represented by nouns or noun phases, as in Figure 4.2. C++ allows us to use rather simple naming schemes for attributes and methods since these names have *class scope*, where the same names can be reused in other classes. In this sense the **DrawWindow** method of the **TextWindow** class is not in conflict with other methods called **DrawWindow** that could be later defined for other classes. By the same token, the thickness attribute can also be reused in reference to other types of graphic objects.

Simplified class diagrams in which attributes and methods are not explicitly listed can be useful in showing class relations and inheritance. Consider a system with two types of window objects, one representing windows that contain nothing but text, a second one for windows that include a bitmap. The first type could be designated as a **TextWindow** and the second one as a **GraphicWindow**. The class structure would be depicted in the class diagram in Figure 4.3.

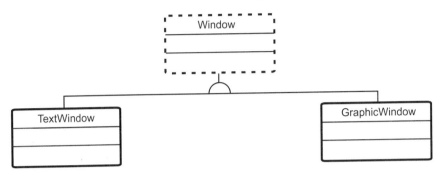

Figure 4.3 *Sample Inheritance Diagram for Window-Type Classes*

Note that in Figure 4.3 **TextWindow** is a subclass of **Window**, as is **GraphicWindow**. Also that **Window** is an abstract class, which implies that its methods are not implemented. Also that at run time we could instantiate objects of type **TextWindow** or of type **Graphic-Window**; however, **Window** objects could not exist since the abstract nature of the base class precludes this possibility. A more detailed diagram of the classes is shown in Figure 4.4.

In Figure 4.4 a **GraphicWindow** class is a subclass of **Window** which adds functionality to the base class. The new functionality is in the form of three new attributes which locate the bitmap on the viewport and a new method to draw the bitmap. The basic coordinates and characteristics of the window itself are defined in the base class, since these attributes apply to any window object.

4.1.1 Searching for Objects

The search for objects should not begin until the analyst has gained some familiarity with the problem domain itself. An analyst that is unfamiliar with an air-traffic control system should not be searching for air-traffic control objects. Instead, the first step should be an attempt to understand the system's fundamental characteristics. It is futile to attempt to identify objects and classes in a technology that is unfamiliar.

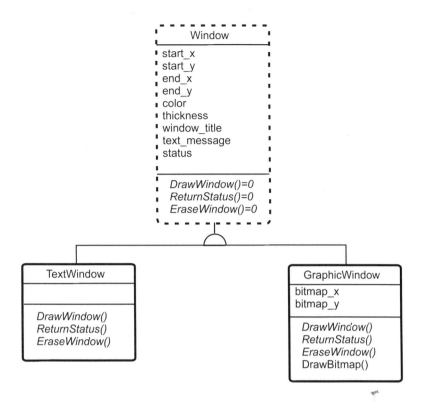

Figure 4.4 *Refined Diagram for Window-Type Classes*

The following are the main sources of information about the problem domain:

1. Published materials and the Internet

2. Firsthand observation

3. Consultation with domain experts

4. Client documents

The search for published material usually leads to libraries, bookstores, and the Internet. Firsthand observation consists of familiarizing ourselves with a system by participating in its operation. For example, to analyze an air-traffic control system we may begin by sitting in the air-traffic control tower for several days while observing the operation of the air-traffic controllers. Domain experts are often the source of valuable and unique information. Many systems are totally or partially unpublished, part of trade or government secret, or are considered confidential. In these cases published materials may be of little use. Our only option is to locate individuals with knowledge and expertise and to have them describe or explain the system to us. Client documentation can also be a valuable source of information. Expert analysts make it a standard practice to request a detailed document from the client. This document should identify the system and its purpose to the greatest possible detail.

4.1.2 Neat and Dirty Classes

In some contexts classification is a clear and neat process, but not in others. When conceptual objects correspond to real-world objects the classification process is often simple and straightforward. For example, when the task is to define a mini CAD program, classification could turn out to be relatively uncomplicated. In this case the screen objects give rise to classes, such as drawings, composed of lines, curves, geometrical figures, and text.

On the other hand, classification may be somewhat less clear when the task is to design an editor or word processing program. In this case we may start thinking of program operations as objects. But is it reasonable to consider operations such as inserting, replacing, and deleting text as physical objects? What about the user's text file? However, since the text file is stored as an array of characters we may be tempted to think of it as an attribute. One possible classification is shown in Figure 4.5.

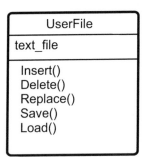

Figure 4.5 *Possible Class Diagram for a Simple Text Editor*

Other projects may be even more difficult to classify. For example, assume the task is designing and coding a virus-detection utility. In this case are the viruses the objects? Would this mean that if no viruses are found the program executes without instantiation? Or is the search itself an object? In this case whatever kind of classification is developed will probably be unsatisfactory, and the classes themselves will be untidy and unreal. What happens is that this is probably one of those cases, mentioned in Section 3.5, that is best handled outside of object orientation.

4.2 Finding Classes and Objects

The skills of an object-oriented analyst include the individual's ability to locate objects and to derive valid and useful classifications. In this respect there is no substitute for experience with various types of problem domains. However, there are some circumstances, patterns, and constructs that the analyst can use to locate possible objects. One proposed methodology consists of searching through the elements of class associations, mechanisms and devices, related systems, preserved data, roles played, sites, and organizational units.

4.2.1 Looking at Class Associations

In Section 3.3 we described a notation for representing two types of class associations: the *Gen-Spec* and the *Whole-Part structure*. This first type refers to a generalization-specialization relation that corresponds to one class being in a "kind-of" association with a parent or base class. The second type refers to an association where a class is "a-part-of" a parent or base class. The notation for class associations is often taken to imply an inheritance configuration whereby the public elements of the base class become accessible to the derived class. Although this assumption is valid during analysis, we should mention that Whole-Part associations are often implemented without using class inheritance. This topic is discussed in detail in Chapter 11.

Associations (also called structures) can be used to identify objects in the problem domain and to uncover levels of complexity in the class structures. The method consists of looking at object associations within the problem domain. For example, in Figure 4.3 we found that two types of windows, called **GraphicWindow** and **TextWindow**, were subclasses of a general **Window** type. A detailed class diagram was later derived from these associations.

Gen-Spec Structures

The name of a specialization is usually derived from its generalization. In this manner **TextWindow** and **GraphicWindow** are specializations of the **Window** type (see Figure 4.4). In a Gen-Spec structure the bottommost classes are concrete classes, from which objects can be instantiated. The higher-level classes can be concrete or abstract. Often class structures are flexible and can be expressed in different ways. For example, we could redo the class diagram in Figure 4.4 so that a concrete class **Window** serves as a generalization with a possible specialization in the form of a **GraphicWindow**. This scheme is shown in Figure 4.6.

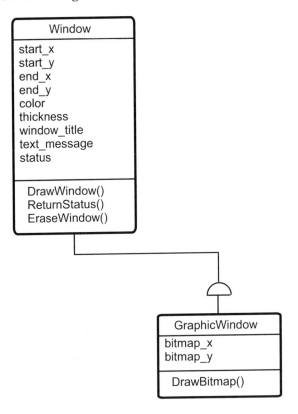

Figure 4.6 *Alternative Structure for Window-Type Classes*

Note that Figure 4.6 depicts a class structure in which the methods **DrawWindow()**, **ReturnStatus()**, and **EraseWindow()** are actually implemented in the base class. Therefore they need not be re-implemented in the derived class, except if these methods need update or modification.

Once we have identified a generalization-specialization structure, perform tests to ascertain whether the structure is both valid and necessary.

1. Does the subclass respond to the "is-a-kind-of" relation regarding the parent class?

2. Does the subclass add attributes or methods to the parent class?

3. Is the structure actually within the problem domain as it pertains to proposed system? In other words: is this structure really necessary to represent the problem at hand?

4. Is the structure within the system's responsibilities? Often a structure that actually exists in the problem domain turns out to be unnecessary in the model since the proposed system does not perform any function related to it. For example, we may recognize that a graphic window (see Figures 4.3 and 4.6) could contain vector drawings as well as bitmaps. However, if the system to be developed deals only in bitmap graphics, then the introduction of vector graphics would be an unnecessary complication since it falls outside of the system's responsibilities.

5. Are there lines of inheritance between the subclass and the parent class? A generalization-specialization structure in which no methods are inherited from the parent class should be questioned since it is inheritance that makes the structure useful.

6. Would it be simpler to use an attribute that qualifies a type than a Gen-Spec structure? For example, a system that deals with vehicles has to distinguish between autos, motorcycles, and trucks. This could possibly be accomplished by a Gen-Spec structure in which **Vehicle** is a base class and **AutoVehicle**, **MotorcycleVehicle**, and **TruckVehicle** are subclasses. Alternatively, the system could be modeled using a **Vehicle** class with a **vehicle_type** attribute. Both alternatives are shown in Figure 4.7.

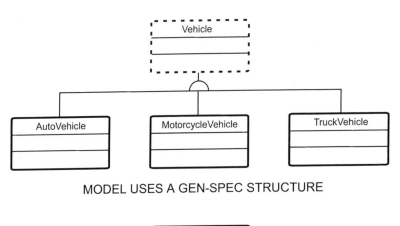

MODEL USES A GEN-SPEC STRUCTURE

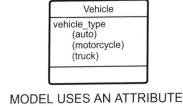

MODEL USES AN ATTRIBUTE

Figure 4.7 *Two Modeling Alternatives*

The general rule used in determining which model is to be preferred is that a generalization-specialization structure should not be used for extracting a common attribute.

Multiple Inheritance in Gen-Spec Structures

The common case in a Gen-Spec structure is that a class inherits from a single ancestor. However, Coad and Yourdon distinguish between a Gen-Spec structure used as a hierarchy and one used as a lattice. The hierarchy is the most common form of the structure and corresponds to the examples used previously in this chapter. In this sense the topmost model in Figure 4.7 represents a hierarchy of the Vehicle class. The notion of a hierarchy corresponds to single inheritance in object-oriented languages. A lattice, on the other hand, corresponds with multiple inheritance, which occurs when a class inherits attributes or methods from more than one ancestor.

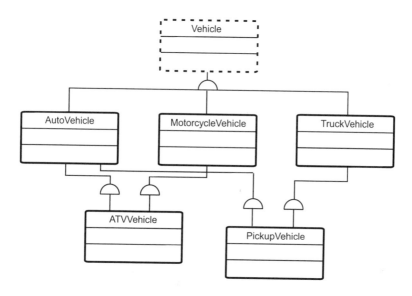

Figure 4.8 *Gen-Spec Structure Lattice*

For example, in the **Vehicle** class structure of Figure 4.7 we could define two additional subclasses. The class **PickupVehicle** could have some of the properties of an **AutoVehicle** (carries passengers) and some of the properties of a **TruckVehicle** (transports cargo). Or an **ATVVehicle** may inherit some properties from the **AutoVehicle** class and others from **MotorcycleVehicle**. Figure 4.8 shows the resulting lattice-type diagram.

Whole-Part Structures

The triangle markings in Figure 3.4 represent a Whole-Part structure which corresponds to the concept of an "is-a-part-of" class relation. Sometimes the Whole-Part notation is supplemented with digits or codes to represent the number of elements that take part in the relation. For example, it may help the model if we clarify that a vehicle can have four wheels but only one engine, or that a wheel can belong to only one vehicle, but a person can own more than one vehicle. A comma separates the low from the high numerical limits. The letter "m" is often used as a shorthand for "many." Figure 4.9 shows a Whole-Part structure regarding some components of an **AutoVehicle** class.

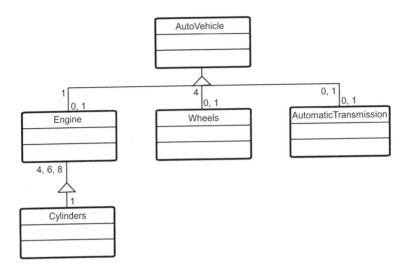

Figure 4.9 *Whole-Part Structure*

Note that the digits in Figure 4.9 add information to the model. For example, we can tell that an auto vehicle has one engine, four wheels, and zero or one automatic transmission. Also that engine, wheel, and automatic transmission can exist independently of the automobile, but that cylinders do not exist outside of the engine; and finally that an engine can have either four, six, or eight cylinders.

There are certain common constructs and relationships that can be investigated when searching for Whole-Part associations. In the example of Figure 4.9 the construct can be described as an assembly-components relationship. Another common case can be described as a container-contents relationship. For example, the driver of an automobile is not one of its components, but may be considered to be in a container-contents relationship. A third common construct is the collection-member relationship. For example, the collection coins has the members quarter, dime, nickel, and penny. Or the collection hospital has the members patient, nurse, doctor, and administrator.

The following tests can be performed to ascertain whether a Whole-Part structure is valid and necessary:

1. Does the subclass correspond to the "is-a-part-of" relation regarding the parent class?

2. Does the subclass add attributes or methods to the parent class?

3. Is the structure actually within the problem domain as it pertains to proposed system? Is this structure really necessary to represent the problem at hand?

4. Is the structure within the system's responsibilities?

5. Would it be simpler to use an attribute that qualifies a type rather than a Whole-Part structure?

Compound Structures

It often happens that a structure contains both Gen-Spec and Whole-Part class relationships. For example, the structures in Figures 4.8 and 4.9 would give rise to the compound structure shown in Figure 4.10.

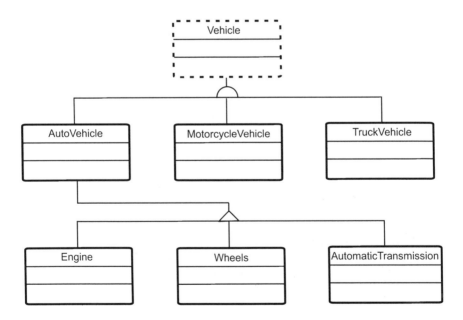

Figure 4.10 *Compound Structure*

4.2.2 Looking at Mechanisms and Devices

Another element of the search for classes and objects is the location of mechanisms and devices within the problem domain. For example, in modeling a burglar alarm system we may notice that it includes devices such as sensors to be placed in possible entry points, audible warnings that sound when a security breach is detected, switches for enabling and disabling the system, and input/output hardware such as a keypad for entering passwords and displays for echoing input and reporting system status. In this case the devices and mechanisms that are within the system's responsibilities are all candidates for classification. In the case of the burglar alarm system we should examine the possibility of having a class named **Sensor**, a class named **AudibleAlarm**, a class named **OnOffSwitch**, and so on.

4.2.3 Related Systems

At the fringes of a system's responsibilities we can sometimes detect other systems with which it interacts. The interaction could be hard-wired (if both systems are mechanically connected), through a communications link, or can result from human-computer interaction. Any associated or related system should be considered as a possible candidate for classification if it is within the base system's responsibilities and if it forms part of the problem domain. For example, if the burglar alarm system mentioned in Section 4.2.2 is connected to a local police alert system, then perhaps some elements of the police alert system should be included in the model.

4.2.4 Preserved Data

Another possible source of class and objects are the data or events that must be preserved or remembered by the system. Events preserved for historical purposes, modifications to data bases, and legal documents are all included in this category. For example, a computer system that uses a telescope to scan the sky for unknown celestial objects must somehow record and remember the position of a new comet in a possible collision path with Earth. The file used to store the time, date, celestial coordinates, and photographic image of the newly detected object is a possible candidate for classification. A more mundane example would be the transaction data stored by a automated teller machine.

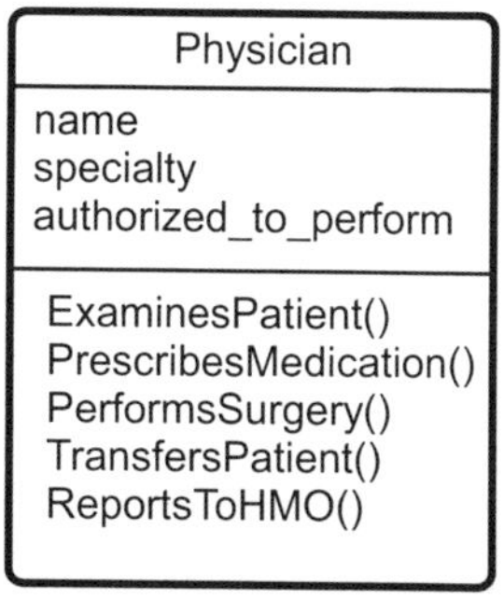

```
┌─────────────────────────────┐
│          Physician          │
├─────────────────────────────┤
│ name                        │
│ specialty                   │
│ authorized_to_perform       │
├─────────────────────────────┤
│ ExaminesPatient()           │
│ PrescribesMedication()      │
│ PerformsSurgery()           │
│ TransfersPatient()          │
│ ReportsToHMO()              │
└─────────────────────────────┘
```

Figure 4.11 *Class Depicting Human Interaction*

4.2.5 Roles Played

Individuals play roles within organizations and these roles are another possible source of classes that should be examined. For example, a Health Maintenance Organization (HMO) has individuals playing the roles of physicians, nurses, patients, administrators, and staff. It is likely that a model of this HMO will consider these roles as classes. Figure 4.11 shows one possible (rather loose) interpretation of the interaction of the class Physician within a fictitious HMO.

4.2.6 Operational Sites

Operational sites or physical locations within the system's responsibilities are often a source of classes. For example, a hypothetical satellite image processing system includes a site in New Mexico where the image data is downloaded from the satellites; a second site in South Dakota receives this raw data and reformats it into specific image files, which are then transmitted to a third site in California which distributes the image files to the system clients. In this case the New Mexico, South Dakota, and California sites perform different functions and could therefore be considered as candidates for classification.

Another example: the quality control department of a food product manufacturer consists of an office and a laboratory. The food product samples are collected in eight manufacturing plants throughout the state. In modeling this system we may have to decide if the classification is based on ten sites, one of which is the lab, one the office, and the other eight sites are manufacturing plants, or if the model can be rationalized to three classes by combining all eight manufacturing plants sites into a single class. In this last option an attribute could be used to designate each one of the individual plants. This case is shown in Figure 4.12.

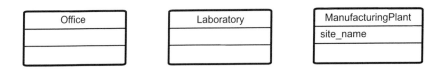

Figure 4.12 *Example of Site-Based Classification*

4.2.7 Organizational Units

Organizations are divided into units that perform different tasks and assume distinct responsibilities within the system. At modeling time these organizational units are also strong candidates for classification. For example, a manufacturing division includes departments called engineering, production, quality control, and shipping. These organizational units should be considered as possible classes.

4.3 Testing Object Validity

Once we have developed a basic classification scheme for the problem at hand it is a good idea to challenge its validity and soundness. There are certain requirements usually associated with objects which can serve to test their legitimacy and significance. In challenging proposed classes and objects the following questions are pertinent:

1. Is there information that the system needs to remember regarding this object?

2. Does this object provide some method or processing operation?

3. Is there more than one attribute associated with this object?

4. Will more than one object be instantiated from the class?

5. Do the attributes always apply to the object?

6. Do the methods always apply to the object?

7. Are the objects related to the problem domain or to a particular implementation?

8. Are the results a simple calculation or derivation?

   In the following sections we proceed to examine each of these questions separately.

4.3.1 Information to Remember

   For an object to be individually remembered by the system it must be associated with one or more related attributes. In this sense an instance of the class **Clerk** must have a name, and instance of the class **Office** must have an address and a set of specific functions, an instance of the class **AutoVehicle** must have a model and a serial number, and so on. An object that is not associated with any attribute should be questioned since it could be irrelevant to the system, even though it may be an object in the real world. Although an object could have methods but no attributes, this case should always be investigated before it is accepted as an exception to the general rule.

4.3.2 Object Behavior

   A class with no methods is suspect of a classification error. Even an abstract class has methods, although these methods are not implemented. If we accept that, in principle, attributes should not be accessible from outside the class, then the fact that an object is affiliated with one or more attributes implies that there are one or more methods to access these attributes. A careful investigation is necessary if an object has attributes but no methods. Some authors consider that classes with methods but no attributes are a result of functional-style thinking and should be reconsidered.

4.3.3 Multiple Attributes

   While a class with no attributes is suspect of incorrect classification, one with a single attribute may indicate a poorly conceived classification. In this case the analyst could use an attribute (typically in the parent class) instead of a full-fledged object.

4.3.4 Multiple Objects

The fundamental notion of classification implies that a class is a type which usually consists of more than one individual. In this sense we can correctly conceive the class **FootballPlayer** or the class **Quarterback**. Multiple objects of either class can be instantiated. However, the class **JohnSmith**, of which only one object can be instantiated, should set off an alarm indicating the need for further investigation. On the other hand, often we must create a class with only one possible object. For example, a satellite image processing system may have a class **ReceivingStation** with a single object. However, in this case we may decide to validate the class considering that another receiving station could be built. The decision about the validity and suitability of a class with a single object must be made considering the problem domain.

4.3.5 Always-applicable Attributes

The general rule is that the attributes in a class apply to all objects instantiated from the class. For example, suppose that the class **AutoVehicle** includes the attributes manufacturer, model number, and size-of-bed. All objects generated from the class include the first two attributes; however, the size-of-bed attribute does not apply to those vehicles that are not trucks. The fact that an attribute is not applicable to all objects instantiated from the class suggests that there is a possible class structure yet undiscovered. In this example perhaps we could use the Gen-Spec structure in Figure 4.7.

4.3.6 Always-applicable Methods

The fact that there are methods in a class that do not apply to all possible instantiations indicates that there is room for improvement in the classification. Perhaps there is a class structure that has not yet been considered. This is unrelated to how simple or elaborate a particular method is, but it is linked to the fact that methods are expected to be applicable to all possible objects. For example, consider a class named **HospitalEmployee** that includes doctors, nurses, and administrators. This class has a method named **PerformMajorSurgery** that is applicable only to doctors, but not to nurses or administrators. The fact that a method does not apply to all objects that can be instantiated from the class strongly suggests a missing class structure.

4.3.7 Objects Relate to the Problem Domain

Many beginning analysts find it difficult to isolate themselves from implementation concerns during the analysis phases. Due to inattention, matters that pertain to implementation often permeate the model. Suppose a system deals with licensing of automobile drivers. Because the system must digitally store each driver's personal data we may be tempted to create a class called **DriverDiskFile**. But, in reality, the concept of a disk file pertains to the solution set. From the problem set's viewpoint the class that stores driver data could be better named **DriverInfo**. How this information is stored or preserved in the computer hardware is outside the scope of the model at the analysis stage.

An important conclusion is that the choice of processing operations, of hardware devices, of file formats, and of other computer-related factors should not be made during the analysis phase. The specific methods, systems, or devices that are used in implementing the solution are inconsequential at this stage. Therefore, a class that represents a solution-related element should be carefully investigated. Exceptionally, we may find that project specifications require the use of a particular algorithm or method of computing. For example, the client of a graphics package requests in the specification documents that lines be drawn using Bresenham's algorithm. In this case the algorithm becomes a domain-based requirement and its inclusion in the model is valid and appropriate. On the other hand, if no mention of a specific algorithm is made in the specification, then it would be premature to decide what method is to be used for drawing lines at the analysis phase. A good general rule is that all implementation matters are best postponed until design or implementation, except if the problem domain specifically mandates it.

4.3.8 Derived or Calculated Results

Finally, we should investigate those objects that represent a mere calculation or that are derived by manipulating stored data. For example, suppose a payroll system must issue a printed report of all salaries and wages disbursed during the period. In this case we may be tempted to create a class, perhaps called WeeklyPayrollReport, to represent this document. However, since this document is directly derived from stored data it could be an improper classification. An alternative and more satisfactory solution is to make the generation of a payroll report a method in the class that stores the pertinent information, rather than an object by itself.

4.4 Subsystems

The complexity of a model sometimes gets out of hand. According to Coad and Yourdon a system containing 35 classes is of average size, while one with about 110 classes is considered large. It is also common for the problem domain to include several subdomains, each one with up to 100 classes. With this level of complexity the fundamental features of the problem domain may become difficult to grasp, and, therefore, to explain to clients and users. A convenient mechanism for reducing model complexity is its division into subsystems, sometimes called *subjects* in object-oriented analysis literature.

Subsystems do not reduce complexity by simplifying the model but rather by progressively focusing on its different components. For example, suppose a model depicts a full-featured graphics library, shown in Figure 4.13.

In such cases the resulting model can be elaborate and complicated. However, by noticing that the graphics operations refer to drawing geometrical figures, to displaying text, and to interacting with a mouse, we are able to decompose it into three independent subsystems. Each of these subsystems can then be treated as a logical entity, even though they may share functions or interact with each other. In Figure 4.14 we have repositioned some of the classes and added rectangles to enclose the subsystems. Each rectangle is labeled with the subsystem's name. Some authors use numbers to designate subsystems. In either case the result is a more manageable model.

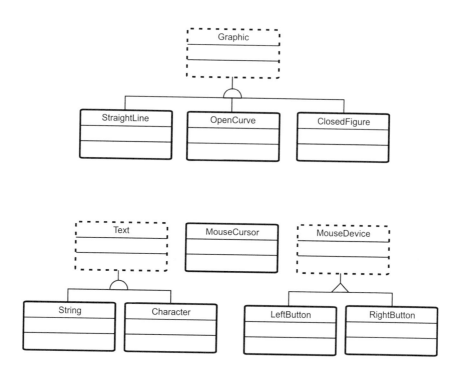

Figure 4.13 *Classes and Structures of a Graphics Toolkit*

4.4.1 Subsystems as Modules

In Section 1.2.3 we discussed the concept of a program module as a logical unit of division based on structural or functional considerations. The concept of a program module should not be equated with that of a procedure, a subroutine, or a disk file, although occasionally they may coincide. This viewpoint determines that modularization should not be considered as an implementation issue, but as one related to system analysis and design.

In this sense the notion of a subsystem is quite compatible with that of a module. Therefore subsystems identified during the analysis stage can become modules during the design stage. But for this to happen the subsystem must meet the same requirements demanded of modules.

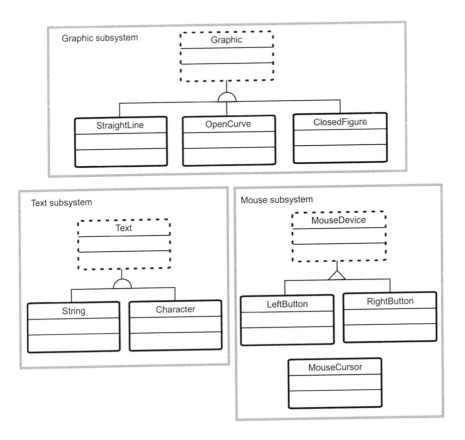

Figure 4.14 *Graphics Toolkit Subsystems*

Subsystem Cohesion

Regarding modules, *cohesion* or *binding* refers to the relationship between its internal elements; the same applies to subsystems. A subsystem in which the contained classes are strongly related has high cohesion. Sometimes we include a class into a subsystem simply because there is no better place for it. Inclusion of an unrelated class reduces subsystem cohesion. However, this does not mean that all classes in a subsystem must be intimately linked, but rather that they must be strongly related in the problem domain. For example, in Figure 4.14 the **Mouse** subsystem contains the class **MouseCursor** which is not part of any class structure. However, because this class is closely related to the problem domain of mouse functions it fits well in the subsystem.

Using conventional terminology we can say that a subsystem in which the classes are related loosely can show only *coincidental cohesion*, while one in which the classes are related logically show *logical cohesion*. Cohesion levels are difficult to quantify, but the functional strength of a subsystem depends on it having high cohesion.

Subsystem Coupling

The concept of *coupling* is a measure of the degree of interconnection between subsystems. In this sense two closely coupled subsystems have a high degree of interaction and interdependence, while loosely coupled subsystems stand independently of each other. Subsystems with high coupling are difficult to understand, analyze, and reuse separately; therefore, high coupling is generally considered an undesirable property. On the other hand all subsystems are usually coupled in some way since they must interact in producing a common functionality. It is difficult to imagine a system in which all its component subsystems are totally uncoupled.

In general, good subsystem structure should have a high cohesion and a low coupling. The classes must be closely related within the subsystem and there should be a minimum interdependency between subsystems.

4.5 Attributes

An attribute is a data element within a class, and each different object instantiated from a class is associated with a unique set of values for its attributes. For example, in Figure 4.11 each object instantiated from the class **Physician** has a unique **name**, **specialty**, and **authorized_to_perform** attribute value. This unique set of values is sometimes referred to as the object's *state*.

One of the fundamental rules of object orientation is that attributes should not be directly accessible from outside the class. The only way to obtain or change the value of an attribute is by using a method that performs this function. However, many programming languages do not impose this rule; for example, in C++ it is possible to declare an attribute to be of public access type and thus make it visible to other classes and to client code. Nevertheless, making attributes visible outside the class violates the principles of encapsulation and data abstraction, which, in turn, defeats one of the fundamental purposes of the object-oriented paradigm.

While classes and structures are relatively stable over the lifetime of a system, attributes are likely to change. In refining or expanding the functionality of a class we often have to introduce new attributes and methods. For example, the **Physician** class in Figure 4.11 may be refined by introducing attributes to reflect the individual's social security number and home address. In this case encapsulation requires that new methods be developed to access the new attributes.

4.5.1 Attribute Identification

During the initial stage of analysis we often draw diagrams of classes and structures excluding attributes and methods, whose definition is postponed until we become more familiar with the basic elements of the model. However, the analysis phase is not complete until we have identified attributes and methods for every class.

The fundamental notion of an attribute relates to what the containing class is responsible for knowing. For example, an analyst defining an **Employee** class may be tempted to include sex as an attribute. However, if the system does not use the employee's sex in any of the processing operations performed by the class, and if this attribute is not required in defining an object's state, then it is outside of the system's responsibilities and should not be included. If the attribute later becomes necessary it can be added at that time. Attempting to predict, at analysis time, the attributes or methods that may become necessary in the future is usually a bad idea. The result is often a system overloaded with useless elements which serve only to complicate it and add to its cost. It is much more practical to make generalized allowances that will accommodate growth or modification, rather than attempt to guess all the requirements that could become necessary.

In identifying attributes we may ask the following questions:

1. How is the object described?

2. What properties are associated with the object in the problem domain?

3. What properties associated with the object are necessary for implementing the system's responsibilities?

4. What properties of the object need to be remembered over time?

5. What states can the object be in?

Not all of these questions are pertinent for all objects and, in some cases, more than one question can have the same answer. At the same time some objects are conceptually very simple, while others are complex. For example, the **LeftButton** object of a mouse device (see Figure 4.14) is a rather simple one. It appears that questions number 3, 4, and 5 are pertinent in this case. Specifically, the system's responsibilities may require that it be known if the left mouse button has been pressed (button down) or released (button up). The property to be remembered over time is the button's current status, which is also the object's possible state. Therefore, it appears that one attribute that encodes the state of the left mouse button as currently being down or up may be sufficient in this case.

On the other hand, an **Employee** class that keeps track of the individuals in the employment of an organization may require attributes such as **name**, **address**, **social_sec_number**, **date_of_employment**, **hourly_wage/salary**, **hours_worked**, **taxable_income**, and many others. Several ethical and legal issues may be considered at this time. For example, if it is illegal to base any employment decision on the employee's age, should the individual's date of birth be stored as an attribute? If a company has no other reason for knowing an employee's age, could the fact that this information is stored with other employee data be used against the company in an age discrimination dispute? The following argument could be made in this case: why would a firm incur the expense of storing data that it does not intend to use?

The decision to include or exclude an attribute is usually made jointly by client and analyst. The safest advice is not to include attributes that are outside of the system's current responsibilities. Crystal ball-based system analysis can be counterproductive.

4.5.2 Attributes and Structures

Occasionally we may be uncertain regarding which class of a Gen-

Spec structure should contain a particular attribute. For example, when assigning attributes to the classes depicted in the **Text** subsystem (shown in Figure 4.14) we may decide that each text string or character will have a particular letter style and point size. Should these attributes appear in the classes **String** and **Character**, or on the parent class **Text**? The general rule in this case is to position the attribute at the highest point in the class structure applicable to all specializations. Therefore the attributes should appear in the class **Text**, as shown in Figure 4.15.

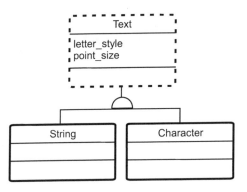

Figure 4.15 *Attribute Positioning in a Gen-Spec Structure*

4.6 Methods or Services

A system is functional and useful by virtue of the processing operations that it performs: a system must do *something*. A perfect structure of classes and attributes, with no methods, is worthless. The specific behavior that an object must exhibit is called a *service*. Service is synonymous with processing operations and coincides with a class' methods.

4.6.1 Identifying Methods

The analyst can follow several routines in order to identify the methods associated with each class. In this respect the following questions could be useful:

1. What are the object states?

2. What are the required services?

Object States

When an object is created it is associated with a set of attribute values that define its state. These attributes can change from the time the object is created until it is released. Every change in attribute values defines a new object state. We can determine an object's state by examining the range of values that can be assigned to each attribute in the light of the system's responsibilities. From this analysis we can construct a simple diagram showing the various states which are defined for the object as well as the transitions between states. For example, regarding the **MouseCursor** object in Figure 4.14 we may define that the system's responsibilities include knowing if the cursor is on or off; if on, its current screen position. The class can now be refined by drawing the state transition diagram. Later on we can use the state transition diagram to deduce the class' methods. The preliminary steps are shown in Figure 4.16.

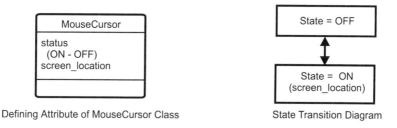

Defining Attribute of MouseCursor Class   State Transition Diagram

Figure 4.16 *Attributes and Object State Diagram*

Required Services

From the object states and the object attributes it is possible to deduce the required services or methods. Here again, the services to be considered should be those within the system's responsibilities. Several categories of algorithmically-simple services should always be investigated. These are usually called *Create, Connect, Access,* and *Release*:

1. Create. This service is used to create and optionally initialize an object. When no particular initialization is required the Create service is often implicit. However, if an object's creation requires the initialization of attributes it should be distinctly defined. This approach is consistent with the operation of constructor functions in C++.

2. Connect. This type of service is used to establish or break a connection between objects. It corresponds to the notion of an instance connection described in Section 4.7.

3. Access. This type of service assigns values to attributes or returns attribute values. Its existence results from the principles of encapsulation and data abstraction, which require that attributes not be accessed from outside the class.

4. Release or Destroy. This service destroys the object. It corresponds to destructors in C++.

Much of the required behavior of an object can be performed by the Create, Connect, Access, or Destroy services. In many systems these algorithmically-simple methods account for 80 to 95 percent of the required functionality. However, algorithmically-complex methods are also often required. They usually correspond to the types Calculate and Monitor.

1. Calculate. This type of service uses the attribute values in the object to perform a calculation.

2. Monitor. This type of service is usually associated with an external device or system. Its functions relate to input, output, data acquisition, and control.

The methodology to follow in defining the required services consists of first examining the object for the four algorithmically-simple service types (Create, Connect, Access, and Destroy) and then for the two algorithmically-complex types (Calculate and Monitor). All object methods fall into one of these categories. For example, examining the **MouseCursor** class in Figure 4.17, we can identify two algorithmically-simple services. An access-type service is used to determine whether the cursor is in the ON or OFF state. A Connect-type service is used to establish a link between the MouseCursor object and the service that monitors the cursor movement on the screen. Figure 4.17 shows the corresponding class diagram.

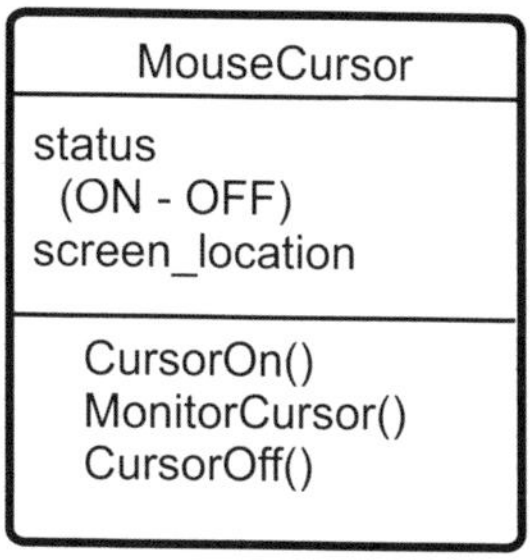

```
┌─────────────────────────┐
│       MouseCursor       │
├─────────────────────────┤
│ status                  │
│  (ON - OFF)             │
│ screen_location         │
├─────────────────────────┤
│ CursorOn()              │
│ MonitorCursor()         │
│ CursorOff()             │
└─────────────────────────┘
```

Figure 4.17 *Defining Services for the MouseCursor Object*

4.7 Instance Connections

While structures depict associations between classes, instance connections, as the name suggests, show associations between objects. Since objects cannot be instantiated from abstract classes, there can be no instance connection to or from an abstract class. In the analysis phase an instance connection reflects a mapping between objects in the problem domain. Note that while instance connections denote association they do not imply inheritance. Also that instance connections are a weaker type of association than a Whole-Part or Gen-Spec structure. Like all other elements of system analysis, all instance connections should be within the system's responsibilities.

4.7.1 Instance Connection Notation

Instance connections are shown in class diagrams as solid lines between objects. Optionally, instance connection lines can be labeled to show the nature of the association. Coad and Yourdon consider that these labels are usually unnecessary. The notation includes numbers that indicate the upper and lower bounds of the object association. Figure 4.18 shows an example of instance connection notation.

In Figure 4.18 we note that each driver can have zero or one license, and that each license must correspond to a single driver. In the first case the numerical constraint is separated by a comma to indicate a range. When there is no explicit upper bound the letter m can be used to replace the word "many."

Figure 4.18 *Example of Instance Connection Notation*

4.8 Message Connections

While an instance connection represents a mapping between objects in the problem domain, a message connection refers to messages being sent between objects. In this context the term "sender" and "receiver" are often used. The purpose of the message is to obtain a processing operation which must be defined in both the sender's and the receiver's specifications. Trivial and literal messages are not included in this convention. Message connections occur when an object instantiates an object of another class, or when an object uses methods defined in another class.

4.8.1 Message Connection Notation

Coad and Yourdon notation uses gray lines to indicate message connections. In hand-drawn diagrams we could substitute them by dashed lines. To illustrate a message connection suppose a graphics package with a class **StraightLine** and a class **Polygon**. Each **StraightLine** object has a start point, an end point, and a thickness attribute. A **Polygon** is drawn by instantiating several objects of the class **StraightLine**. Figure 4.19 shows the objects and the corresponding message connection notation.

Note that the arrow in Figure 4.19 points from the sender to the receiver of a message. This implies that the sender takes some specified action to which the receiver replies by returning a result to the sender or by performing a predefined function. Although typically the message connection takes place between objects, it is also possible to make the receiver a class, in which case it responds by instantiating a new object. An alternate notation uses a multipointed arrow in the case where more than one object is a receiver. Note that human interactions with a system (usually in the form of commands or requests) can often be depicted by means of message connection symbols.

4.9 Final Documentation

Once the analysis has concluded we must put together the corresponding documents. The most important one is normally the class diagram. However, in substantial projects it is often necessary to reduce complexity by layering the class diagram, as follows:

1. A layer indicating the various subsystems

2. A layer for each subsystem indicating inheritance in the form Gen-Spec and Whole-Part structures

3. A layer showing attributes and services for each class

4. A layer depicting instance and message connection for each object

In addition to the class and object diagrams, other documents are usually associated with the analysis phase, namely:

1. A description of class and object specifications

2. State transition diagrams

3. Documents describing system constraints and critical threads of execution

Figure 4.19 *Example of Message Connection Notation*

Chapter 5

Object-Oriented Design

5.0 Elements of System Design

Although the analysis phase of object-oriented development is currently a well-defined set of rules and activities (such as those proposed by Coad and Yourdon), the same is not true about the design phase. Monographs and textbooks on object-oriented design often leave us with the feeling that the subject matter is a rather amorphous collection of operations, which appear to be more extensions of those in the analysis phase than a new and specific task. We believe that the reason for the fuzziness of the design phase is not related to lack of talent or vision on part of the writers, but to their ambition to make the analysis phase independent from machine specifications, implementation issues, and programming environments.

In the context of software engineering, *design* refers to *program design*, and programs are concrete (although intangible) products. Therefore, adopting a high level of abstraction for the purpose of achieving a greater generality can lead to models that are of little practical use. At coding time programmers need design documents that conform to the development environment. For example, if a program is to be coded in a strongly typed language, the design phase should address specific data types. On the other hand, if the project is to be coded in a loosely typed or untyped language then data type decisions in the design phase are both unnecessary and unadvisable. In this sense a programmer working in C++ may find it convenient if the designer defined the variables that would be integers, those that would be arrays, and the ones that would be reals. By the same token, a programmer working in Lisp or Prolog would find concrete data types meaningless and confusing.

We realize that our hands-on approach to object-oriented design may not be acceptable to those more theoretically inclined, and we admit that it is not a universally applicable methodology. Our justification for adopting this rather pragmatic approach is that it gives developers who have already committed to object orientation as a paradigm, to C++ as a development environment, and to the PC as a host machine a more tangible and practical approach to the design phase, and that it provides a smoother transition path from analysis to coding.

5.0.1 A Transitional Phase

In the Introduction we mentioned that this book's approach to object-oriented development is geared towards the smaller project. Therefore we have been more concerned with practicality of the proposed methods than with their theoretical correctness. Our book assumes that the project will be developed in C++ and that the target environment is a Personal Computer. This means that we have already committed to a particular hardware platform and to a development environment. In this context our vision of program design in general, and of object-oriented design in particular, is a transition from analysis to coding. We start the design phase with a series of documents and diagrams that were developed during analysis. At the conclusion of the design phase we should be ready to start producing code.

Furthermore, the design phase should facilitate the partitioning of the coding task among several programmers, with a reasonable expectation that their various efforts will integrate into a finished product. Rather than avoiding environment and platform considerations, we propose that these decisions are the most important ones that must be addressed during design. In fact, we begin design by defining the hardware platform and the software environment for the project. The following is a list of the critical tasks that must be performed during the design phase:

1. Definition of the hardware and operating system environment

2. Definition of the user interface and software development environment

3. Adoption of naming conventions and standard headers

4. Identification of program modules. Refinement of the modular structure to suit the development environment

5. Definition of data types and structures

6. Description of algorithms, flowcharts, and pseudocode for the critical processes. Possibly also of the partial prototypes and code fragment that will be used to ascertain the functionality and appropriateness of the selected algorithms

7. Refinement of classes and objects

8. Definition of language-specific inheritance structures from the classifications performed during the analysis phase

9. Convention for error handling and exceptions

10. Code documentation, comments, and semiformal specifications conventions

This list does not imply that we must perform these operations in any given order, nor that we cannot undertake any one task until the preceding ones are completed. For example, we may decide to postpone a decision on the development environment (list entry number 2) until the details of program design are defined. Or we may find it more convenient to defer the definition of data types and data structures (list entry number 5) until after the fundamental classes are refined (list entry number 7) and the inheritance structures established (list entry number 8). Furthermore, it is feasible that some of the listed tasks are not applicable or unnecessary in a particular project. For example, for a project that requires simple and straightforward coding we may decide not to define algorithms or partial code prototypes mentioned in list entry number 6.

A more useful scenario is one in which the various tasks are initially visited and then revisited several times during the design phase. In one case we may initially decide that the hardware platform requires a 66 Mz 486 PC, 16 Mb of RAM, and a 1.2 gigabyte hard drive, running Windows 3.1. Later in the design we may observe that the proposed machine does not ensure minimal performance requirements. Therefore the hardware specifications are upgraded to a 120 Mz. Pentium PC, with 32 Mb of RAM, running Windows 95. In a final consideration we may decide to maintain the requirements regarding CPU and

RAM, but reconsider that Windows 3.1 would also serve as an operating system. The one important consideration is that design decisions are flexible by nature, and commitments are subject to frequent revisions and modifications. It is not unusual that a project well under way must be redesigned in order to accommodate new hardware or software developments. The one unacceptable alternative is a program or system that is already obsolete the day that it is released.

5.1 Hardware and Operating System

In the analysis phase we intentionally avoided implementation decisions. At that time our purpose was to produce a model of the problem domain that was not influenced by particular hardware preferences or by the preselection of a development platform. An exception to this rule is when implementation considerations are part of the specification. For example, if a client requires an application that executes in Windows 95, then it would be futile to exclude this requirement during the analysis phase. In this case the fact that the program is to execute under Windows 95 should be a major design consideration. However, the more common case is that during the analysis phase no effort is made to define hardware environments or software development tools.

In this book we start from the assumption that our program executes in a Personal Computer. This presumption somewhat defines the system hardware. In some very flexible and undemanding projects the general machine specifications may suffice. But in many cases we have to make further refinements in the hardware requirements and in the operating system choice. Suppose that the project at hand is a satellite image processing application that stores image data, performs enhancement operations on this data, and displays the results on a graphics screen. In this case program designers have to define the minimum graphics requirements for the application, which, in turn, determines a minimal hardware configuration, and may even affect the possible choice of operating systems.

5.1.1 PC Hardware Components

The following list includes some of the more important hardware components of the PC. It is intended to be used more as a checklist than as a template.

1. Central processing unit
   a. number of processors in system
   b. CPU specifications and manufacturer
   c. CPU speed
   d. amount of level 1 cache memory

2. Motherboard
   a. number of CPUs
   b. chipset
   c. on-board controllers
   d. expansion slots
   e. BIOS
   f. input/output ports
   g. RAM expansion
   h. bus architecture

3. System memory resources
   a. RAM
   b. level 2 cache

4. Storage
   a. floppy drives
   b. hard disks
   c. CD ROM drive
   d. other storage and backup devices

5. Video system
   a. monitor
   b. video controller
   c. video memory and expandability
   d. support for standard video modes

6. Peripheral components
   a. networks
   b. keyboard and mice
   c. hardcopy devices

In this list we have intentionally omitted many of the hardware details. Often the system designers have to go beyond these fundamental elements. For example, the design of a high-end CAD system could require specialized input and output devices together with a video system that exceeds normal requirements.

5.1.2 System Architecture

In the context of computer hardware and operating environments the term "architecture" refers to a particular arrangement of components that suits a specific purpose. One of the first elements that defines a system architecture is the number of machines and their connectivity. In PC systems the following are the most common cases:

1. System consists of a single machine

2. System consists of several unconnected machines

3. System consists of several connected machines

In the third case we must further define the characteristics of the network. Although there is no reason why PCs cannot be used in wide area networks, the more common case is that of a local area network. At the design stage LANs can be defined in the following general terms:

1. Number of servers and clients

2. Network topology

3. Access procedures

A second architectural element relates to the software environment. Current day PC systems fall into one of the following types:

1. Turn-key system

2. DOS system

3. Windows system

4. Unix system

Turn-key Systems

Turn-key or dedicated systems are specialized machines designed to perform a single function. Sometimes they contain a small operating system in ROM and powerup directly to an application, thus the name "turn-key." Because turn-key systems are configured for a single purpose they can be optimized to perform a selected set of functions. Another advantage is that before the system is delivered all software and hardware components are installed, initialized, and tested. Also, users have few reasons for changing system settings since the machine cannot perform other tasks. The major disadvantage is that a dedicated system cannot be used for other purposes. Nevertheless, PC system designers often fail to consider the possibility of a dedicated or turn-key system since the PC is regarded as a universal machine. For many applications a turn-key system is a more suitable option than a general-purpose machine.

DOS Systems

DOS was the original operating system for the PC and remains its major software workhorse. Programmers working in the DOS environment have easy access to all hardware devices and related machine features. The operating system places no restrictions on the programmer's power. Therefore it is possible to access all components directly in order to produce any desired functionality that lies within the machine's capabilities. But with this power come risks and responsibilities, since badly designed or coded DOS programs can raise havoc with the machine hardware settings, the installed software, and the user's data files. Another factor to consider is that developing sophisticated software for the DOS environment may entail considerable difficulty. For example, designing and coding from scratch a DOS graphical user interface, with the corresponding video and mouse controls, can be a major undertaking; although toolkits, programming support packages, and DOS frameworks are available to ease this task.

Windows Systems

Windows is a graphical environment with multitasking capabilities that operates the CPU in protected mode. Major versions in common use are Windows 3.1, Windows 95, Windows NT, and OS/2 Warp. Windows 95 has better performance than Windows 3.1 but requires a 486 or higher CPU. It also claims a more friendly user interface. OS/2, the IBM version of Windows, has many features of interest to the programmer, however, this operating system has achieved little popularity.

Unix Systems

Unix is a mainframe operating system but in recent years software emulations for the PC have become available; Linux and Freebsd are probably the best known ones. Although very few desktop PCs operate under it, a unix PC is an attractive option in some cases. For example, a high-end PC running Linux or Freebsd can be used as a network server for a small LAN.

Protected mode execution provided by Windows, OS/2, and Unix is safer than real mode, since applications have limited access to critical system resources. This makes it more difficult for code to have damaging effects on hardware or software systems. On the other hand, the Windows programmer is limited to those functions provided by the operating system, and, in general, cannot exceed this functionality. An additional possible disadvantage of programming in Windows or OS/2 is that some applications run slower than in DOS.

Choosing a System

The choice between a dedicated or turn-key system, a DOS, a Windows, or a Unix environment is often not an easy one. Each option entails advantages and disadvantages. Personal preference or previous skills in the development team can tip the scale in favor of a system that may not be the best choice. The following guidelines may help in reaching a decision.

1. Systems that require special or unusual hardware or software configurations, in machines that are not needed for other purposes, are candidates for a turn-key system. The fact that turn-key systems are usually more stable and dependable should also be considered.

2. Systems that require special functionalities, access to hardware devices, or high levels of performance or programmer control are candidates for DOS. The decision to use DOS should take into consideration the availability of special programming facilities and the skills of the development team. Hardware programming usually requires assembly language, and assembly language programmers are in short supply nationwide.

3. Windows systems are usually associated with a graphical user interface and with software that can conform to the behavior and performance assured by the operating system environment. Windows programs have access to a host of standard GUI functions that facilitate coding. Windows libraries, toolkits, and frameworks can provide additional assistance.

4. Coexistence with other software can be a determining factor. For example, a new program that must interact with an existing one operat-

ing in a particular environment will make this environment a strong candidate.

5.2 User Interface Design

Selection of an operating system can facilitate the development of a user interface. However, the problems associated with the design of a user interface often extend beyond the services provided by an operating system. That is, when the program requires input or output services not furnished by the operating system of choice.

An example could be a CAD application requiring access to an elaborate input device (such as a graphic tablet); it must drive a specialized output device (such as a plotter). In this case both components of the user interface, input and output, are critical elements in the program's design and may include many features and details which are outside the services normally provided by operating system functions. Another example of the user interface becoming an issue to be addressed separately during design is a DOS application that includes a graphical user interface. In this case the DOS operating system and the conventional DOS programming environments do not furnish GUI services; therefore, the user interface becomes a design to be addressed separately.

5.2.1 Interface Component Protocol

Whether using standard or customized services, define an interface protocol that applies to the entire development process and that is adopted by all members of the coding team. A consistent format should be used for displaying error messages, prompting user input, and for controlling visual program elements such as windows, scrollbars, and buttons. Cursors and icons should also be defined and adopted as a project standard. In some development environments the interface protocol is defined by the operating system services. In cases in which the interface is customized the designers have to define the components both graphically and literally.

One possible approach to interface standardization is to provide a common access hook for all code. For example, upon detecting an error condition, a program element calls a general error message handler routine and passes to it a message string and an action code. The error handler displays the string in a standard error message box and takes the corresponding action.

5.3 The Software Development Environment

Today most programs are created using rather sophisticated development tools. The selection of the most adequate tools for the project at hand can facilitate or hinder the program designer's tasks, a decision whose consequence later overflows into the coding stage. Suppose a Windows application that includes an auxiliary word processor program. The task of designing and coding a word processor is a major chore. However, the Borland Visual Solution Pack, a framework for Windows development, includes a WYSIWYG word processor application that can be integrated into user code with minimal effort. In this case we can considerably reduce design and coding effort for our project by choosing a development environment that is compatible with the Visual Solutions Pack. Similar facilities are available from Microsoft and other software vendors.

The popularity of the so-called *visual* development tools is related to the fact that they provide an effective code reuse mechanism that simplifies development. Coding the operations and functions that are unique for a particular application is usually a big enough job in itself. Any help that we can get from reusing code is welcomed. Code reuse is achieved by means of programming libraries, toolkits, application frameworks, and even by simple scavenging through programmer's cookbooks or through our own sources. Chapter 8 is devoted to code reuse mechanisms and techniques.

In addition to programming facilities, several other factors influence the choice of development environments. Since, in the context of this book, we have already decided on C++, we must next pick a particular compiler, its associated development tools, and the compatible plug-ins. The following considerations can be examined:

1. Compatibility with other executables. This factor must be taken into consideration when the design calls for using existing code or interfacing with other applications.

2. Compatibility with development tools. This refers to the use of compilers, assemblers, programming toolkits and applications frameworks.

3. Compatibility with low- or high-level languages. This applies to projects that are developed in a multilanguage environment. In this case the selected software environment must be friendly to the other languages. One factor to be considered is that some vendors ensure and support compatibility with their own products. For example, a Microsoft version of C++ easily interfaces with assembly language code developed using Microsoft MASM. By the same token, a Borland C++ compiler code interfaces with assembly language code generated with Borland's Turbo Assembler. Multilanguage programming is discussed in Section 13.2.

4. Preferences and skills of the development team. The fact that members of the development team have skills in a particular environment is an asset that can be capitalized, assuming no other drawbacks. Even subjective preferences should be favored when no other factors advise against it. People work better with the tools they are used to and like.

5. Cost, availability of resources, or compatibility with existing systems. All other factors being equal it is reasonable to favor the less costly development environment, the one already available, or the one that is compatible with existing hardware and software.

6. Client's preference and maintenance considerations. Sometimes it is a good idea to consult a client regarding preferences in the development environment. If a program is to be maintained or updated by another organization, that organization's preference should be a factor in the choice.

5.4 Naming Conventions

During the coding phase we create many smaller program components, most of which were not specifically addressed during design. The programming team should have a naming agreement for all program elements. Without a naming convention the project can become difficult to understand and maintain. The following program components should be considered for naming rules:

1. Sources, executables, libraries, modules, and programming support files

2. Classes and objects

3. Variables, constants, and data structures

4. Methods, functions, and subroutines

Deciding what should be in a name is no trivial task. For example, a name structure suitable for a program module may not be adequate for a variable. In the following sections we will address naming requirements for each of the listed elements.

5.4.1 Filenames

The allowable length and the structure of a filename vary in different operating systems. MS DOS, for example, limits filenames to eight alphanumeric characters plus an extension with up to three additional characters. Unix and Windows 95, on the other hand, allow longer filenames and extensions. The actual filename structure is usually predetermined. However, in some cases development takes place in multiple operating system environments. For example, a Windows 95 application may be developed using some DOS programming tools. In this case it is safer to adopt the filename rules of the more restrictive operating system. In addition to field length, the filename format may also define the use of terminators and establish rules for capitalization.

Once we have decided the filename format we should consider the rules to be used in name generation. The development environment generally allows extensions to filenames, often used to identify the various file types. For example, PC executable files have the extensions EXE or COM, while C++ source files have the extension CPP. This eliminates the need to use the filename character field to define program elements that can be deduced from the extension. Other items of information often provided by the operating system are the file's date and time of creation.

Note that not all filename data fields apply to all file types. For example, module names usually need not appear in the executable. Therefore, the adopted naming convention for one type of file may be different than the one for another type. The following list mentions other data elements to be considered:

1. The filename can contain elements specific to the development project. For example, a project developing satellite image processing soft-

ware could be identified by the initials SIP. In this case we may require that every filename in the project start with the SIP character field.

2. The filename can identify a particular member of the development team or a subteam. In this case we could require a two-character field that identifies the developer. For instance, Mary Smith would use the field code MS in all the files which she creates. The filename would now appear as SIP_MS

3. Programs are usually divided into modules. The filename convention can include information about the program module. A digit or digit field can be used to identify the module. For example, an editor program may include the modules: monitor, insert, replace, delete, and store. In this case we could use the letter M, I, R, D, and S to identify the module. The filename for the replace module would now be: SIP_MS_R.

4. A module is usually stored in more than one disk file. The naming convention may reflect each source file of the module. A simple approach is to use the module name field as a root and add a numerical code for each source file or submodule. For example, if the filename for the module is SIP_MS_R, then the first source file would be SIP_MS_R1.

5. A program version can also be reflected in the filename. For example, the executable for the second alpha version of the mentioned program could be named SIP_A2.

5.4.2 Standard Headers

It is usually difficult to record all the needed information within a filename, no matter how much we compress and encode the data. A standard header can be used in source files to remedy this. The following is a list of some items of information often included in standard headers:

1. Date of file creation

2. Name of author or authors

3. Copyright notice

4. Filename

5. File update history, including dates and modifications

6. Associated modules and support files

7. Development tools and resources

8. Hardware and software requirements

9. Testing history and bug fixes

Some of these elements should appear in any program header; others depend on the project's type and complexity. The following is our program header template for C++ source files:

```
//******************************************************************
//                           PROGNAME.CPP
//          Copyright (c) 199? by Skipanon Software Associates
//                        ALL RIGHTS RESERVED
//******************************************************************
// Date:                        Coded by:
// Filename:                    Module name:
//                              Source file:
// Description:
//
//******************************************************************
// Libraries and software support:
//
//******************************************************************
// Development environment:
//
//******************************************************************
// System requirements:
//
//******************************************************************
// Start date:
// Update history:
//          DATE              MODIFICATION
//
//******************************************************************
// Test history:
//    PROTOCOL          DATE        TEST RESULTS
//******************************************************************
```

5.4.3 Names of Program Components

Naming conventions can include classes, data types and structures, methods, and other programmer-defined elements. The actual naming rules depend on the information items that we want represented in the name, on the rules imposed by the programming environment, and on style considerations. For example, we may decide that class names should use an alphanumeric code that identifies the module in which the class resides; or that variable names are in lower case, using underscore symbols to separate words, while functions and method names start with an initial cap; and that capital letters are used to separate individual words in functions. This or any other naming scheme is acceptable as long as it is legal in the programming language, the names represent the data items considered important, and it follows the fundamental conventions in C++ coding style.

The principal analyst or project manager is responsible for enforcing the adopted naming conventions and for monitoring their use by the individual members of the programming team.

5.5 Modularization

The word module is used inconsistently in the literature. In the context of this book a *module* is a logical unit of program division based on structural, functional, or logical considerations. A module is not a procedure, a subroutine, or a disk file. In Chapter 4 we saw that the notion of a subsystem coincides with that of a program module. Also, subsystems and modules share the properties of high cohesion and low coupling. Therefore, the subsystems identified during the analysis phase are strong candidates for program modules in the design phase. If no subsystems were identified during analysis, then either the project is structurally very simple, or the analysis was not performed to the necessary level of detail.

Modular division should precede the coding phase since modules provide a convenient unit for division of labor. In practice, coding tasks are often distributed to individual programmers or to programming teams based on the identified modules. The high cohesion and low coupling features of good modularization support this approach. If a project to be coded by several programmers presents no modular units in the design state, then the division of responsibilities during the coding state becomes more difficult. If modules do not exist naturally, then we have to invent them. Any unit of program division that is consistent with the rules of good modularization can be used.

5.5.1 Modularization Refinements

Often, modules derived directly from the subsystems identified in the analysis phase are well suited to our purpose, although occasionally they must be further refined or extended. One reason for these refinements could be practical constraints imposed by the module size. For instance, a very large module may have to be partitioned to several programmers during the coding phase. In this case modular subdivision is an issue that should be addressed during design.

Submodules and Source Files

Most analysts and project managers like to keep file sizes within reasonable limits. Large source files are difficult to manage and require long compile- or assembly-times. In most projects a size limitation should be placed on source files. The limit can be expressed in the file's byte size, in a source line count, or in any other unit that can be conveniently estimated with the development tools at hand. The file size in kilobytes is usually calculated by the operating system and can be readily checked by the programmer. Some editors display a source file line count that can be used as a unit for measuring file size.

Partitioning into several source files does not entail additional modularization. A module is a logical concept but a disk file is a mere unit of storage. A module can be contained in as many disk files as is necessary or convenient. We usually call the disk files submodules or sources. One issue that arises in dividing a module into subunits is a naming convention for the individual files. This problem was addressed in Section 5.4.1.

The General Support Module

No matter how well thought-out the modularization for a project, program elements will appear during the coding phase that do not fit well into any of the existing modules. This is the case with general purpose routines, such as error and exception handlers, and support functions that provide programming services, such as a mouse interface, a display operation, a keyboard filter, or a memory management routine. Support modules that serve as a catch-all for general purpose code and other program elements that do not fit well into any of the established modules should be created. The rationale behind the catch-all module is that it may not be a rigorous construct, but that it is better to have a vessel in which to place these loose program elements than have them distributed all over the code, thus contaminating the integrity of the entire program.

5.6 Critical Data Elements

In a project of even modest complexity it is impossible to anticipate all the data elements that will become necessary during its implementation. In most cases it is futile and even wasteful to attempt it. However, in many projects there are critical data elements that take on a special importance. For example, a typical word processor program manipulates the user text file as a complex memory structure that includes ASCII characters, as well as control and terminator codes. Most programmers working on the word processor project would write code that accesses this large and complicated data construct, adds to it, deletes from it, or manipulates it in various other ways.

In this case the user text file is a critical data element in the project, and its structure and operation should be carefully considered during design. In structured programming we used to look into external data components in order to identify the critical structures. When using object-oriented methods we often encapsulate a critical data component within a class that provides limited access to the actual structure. The object-oriented approach is safer but also more complicated.

At design time the following steps are useful regarding critical data elements:

1. Locate and identify the critical data elements

2. Decide how the data elements will be represented in the code

3. Define, in detail, the actual representation

The first step consists of a search for data components that are critical to the program. The second step is a decision whether the critical data component will be an external program element (as in conventional structured programming) or if it will be encapsulated in a class structure. If an external data structure, accessible to all code, then merely define its architecture. If an encapsulating class, then identify and describe the methods that provide access to the hidden data construct. In the third step the actual data construct must be defined with as much detail as is feasible and practical at this stage.

5.7 Critical Processing Elements

Some projects can be implemented with straightforward, conventional code, while others contain subtleties or complications of execution that must be addressed in the design. It is impossible to predict all program elements that may originate critical processing operations. The following list covers only the most fundamental and obvious ones:

1. Code with critical requirements in execution time

2. Code with critical requirements in numeric precision

3. Routines that access hardware resources directly

4. Routines that perform uncommon operations or that violate system constraints or restrictions

5. Code that performs multitasking or multiprocessing tasks or others not supported by system facilities

Each of these, as well as many others that arise in practical programming, may give rise to critical processing operations that should be addressed in the design phase.

5.7.1 Algorithm Identification

Execution requirements can be separated into three broad categories: performance requirements, precision requirements, and operational context requirements. Either one of these may determine the need for identifying a particular algorithm in the design phase. In some cases more than one requirement applies. One such case is a processing routine that has to ensure both the performance and the precision of a calculation, or a routine that must solve a new problem and do so within a given performance constraint.

In some fortunate cases algorithm identification can be resolved by browsing through textbooks or periodical publications. However, in those cases where no canned solution is available the designers must tackle the task of inventing a new solution path. The problem for finding solutions for not-yet-answered questions has been addressed by Polya (see bibliography) and others. The whole field of heuristics is devoted to this difficult and often perplexing chore.

5.7.2 Flowcharts and Pseudocode

Once we have a notion of the solution path for a critical processing operation, the next step is usually to break it down into a sequence of logical processing steps. Later on we will be able to follow these steps in implementing the solution in code. Two tools are frequently used in this phase: flowcharts and pseudocode. Either one is suitable and both can be used simultaneously.

Note that we indicate the use of flowcharts and pseudocode for critical processing operations. By no means do we suggest that every program element should be flowcharted or pseudcoded at design time. Flowcharts and pseudocode are code development tools and they should be used, predominantly, during the coding phase.

5.7.3 Partial Prototypes

Sometimes we must ascertain the validity of a proposed algorithm by means of coding experiments, also called *partial prototypes*. These experiments are designed to tell us if the solution is a valid one or if we must continue searching and investigating. In some cases these tests and prototypes can be postponed until the coding phase; in others, it becomes important to determine if a possible solution actually works in code before we make other decisions or commitments.

There is much to be said for the judicious use of partial prototypes and code experiments. These efforts can help us keep the design on a realistic foundation and allow the designers to visualize the final product. Furthermore, the coding time and effort that goes into performing these tests are usually not wasted, since they are reused in the final program.

5.8 Refinement of Classes and Objects

The project's fundamental classes and objects are identified and interrelated during the analysis phase. At design time the system analyst should have available the diagrams, charts, and textual descriptions that were developed during analysis. These documents define the project's classes, inheritance paths, and class associations. However, during the analysis phase we have the option of deferring many details and particulars until the design phase. On the other hand, it is often difficult to decide how much detail of class structure and composition we are to incorporate during the analysis phases. The following considerations are pertinent:

1. The type of project

2. The skill level of the programming team

3. The personal style of the principal main analyst or project manager

There are two possible extremes. In one extreme case we model the problem domain with the highest possible level of detail, including all class attributes and methods. At the other extreme we adopt a barebones classification, which depicts only the coarsest level of detail. In the first case we present the programmers with a detailed structure which they must follow in the coding, leaving little to their creativity and imagination. In the second case we present them with a rough sketch and let the programmers fill in all the details at coding time.

Highly technical projects, with strict requirements and formal or semiformal specifications, lend themselves to a very strict and detailed classification during design. More flexible projects, specified in more general terms, can give programmers greater freedom of implementation. By the same token, more competent and experienced programming teams can be trusted with greater autonomy at implementation time, while those with less talent and skills are usually subject to more stringent guidelines.

5.9 Language-specific Concerns

Class diagrams show attributes and methods for each class, lines of inheritance between classes, class associations in Gen-Spec and Whole-Part structures, instance and message connections, and the position of classes within subprograms. All of these characteristics and relationships must be addressed at coding time, not in theoretical or schematic terms, but in lines of code written in a particular programming language. The designers must make sure that the coders interpret these class characteristics and associations correctly. Therefore, the diagrams, sketches, and descriptions must be revised and re-evaluated according to implementation characteristics. In our case, we must make sure that the properties and characteristics in the class diagrams and other analysis documents are interpreted correctly in C++ code.

Fortunately, C++ has a rich set of object-oriented mechanisms which allow the straightforward implementation of abstract classes, virtual functions, and single or multiple inheritance. The C++ mechanism for achieving these class associations are constructors and destructors, overloading, and early and late binding. Nevertheless, there could be some possible variations in implementation that must be addressed during design. One such case arises in multiple inheritance. In Chapter 9 we discuss options for implementing common patterns of inheritance in C++.

5.10 Error and Exception Handling

What to do when an error condition is detected or when an exception occurs can also be a design concern. A program must provide a seamless and uniform response to errors and exceptions. This is particularly important regarding the handling of similar error conditions. For example, it would be unacceptable if upon detection of a division-by-zero exception some program code would be recovered by posting an error message to the user, while other program code would cause execution to abort.

The first consideration is to provide a uniform interface for the error handler. One possible approach to interface standardization is to design common access hooks. In the case of an error handler, application sources can pass an error message string and an action code to the handler. The handler in turn displays the error message string and executes the action that corresponds to the passed code. In C++ implementations the handler could take the form of a class, perhaps called **ErrorResponse**. Application code responds uniformly to any error condition by instantiating an object of the **ErrorResponse** class.

A second consideration relates to ensuring a uniform response to the same error condition or to similar ones. This requires analysis of the anticipated errors and exceptions and a decision on the most adequate action for each one. The action itself is usually determined by the application and its specifications. One program may be able to recover from an error in a manner transparent to the user, while in another program the same error could force termination of execution.

5.11 Documentation Conventions

Before coding begins each programmer should know about the expected documentation styles and requirements. In Section 2.2.3 we referred to assertions notation, a special style of program comments that appears to be gaining favor. Assertions notation reduces ambiguity and inconsistency of specifications while not requiring any special mathematical or logical expertise. If assertions notation is to be used in a project, all programmers should be informed about this requirement and trained in its use.

Coding style changes among programmers. One element of the coding style is the use of comments. Although the program development environment should be capable of accommodating different coding styles, some extremes may be unacceptable. For example, it would be undesirable for one portion of a program to be profusely commented while another one totally lacks comments. In Section 5.4.2 we discussed the use of standard program headers. Documentation conventions should also include comment levels expected of all programmers.

Some lead analysts or project managers require written progress reports from the members of the programming team. These reports are often issued at fixed time intervals, usually on a weekly, biweekly, or monthly basis. It is a good idea to define a format for the progress reports or to provide a form to be used by the programmers.

PART III

C++ Programming Mechanics

Chapter 6

Indirection

6.0 Indirection in C++

The extensive use of addresses and indirection is one of the most unique and powerful features of C, and of its descendant language C++. Although several imperative languages implement pointer variables, as is the case with Pascal, Ada, Fortran 90, and PL/I, few do it with comparable flexibility and power. The uniqueness of C and C++ in regards to pointers relates mainly to how the languages handle pointer arithmetic, as well as to some unique features, such as pointers to **void**, pointers to functions, pointers to objects, and pointers to pointers.

In C the use of pointers includes accessing variables and arrays, passing strings, implementing data structures such as stacks and linked lists, and facilitating heap management. In C++ the use of pointers is imperative in inheritance and run-time polymorphism. For this reason the C++ programmer needs much more than a superficial understanding of pointers and indirection. Only with thorough understanding of pointers will the C++ programmer be able to take advantage of all the power and flexibility of object orientation.

In this chapter we discuss the topic of indirection in general. Its purpose is to serve as a review and to focus the reader's attention on certain aspects of indirection that later take a particular importance in object-oriented programming. Indirection as an object-oriented programming tool is discussed in depth in Chapter 7.

6.0.1 Pointer Phobia

Most beginning programmers agree that there is something intimidating about pointers. Those of us who teach programming can attest to the difficulty with which the notion of indirection is grasped by beginning students of high-level languages. On the other hand, students of assembly language usually master the same notions with little effort. The reasons why similar concepts are easily learned in one environment, and the cause of great consternation in another one, perhaps relate to how indirection is implemented in code. The fact that low-level indirection is not difficult to learn has led Dr. Robert Gammill of North Dakota State University to propose teaching C and assembly together.

In x86 assembly language indirection is achieved in code by using bracket symbols to enclose the machine register that serves as a pointer. The student quickly learns to associate brackets with pointers. The fact that brackets are used for nothing else and pointers can be implemented in no other manner facilitates the learning process. In addition, the programming terminology and the instruction mnemonics are self-explanatory and consistent. In this manner the LEA instruction (Load Effective Address) can be used to initialize a pointer register. The mnemonics indicate that the register has been loaded with an address. Later on, the indirection symbols [] show that the code is using the register as a pointer. The following code fragment serves as an example:

```
DATA    SEGMENT
; A memory area named BUFFER is reserved and initialized with a
; text string, terminated in NULL
BUFFER1      DB      'This is a test',0

; A second buffer is created and left uninitialized
BUFFER2      DB    20 (DUP '?')
DATA    ENDS
;
CODE    SEGMENT
        .
        .
        .
; The SI register is first set up as a pointer to the memory area
; named BUFFER1
        LEA    SI,BUFFER1     ; SI holds the address of the first
                              ; memory cell in the area named
                              ; BUFFER1
        LEA    DI,BUFFER2     ; A second pointer register is set up
                              ; to the area named BUFFER2
```

```
MOVE_STRING:
        MOV    AL,[SI]        ; The pointer register SI is used
                              ; indirectly to access the first byte
                              ; stored in BUFFER1, which goes into
                              ; AL
; Assert: AL holds a character or a NULL
        MOV    [DI],AL        ; The character is stored in BUFFER2
        CMP    AL,0           ; AL is tested for a string terminator
        JE     END_OF_MOVE    ; Go if AL holds the string terminator
        INC    SI             ; Pointer is bumped to next character
        INC    DI             ; and so is the second pointer
        JMP    MOVE_STRING    ; Execution returns to the loop start
; When execution reaches the END_OF_MOVE label the string in
; BUFFER1
; has been copied into BUFFER2
END_OF_MOVE:
        .
        .
        .
```

The following C++ program uses pointers to transfer a string from one buffer into another one. The processing is similar to the one performed by the assembly language code previously listed.

```cpp
//******************************************************************
// C++ program to illustrate data transfer using pointers
// Filename: SAM06-01.CPP
//******************************************************************
#include <iostream.h>

main() {
  char buffer1[] = "This is a test";  // buffer1 is initialized
  char buffer2[20];                   // buffer2 is reserved
  char* buf1_ptr;                     // One pointer variable
  char* buf2_ptr;                     // A second pointer variable

// Set up pointers to buffer1 and buffer2. Note that since array
// names are pointer constants, we can equate the pointer
// variables to the array name. However, we cannot say:
// buf1_ptr = &buffer1;
  buf1_ptr = buffer1;
  buf2_ptr = buffer2;

// Proceed to copy buffer1 into buffer2
  while (*buf1_ptr) {
    *buf2_ptr = *buf1_ptr;     // Move character using pointers
    buf1_ptr++;                // Bump pointer to buffer1
    buf2_ptr++;                // Bump pointer to buffer2
    }
  *buf2_ptr = NULL;            // Place string terminator

// Display both buffers to check program operation
  cout << "\n\n\n"
```

```
    << buffer1 << "\n"
    << buffer2 << "\n\n";
  return 0;
}
```

The C code has several peculiarities; for example, the statements

```
char* buf1_ptr;
char* buf2_ptr;
```

declare that **buf1_prt** and **buf2_ptr** are pointer variables to variables of type **char**. If the statements had been:

```
char *buf1_ptr;
char *buf2_ptr;
```

the results would have been identical. Students are often confused by these syntax variations. Placing the asterisk close to the data type seems to emphasize that the pointer is a pointer to a type. However, if we were to initialize several variables simultaneously we would have to place an asterisk before each variable name either in the form:

```
char* buf_ptr1, * buf_ptr2;
```

or in the form:

```
char *buf_ptr1, *buf_ptr2;
```

either syntax seems to favor the second style.

Once a pointer variable has been created, the next step is to initialize the pointer variables (in this case **buf_ptr1** and **buf_ptr2**) to the address of the first byte of the data areas named **buffer1** and **buffer2**. A student familiar with the use of the **&** operator to obtain the address of a variable would be tempted to code:

```
buf1_ptr = &buffer1;    // INVALID FOR ARRAYS
```

However, in C and C++ an array name is an address constant. Therefore, this expression is illegal for arrays, but legal and valid for any other data type. In the case of an array we must initialize the pointer variable with an expression such as:

```
buf1_ptr = buffer1;
```

We again overload the * symbol when we need to address the characters pointed to by the pointer variable, as is the case in the expressions:

```
while (*buf1_ptr) {
```

```
*buf2_ptr = *buf1_ptr;
buf1_ptr++;
buf2_ptr++;
}
*buf2_ptr = NULL;
```

The result is that even in the simplest cases, such as the one discussed, the treatment of pointers and indirection by C and C++ can be confusing and inconsistent. The fact that these concepts are much clearer in assembly language may tempt us to use assembler in order to explain indirection in C++. The problem with this approach is that those that are fluent in assembler are not likely to have problems in understanding indirection in C++, which means that using assembler to explain C pointers may be like preaching to the choir.

6.1 Indirect Addressing

In the x86 family of Intel microprocessors indirect addressing is supported by the hardware. The assembly language code listed in Section 6.0.1 shows instructions to load the effective address of a memory operand (LEA), and the use of the [] symbols (sometimes called the indirection indicators) in accessing memory via a pointer register. The registers SI, DI, BX, and BP, as well as their 32-bit counterparts ESI, EDI, EBX, and EBP, can be used as pointers. In addition to indirect addressing of memory operands, the x86 CPUs support indirect jumps and calls that transfer execution to the address contained in any general register.

The x86 assemblers also support various refinements to indirection, such as based, indexed, and based-indexed addressing. In these cases the processor calculates the effective address using the contents of more than one register, as well as optional immediate data contained in the instruction opcode. In addition, the so-called string instructions implicitly use indirect addressing. In conclusion, x86 hardware supports indirect addressing quite well.

6.2 Pointer Variables

In high-level languages a pointer is a variable used for storing a memory address or a special value, sometimes called "nil." The value **nil** indicates that the stored value is invalid and cannot be legally dereferenced. A pointer variable can be used to access the contents of the memory cell or cells whose address it contains. This way of accessing memory through an address stored in another memory location is called *indirect addressing*. Assembly languages rely heavily on indirect addressing for accessing memory operands. Figure 6.1 is a symbolic representation of indirect addressing by means of a pointer variable.

In Figure 6.1 the pointer variable holds the value 0x010A, the address at which the value 9 is stored. By using the pointer variable we can access this value stored at memory location 0x010A indirectly. However, in the x86 architecture, pointer variables have no special tag to identify them. Therefore, memory location 0x0104 in Figure 6.1, which holds the value 0x100, could be a pointer variable or not. The same can be said of any other memory location in the system's address space. It is up to the programmer and the compiler to keep track of pointers.

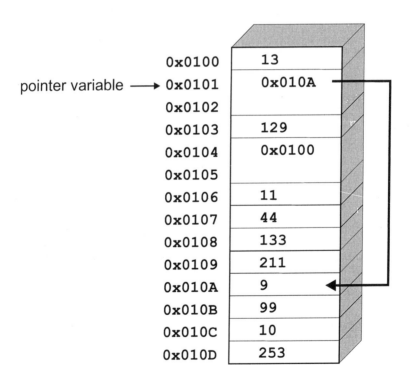

Figure 6.1 *Visualization of Indirect Addressing*

6.2.1 Dangling Pointers

A *dangling pointer* is a pointer variable that contains an invalid or deallocated address. Dangling pointers are a danger because the referenced memory area can contain a constant, invalid data, or garbage. Since pointers can be used to direct program execution, a dangling pointer could be the cause of a crash, specially in programs that execute in real mode. In x86 architecture the addresses at the beginning of memory are reserved for the interrupt vector table. Therefore it would be possible, in the x86 machine environment, to assign a zero value to any uninitialized or invalid pointer and check for this value before using it. However, C++ provides no internal checks for dangling pointers, which are the programmer's responsibility.

6.2.2 Pointers to Variables

One use of pointers is in indirectly accessing the contents of variables. Three different operations are available in C++: pointer declaration, pointer assignment or initialization, and pointer dereferencing.

Pointer Variable Declaration

The first step in implementing C++ indirection is usually declaring the variables that will hold pointers. C probably inherited the * as a pointer symbol from the syntax of some older assemblers. C++ is concerned with two elements of pointers: the address of the target variable and its data type. The address is necessary to locate it in the system's memory space. The data type is used in implementing pointer arithmetic, discussed later in this chapter.

The statement

```
int* ptr1;
```

or its alternative syntax

```
int *ptr1;
```

indicates that the variable **ptr1** is a pointer to a variable of int type. Note that this does not refer to the pointer but to the type of the target ariable. The pointer to **void** is a special case of a pointer that can refer to a target variable of any data type. Pointers to **void** are discussed in Section 6.6.

Pointer Variable Assignment

Once a pointer variable is declared, it can be initialized to the address of a target variable that corresponds to the one declared for the pointer. For example, if **ptr1** is a pointer variable to the type **int**, and if **ivar1** is an integer variable, then we assign the address of the target variable to the pointer variable with the statement:

```
ptr1 = &ivar1;
```

The ampersand symbol (&), which in this case corresponds to the *address-of* operator, extracts the address of the target variable and stores it in the pointer. One important exception is the address extraction of arrays. In C and C++ the array name represents the address of the first element of the array, which corresponds to the notion of an address constant. Therefore, if **arr1** is an array of type **int**, we initialize the pointer variable **ptr1** to the address of the array with the statement:

```
ptr1 = arr1;
```

In this case the use of the **address of** operator is not only unnecessary but illegal.

Pointer Variable Dereferencing

The process of accessing the value of the target variable by means of a pointer is called *dereferencing*. For example, dereferencing the pointer variable in Figure 6.1 results in the value 9, which is stored in the target variable. The asterisk symbol (*) is also used in dereferencing a pointer. In this case it precedes the name of the pointer variable and is sometimes called the *indirection operator*. For example, if **prt1** is a pointer to the integer variable **var1**, which holds the value 22, then the following statement displays this value:

```
cout << *ptr1;
```

The following program shows the three operations previously described:

```
//*******************************************************************
// C++ program to illustrate the use of a pointer variable
// by means of its declaration, initialization, and
// dereferencing.
// Filename: SAM06-02.CPP
//*******************************************************************
#include <iostream.h>

main() {
// Declare pointer and target variable
  int* ptr1;                 // Pointer to type int
  int var1 = 99;             // Variable of type int
// Initialize pointer to target variable
  ptr1 = &var1;
// Dereference of var1 using the pointer
  cout << "the value of var1 is " << *ptr1;

  return 0;
}
```

6.3 Pointers to Arrays

An array name represents the address of the first element of the array. When we use the array name as an address we remove the brackets used to enclose the array index. Since an array name is an address constant, the **address-of** operator is not applicable. For example, in the program SAM06-01.CPP listed at the beginning of this chapter, we first created an array and the corresponding pointer variable:

```
char buffer1[] = "This is a test";  // buffer1 is initialized
char* buf1_ptr;                      // One pointer variable
```

then we initialized the pointer variable using the array name

```
buf1_ptr = buffer1;
```

A word of caution can be inserted at this point: because an array name is an address *constant* its value cannot be changed by code. In other words, it can be used to initialize a pointer but it cannot serve as a pointer itself. Therefore, note the following operations:

```
++buf1_ptr;                // legal
++buffer1;                 // illegal
```

A final point to note is that access to array elements can also be achieved by means of the conventional subscript notation, although most compilers internally substitute subscript notation with pointers.

6.4 Pointers to Structures

Some of the lexical elements used in structures, characteristic of C, have been reused in C++ in relation to classes and objects. For this reason it is useful to revisit structures and structure pointers before discussing classes and object pointers.

While all the elements of an array must belong to the same data type, the elements of a structure can be of different types. Accordingly, structures are useful in creating data constructs in which several, often different, data types are related. A typical example of a structure is one used for storing employee data files, as in the following declaration:

```
struct employee_data {
    char emp_name[30];         // array for storing employee name
    char SS_num[12];           // array for SSN
    float wage;                // storage for hourly wage
    float hours_worked;        // storage for time worked
    unsigned int dependents;   // number of dependents
};
```

Once the structure has been declared we can create variables of the structure type. For example, we create instances of the structure **employee_data** with the following structure variable declarations:

```
struct employee_data welder_1;
struct employee_data welder_2;
struct employee_data shop_foreman;
```

Now we can access the structure members by means of the **dot** or **member-of** operator, as follows:

```
strcpy (welder_1.emp_name, "Joseph W. Smith");
strcpy (welder_1.SS_num, "255-47-0987");
welder_1.wage = 18.50;
welder_1.hours_worked = 45.6;
welder_1.dependents = 3;
```

Note that in initializing arrays within structures we used the string copy function **strcpy()**, defined in the **string.h** header, since aggregate array assignment is illegal in C and C++.

C's treatment of structure pointers is based on several unique concepts. One fundamental notion is that a structure is a class declaration which creates a template for instantiating structure variables, but is not a memory object in itself. Therefore, we define a pointer to a structure type, but initialize it to a structure variable, for example:

```
truct employee_data *ed_ptr;   // Pointer to type
ed_ptr = &welder_1;            // Pointer initialization
```

At this point we have created a pointer to the structure variable **welder_1**, of the structure type **employee_data**. We can now proceed to access the structure members by means of the *pointer-member* operator, which consists of a *dash* and *greater than* symbol combined to simulate an arrow. Therefore we can say

```
float wage_of_w1 = ed_ptr -> wage;
```

Furthermore, we can pass the pointer of a local structure to a function, as shown in the following program:

```
//*****************************************************************
// C++ program to illustrate the use of pointers to structures
// Filename: SAM06-03.CPP
//*****************************************************************
#include <iostream.h>
#include <string.h>
// Structure type declaration
struct employee_data {
  char name[30];
  char SS_num[12];
  float wage;
  float hours;
  unsigned int dependents;
};
// Function prototype
void Show_employee(struct employee_data *);
//***************************
//           main()
//***************************
main() {
// Structure variable declaration
  struct employee_data welder_1;
// Initialize structure variables
  strcpy (welder_1.name,"Joseph W. Smith");
  strcpy (welder_1.SS_num, "263-98-0987");
  welder_1.wage = 18.5;
  welder_1.hours = 22.3;
  welder_1.dependents = 3;
// Pointer operations
  struct employee_data *edata_ptr;    // pointer type defined
  edata_ptr = &welder_1;              // pointer initialized to
                                      // variable
// Call function show_employee passing pointer
  Show_employee(edata_ptr);
```

```
  return 0;
}
//**************************
// function Show_employee()
//**************************
void Show_employee (struct employee_data *e_ptr) {
// Note that the function receives a copy of the pointer variable
// edata_ptr
  cout << "\n\nEmployee data: ";
  cout << "\n" << e_ptr -> name;
  cout << "\n" << e_ptr -> SS_num;
  cout << "\n" << e_ptr -> wage;
  cout << "\n" << e_ptr -> hours;
  return;

}
```

6.5 Pointer Arithmetic

In handling pointers the assembly language programmer must take into account the stored data type. For example, if a machine register is set as a pointer to a memory area containing an array of characters, stored at the rate of one byte per element, then the programmer adds one to the pointer which accesses the successive elements in the array. However, if the array is of integers (two bytes per element), then the code must add two to the value of the pointer register in order to access the consecutive array entries. By the same token, we would add four to access doubleword entries, eight to access quadwords, and ten to access successive ten-bytes. This manipulation is, of course, machine dependent; in a machine in which integers are stored in four bytes, the code would have to add four during each successive increment in order to access adjacent values.

The machine dependency on low-level pointer handling compromises the portability of a high-level language and complicates programming. C and C++ automate the scaling of pointers in order to make the size of the stored elements transparent to the code. This automatic pointer scaling is sometimes called *pointer arithmetic*. Three types of operations are permitted in C and C++ pointer arithmetic: addition, subtraction, and comparison. Operations that are meaningless in pointer scaling are also illegal. Therefore multiplication, division, remainder, as well as all other mathematical functions, are prohibited.

Addition and subtraction of pointer variables are typically used in accessing successive array elements. In the program SAM06-01.CPP listed in Section 6.0.1, we bumped an array pointer with the statement:

```
buf1_ptr++;
```

In this case C++ adds 1 to each successive value of the pointer since the array is of type **char**. By the same token, subtraction operations can be used to access preceding entries in the array.

Comparison is a pointer operation with less obvious applications. In comparison we usually relate two or more pointers to the same data construct. For example, in a stack structure we can set a pointer to the stack top and compare it to the current stack position in order to detect an overflow. The following program shows pointer addition and comparison operations:

```
//*************************************************************
// C++ program to illustrate pointer arithmetic by adding all the
// elements in an int array. The end of the array is detected
// by means of a pointer comparison
// Filename: SAM06-04.CPP
//*************************************************************
#include <iostream.h>
main() {
// Variable declarations
   const int ENTRIES = 5;
   int num_array[ENTRIES] = {12, 8, 10, 5, 3};
   int total = 0;
   int *num_ptr;
   num_ptr = num_array;           // Initialize array pointer
// The following loop continues while the address of the pointer
// is less than the address of the end of the array
   while (num_ptr < num_array + ENTRIES)
      total = total + *num_ptr++;
   cout << "\nThe total is: " << total;
   return 0;
}
```

6.6 Pointers to Void

C and C++ provide a mechanism for implementing a generic pointer that is independent of the object's data type. This mechanism is called a *pointer to void*. Most C programmers first encountered pointers to **void** in the context of memory allocation using **malloc()**. However, pointers to **void** are a powerful tool that allows solving problems which are difficult to approach without them. In C++ some of the principal application of pointers to **void** are in accessing system memory areas, in passing addresses to functions that perform operations independently of the data type, in dynamic memory allocation, and in accessing system services.

When initializing a conventional pointer in C++, the programmer must make sure that the pointer type coincides with the target data type. For example:

```
double dbl_var = 22.334455;
int* i_ptr = &dbl_var;          // ILLEGAL EXPRESSION
```

The preceding code fragment would produce a compile-time error since we have declared a pointer to **int** and tried to initialize it with the address of a variable of type **double**. One possible solution is a type cast of the pointer to a double:

```
int* i_ptr;
(double*) i_ptr = &dbl_var;
```

Type casting pointers is allowed in C and C++. After the previous type cast the compiler treats **i_ptr** as a pointer to type double, and it is up to the programmer to ensure that all operations that follow the type cast are consistent and valid.

An alternative approach is to define a pointer to type **void**, which can then be initialized with the address of any variable, array, or structure type. For example:

```
double dbl_var = 22.334455;
int_var = 12;
void* v_ptr;
v_ptr = &dbl_var;
   .
   .
v_ptr = &int_var;
```

A pointer to **void** is capable of holding the address of a variable of type **int** or of type **double**. In fact, a void pointer can hold the address of any variable, independently of its data type. One question that arises is how can C or C++ perform type checking and pointer arithmetic with **void** pointers? Another one is that if **void** pointers work, why do we need typed pointers? The answer to both questions is that **void** pointers have a limited functionality since they cannot be dereferenced. For example, if v_ptr is a pointer of type **void**, then the expression:

```
*v_ptr = 12;               // ILLEGAL EXPRESSION
```

is illegal. Since C++ has no knowledge of the data type of the pointer it cannot use it to change the contents of a memory variable. However, like conventional pointers, void pointers can be type cast:

```
*(int*) v_ptr = 12;        // v_ptr a pointer to type void, pointing
                           // to a variable of type int
```

Although the preceding expression is valid, the fact that pointers to **void** must be type cast before dereferencing somewhat limits their practical use.

A historical note is in order. The first high-level language to implement pointer variables was PL/I. In PL/I the object of a pointer variable can be a static or dynamic variable of any type; therefore, all PL/I pointers are equivalent to the notion of a C++ pointer to **void**. The result is a very flexible but dangerous construct which is the cause of several PL/I pointer problems, mainly related to type checking, dangling pointers, and lost objects. Language designers took into account the problems in PL/I and attempted to solve them by means of typed pointer variables, which simplify type checking and make code safer. Pointers to **void** are implemented for those cases in which a generic pointer is necessary.

6.6.1 Programming with Pointers to Void

Pointers to **void** can be useful in many programming situations. For example, the **malloc()** function is used in C to dynamically allocate heap memory. The prototype for malloc is:

```
void *malloc(size_t size);
```

where **size_t** is defined in STDLIB.H as an unsigned integer and size is the number of memory bytes requested. Note that **malloc()** returns a pointer to **void** since the function need not know the data type to be used in formatting the allocated memory. The caller assigns the allocated memory to any valid unit of storage. The following program shows the use of **malloc()**, and its associated function **free()**, in dynamically allocating and deallocating an array.

```
//*****************************************************************
// C++ program to illustrate void pointers and dynamic memory
// allocation using malloc() and free()
// Filename: SAM06-05.CPP
//*****************************************************************
```

```
#include <iostream.h>
#include <string.h>
#include <alloc.h>
main() {
   char* str_array;                    // Declare pointer to char
// allocate memory for char array - Post error message and exit
// if malloc() fails
   str_array = (char *) malloc(20);
   if (str_array == NULL){
      cout << "\nNot enough memory to allocate array\n";
      return(1);
    }
   // copy "Hello World!" string into allocated array
   strcpy(str_array, "Hello World!");
   cout << str_array;                  // display array
   free(str_array);                    // free allocated memory
   return 0;
}
```

In the program SAM06-05.CPP, **malloc()** returns a pointer to void. Our code type casts this pointer into a pointer to an array of char with the statement:

```
str_array = (char *) malloc(20);
```

Another frequent use for pointers to **void** is in passing pointers to functions that perform operations independently of data types. For example, a routine to perform a hexadecimal dump, such as is commonly found in disassemblers and debuggers, can receive the address of the data element in a pointer to **void**. This makes the code transparent to specific data types. The following program is an example of a hexadecimal dump function that uses a pointer to **void**.

```
//****************************************************************
// C++ program to illustrate use of pointers to void in a
// function that performs a hexadecimal dump
// Filename: SAM06-06.CPP
//****************************************************************

#include <iostream.h>

void Show_hex(void *p, int);       // Function prototype

//***************************
//          main()
//***************************
main(){
// Declare and initialize sample arrays and variables
   int int_array[] = {22, 33, 44, 55, 66};
   char char_array[] = {"abcdef"};
   float float_array[] = {22.7, 445.6, 111.0};
```

```
  long int long_var = 123456789;
  double dbl_var = 267.889911;
  cout << "\nHexadecimal dump: \n";
// Arrays and variables are passed to hex_dump() function
  Show_hex(int_array, sizeof(int_array));
  Show_hex(char_array, sizeof(char_array));
  Show_hex(float_array, sizeof(float_array));
  Show_hex(&long_var, sizeof(long_var));
  Show_hex(&dbl_var, sizeof(dbl_var));
  return 0;
}


//****************************
//    show_hex() function
//****************************
void Show_hex(void *void_ptr, int elements) {
unsigned char digit, high_nib, low_nib;
  for(int x = 0; x < elements; x++) {
      digit = *((char *)void_ptr + x);
      high_nib = low_nib = digit;     // copy in high and low nibble
      high_nib = high_nib & 0xf0;     // Mask out 4 low-order bits
      high_nib = high_nib >> 4;       // Shift high bits left
      low_nib = low_nib & 0x0f;       // Mask out 4 high-order bits
// Display in ASCII hexadecimal digits
      if(low_nib > 9)
          low_nib = low_nib + 0x37;
      else
          low_nib = low_nib + 0x30;
// Same thing for high nibble
      if(high_nib > 9)
          high_nib = high_nib + 0x37;
      else
          high_nib = high_nib + 0x30;
      cout << high_nib << low_nib << " ";
}
  cout << "\n";
  return;
}
```

6.7 Reference Variables

C++ introduced a new way of achieving indirection by means of a mechanism called a *reference variable* or a *reference type*. The syntax for creating a reference is as follows:

```
int var_1 = 456;
int& var_1A = var_1;
```

Now **var_1A** is a reference variable to **var_1**. From this point on we can access **var_1** by means of **var_1A** at any time. This fact leads some authors to refer to a reference as an *alias*, which implies that it is merely another name for the same entity.

Several unique features of references make them useful to the programmer. In the first place, once created, the use of a reference variable does not require the dereference (*) or the address-off (**&**) operators. In addition, the compiler treats a reference variable as a constant pointer that cannot be reassigned, as is the case with array names. After a reference variable has been initialized its address value cannot be again accessed. For example, if **var_1A** is a reference variable, then

```
var1A = 26;
var_1A++;
```

The last statement increments the stored value, so that now **var_1A** holds the value 27. This notational convenience saves the programmer from having to continuously use the * operator to refer to the contents of a variable referenced by the pointer. The fact that reference variables cannot be reassigned serves as a safety device.

One frequent use of reference variables is in passing a scalar to functions so that the function has access to the original variable. The following program illustrates this operation in a rather trivial example:

```
//*****************************************************************
// C++ program to illustrate use of reference variables
// Filename: SAM06-07.CPP
//*****************************************************************

#include <iostream.h>
void Swap(int&, int&);                // Prototype for function

//****************************
//           main()
//****************************
main() {
   int var_1 = 11;
   int var_2 = 22;
   Swap(var_1, var_2);
   // Testing function Swap()
   cout << "\nvar_1 now holds " << var_1;
   cout << "\nvar_2 now holds " << var_2 << "\n";
   return 0;
}
//****************************
//       Swap() function
//****************************
```

```
void Swap(int& x, int& y)
{
 // This function swaps the contents of two variables in
 // the caller's memory space
 int temp = x;
 x = y;
 y = temp;
 return;
}
```

Note that by using reference variables we can simplify the call to the function which appears identical to a call by value. The reference variables are declared in the header line of the function, as follows:

```
void Swap(int& x, int& y)
```

From this point on variable **x** can access the contents of variable **var_1** and the variable **y** can access the contents of **var_2**. The fact that the **call** statement using reference variables does not show that an address is being passed to the function is sometimes mentioned as a disadvantage to their use.

6.8 Dynamic Memory Allocation in C++

In Section 6.6 we described the use of **malloc()** and **free()** in implementing dynamic memory allocation in C. C++ provides more powerful and easier ways of handling dynamic allocation, although **malloc()** and **free()** are still available.

In C, program data can be of three storage classes: static, automatic, and dynamic. The storage class determines a variable's lifetime, which can be defined as the period of time during which an identifier holds a memory allocation. *Static data* refers to global variables and to those declared using the **static** keyword. These variables retain their value throughout program execution. Therefore, the storage space remains allocated until execution terminates. In more precise terms we can say that the lifetime of a static variable is the entire program. An *automatic variable* is one whose storage is allocated within its activation frame. The *activation frame* is either a block or a function. If no storage class specifier is given, automatic storage class is assumed for all local variables (those declared inside a function or block) and static is assumed for all global variables.

There is a difference between a global variable and a local one declared with the **static** keyword. Both have the same lifetime, but the local scope makes the variable invisible to other functions in the program. In some cases this restricted visibility can safeguard against undesirable changes. The visibility rules for identifiers are similar in C and C++. For example, an identifier can be local to a block:

```
if (var_1 > 10) {
    int input_var;
    cin >> input_var;
    .
    .
    .
}
```

In this case the variable **input_var** is visible within the compound statement block of the **if** construct, but not outside of it. Because a function body is a syntactical block, the notion of *block scope* also applies to functions.

6.8.1 Dynamic Data

The main objection to the use of static and automatic variables is that it often leads to wasted memory space. The worst case is with static variables, in which the memory storage persists throughout the program's execution time. In the case of static variables the storage assigned is never released or reused. The storage assigned to automatic variables is usually located in the stack; therefore, it is reused during execution. But a program's control over automatic variables depends upon the activation frame of the function or block. This forces the programmer to declare all variables that *could be* needed at execution time, which also leads to wasted storage.

Suppose that we were designing the data structure to hold the text file of a word processor or editor. One possible option would be to make the text file an external array, visible to all code. However, how large would we make this array? If too small, the user could run out of storage space at execution time. If too large, the system may not find enough free memory to allocate at run time. Another example, this one mentioned by Headington and Riley (see Bibliography), is an array to hold seating assignments in an airline reservation system. If the largest airplane in the fleet had 400 seats, then we would have to define and allocate an array with 400 elements. The remainder of the allocated array would be wasted storage if only 40 of these seats were booked for a particular flight. At the same time, the program would have to be recoded if a new model of aircraft which contained 410 seats were added to the fleet. Problems such as these may lead to a design decision in which static and automatic data structures are assigned the largest possible memory space. The results are often the waste of a valuable resource.

Dynamic data provides a mechanism whereby storage is assigned as needed, at run time. Specific instructions are used to allocate and deallocate memory according to occasional requirements. In this case the array for storing seating assignments in the airline reservation system of the preceding paragraph would be allocated as needed. If only 40 seats were booked, the array would have 40 entries. If a new aircraft were put into service, the array could be configured to hold any number of items as long as there was storage available.

6.8.2 The *new* and *delete* Operators

In C++ the unary operators **new** and **delete** can be used to control allocation and deallocation of dynamic data. These operators are C++ counterparts to **malloc()** and **free()**. The new operator returns a pointer to the allocated memory. If there is insufficient memory to satisfy the request then new returns **NULL**. The delete operator frees the memory allocated by **new**. Their general forms are as follows:

```
ptr_var = new type;
delete ptr_var;
```

where **ptr_var** is a pointer variable, and **type** is a C++ data type. The **delete** operator must refer to a valid pointer created with **new**. One of the differences between **new** and **malloc()** is that **new** automatically calculates the size of the operand. A second one is that **new** does not require an explicit type cast. Finally, both **new** and **delete** can be overloaded. Figure 6.2 is a visualization of the operation of the **new** and **delete**.

Another feature of **new** is that it allows the optional initialization of the allocated storage. For example:

```
int *ptr_var;
*ptr_var = new int (25);      // dynamic variable is initialized
```

When allocating arrays using the **new** operator the general format is as follows:

```
ptr_var = new array_type [array_size];
```

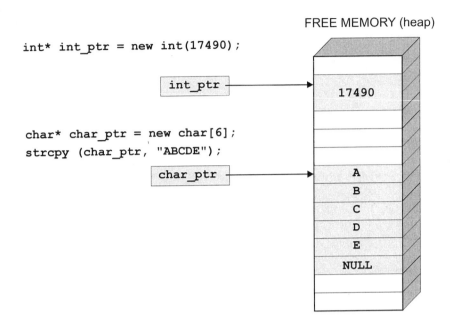

Figure 6.2 *Visualization of C++ Dynamic Allocation*

For example:

```
char *ptr_var;
ptr_var = new char[10];        // Allocate array to hold 10
                               // elements of type char
```

To deallocate this array use the form:

```
delete []ptr_var;
```

Dynamically allocated arrays cannot be initialized.

The following program uses **new** and **delete** to dynamically allocate and deallocate memory for an array. Comparing it to SAM06-05.CPP, which performs the identical function using **malloc()** and **free()**, shows how the coding is simplified by using the **new** and **delete** operators.

```
//*****************************************************************
// C++ program to illustrate dynamic memory allocation using
// new and delete
// Filename: SAM06-08.CPP
//*****************************************************************
```

```
#include <iostream.h>
#include <string.h>
main() {
   char* str_array;                    // Declare pointer to char
// allocate memory for char array - Post error message and exit
// if new() fails
   str_array = new char(19);
   if (str_array == NULL){
      cout << "\nNot enough memory to allocate array\n";
      return(1);
    }
// copy "Hello New World!" string into allocated array
   strcpy(str_array, "\nHello New World!\n");
   cout   << str_array;               // display array
   delete [] str_array;              // free allocated memory
   return 0;

}
```

6.9 Pointers to Functions

In Section 6.1 we mentioned that the Intel x86 microprocessor family used in the PC supports indirect jumps and calls. This indirect access to code is achieved either through a register or memory operand,
or through both simultaneously. One commonly used technique of indirect access to code is by means of a memory resident *jump* or *call table*, which holds a set of addresses to various processing routines. A
offset value is added to the address of the start of the table to determine the destination for a particular jump or call. The following trivial program in x86 assembly language shows the use of a jump table in
accessing one of four possible routines:

```
;*********************************************************************
;*********************************************************************
;                              IND_JMP.ASM
;*********************************************************************
;*********************************************************************
; Program description:
;     Test program for indirect jumps in x86 assembler language
;
;*********************************************************************
;                           stack segment
;*********************************************************************
STACK    SEGMENT stack
         DB       1024 DUP ('?')   ; Default stack is 1K
STACK    ENDS


;*********************************************************************
;                           data segment
;*********************************************************************
```

```
DATA    SEGMENT
; Address table is defined in memory
ADD_TABLE       DW      ACTION1, ACTION2, ACTION3, ACTION4
                DW      0
;
;*************************|
;       text messages     |
;*************************|
USER_PROMPT     DB      'Enter a number from 1 to 4: $'
BAD_ACTION      DB      0AH,0DH,'Invalid input',0AH,0DH,'$'
;
AC1_MSG         DB      0AH,0DH,'Action 1 executed',0AH,0DH,'$'
AC2_MSG         DB      0AH,0DH,'Action 2 executed',0AH,0DH,'$'
AC3_MSG         DB      0AH,0DH,'Action 3 executed',0AH,0DH,'$'
AC4_MSG         DB      0AH,0DH,'Action 4 executed',0AH,0DH,'$'
;
DATA    ENDS
;************************************************************
;                       code segment
;************************************************************
CODE    SEGMENT
        ASSUME  CS:CODE
;
;******************|
; initialization   |
;******************|
ENTRY_POINT:
; Initialize the DATA segment so that the program can access the
; stored data items using the DS segment register
        MOV     AX,DATA         ; Address of DATA to AX
        MOV     DS,AX           ; and to DS
        ASSUME  DS:DATA         ; Assume directive so that
                                ; the assemble defaults to DS

;***********************|
; prompt user for input |
;***********************|
        LEA     DX,USER_PROMPT  ; Pointer to message
        MOV     AH,9            ; MS DOS service number
        INT     21H             ; MS DOS interrupt
; Input character and echo
        MOV     AH,1            ; MS DOS service number
        INT     21H
; At this point AL holds ASCII of user input
; Test for invalid value
        CMP     AL,'4'          ; 4 is highest allowed
        JBE     OK_HIGH_RANGE   ; Go if in range
        JMP     ERROR_EXIT      ; Error if out of range
OK_HIGH_RANGE:
        CMP     AL,'1'          ; Test low range
        JAE     OK_RANGE        ; Go if in range
; Display error message and exit
ERROR_EXIT:     21H             ; TO DOS
;
```

```
;****************************************************************
;                        ACTION PROCEDURES
;****************************************************************
ACTION1:
        LEA     DX,AC1_MSG      ; Pointer to message
        MOV     AH,9            ; MS DOS service number
        INT     21H
        JMP     DOS_EXIT
ACTION2:
        LEA     DX,AC2_MSG      ; Pointer to message
        MOV     AH,9            ; MS DOS service number
        INT     21H
        JMP     DOS_EXIT
ACTION3:
        LEA     DX,AC3_MSG      ; Pointer to message
        MOV     AH,9            ; MS DOS service number
        INT     21H
        JMP     DOS_EXIT
ACTION4:
        LE
        LEA     DX,BAD_ACTION   ; Pointer to message
        MOV     AH,9            ; MS DOS service number
        INT     21H
        JMP     DOS_EXIT
; Convert to binary and scale
OK_RANGE:
        SUB     AL,30H          ; AL now holds binary
        SUB     AL,1            ; Reduce to range 0 to 3
        ADD     AL,AL           ; Double the value
        MOV     BX,0            ; Clear BX
        MOV     BL,AL           ; Offset to BX
        JMP     ADD_TABLE[BX]   ; Jump to table address plus offset
;******************|
;   exit to DOS    |
;******************|
DOS_EXIT:
        MOV     AH,76           ; MS-DOS service request code
        MOV     AL,0            ; No error code returned
        INT  A  DX,AC4_MSG      ; Pointer to message
        MOV     AH,9            ; MS DOS service number
        INT     21H
        JMP     DOS_EXIT
CODE    ENDS
        END     ENTRY_POINT     ; Reference to start label
```

The IND_JMP program operates as follows:

1. A jump table (named ADD_TABLE) is defined as data. At assembly
   time the table is filled with the offset of the four routines referenced
   by name. The corresponding routines are found toward the end of the
   code segment.

2. The user is prompted to enter a value in the range 1 to 4. After testing for a valid input, the code converts the ASCII character to binary, scales to the range 0 to 3, doubles its value so that it serves as an index to the word-size offsets in the jump table, and stores the result in the BX register.

3. An indirect jump instruction (JMP ADD_TABLE[BX]) accesses the address in the jump table that corresponds to the offset in the BX register. Thus, if BX = 0 the routines labeled ACTION1 executes; if BX = 2 then the routine named ACTION2 executes.

One point to note is that the IND_JMP program code performs a check for an input in the valid range. This check is advisable, since, in this type of execution, an invalid offset sends the program into a garbage address which produces an almost certain crash.

6.9.1 Simple Dispatch Table

C++ implements code indirection by means of pointers to functions. Since a function address is its entry point, this address can be stored in a pointer and used to call the function. When these addresses are stored in an array of pointers, then the resulting structure is a call table similar to the one discussed in the preceding section. Jump and call tables are sometimes called *dispatch tables* by C and C++ programmers.

The implementation of pointers to functions and dispatch tables in C and C++ requires a special syntax. First, a pointer to a function has a type which corresponds to the data type returned by the function and is declared inside parentheses. For example, to declare a function pointer named **fun_ptr**, which receives two parameters of **int** type in the variables named **x** and **y**, and returns **void**, we would code:

```
void (*fun_ptr) (int x, int y);
```

The parentheses have the effect of binding to the function name not to its data type. If in this statement we were to remove the parentheses, the result would be a pointer to a function that returns type **void**. Note that the previous line creates a function pointer that is not yet initialized. This pointer can be set to point to any function that receives two **int**-type parameters and returns void. For example, if there was a function named **Fun1** with these characteristics we could initialize the function pointer with the statement:

```
fun_ptr = Fun1;
```

Note that the C and C++ compiler assumes that a function name is a pointer to its entry point; thus, the **address of** (**&**) operator is not used. Once the function pointer is initialized, we can access the function **Fun1** with the statement:

```
(*Fun1)(6, 8);
```

In this case we are passing to the function the two integer parameters, in the conventional manner.

The declaration and initialization of a dispatch table also need a special syntax. Since a dispatch table should not be changed by code, it is a good idea to declare it of static type. For example, the following statement creates an array named **dispatch** that holds the addresses of the functions named **Fun1**, **Fun2**, **Fun3**, and **Fun4**, all of which receive no arguments and return **void**.

```
static void (*dispatch[]) (void) = {Fun1, Fun2, Fun3, Fun4};
```

To access a particular function whose address is stored in the dispatch table we must create a variable to store this offset. For example:

```
unsigned int off_var = 1;
```

Since **off_var** is now initialized to the second entry in the array (recall that array indexes are zero-based) we can access Fun2 with the statement:

```
(*dispatch[off_var]) ();
```

The following program shows the use of a dispatch table in C++ to achieve the same purpose as the assembly language program named IND_JMP listed in Section 6.9.

```
//****************************************************************
// C++ program to illustrate pointers to functions and the use
// of dispatch tables
// Filename: SAM06-09.CPP
//****************************************************************
#include <iostream.h>
#include <string.h>

// Function prototypes
void Action1(void);
void Action2(void);
void Action3(void);
```

```
void Action4(void);

//****************************
//          main()
//****************************
main() {
// Create dispatch table
static void (*add_table[]) (void) = {Action1, Action2, Action3,
            Action4};
// Create variable for offset into table
unsigned int table_offset = 0;
// Prompt user for input
   cout << "\nEnter a number from 1 to 4: ";
   cin >> table_offset;
// Test for invalid user input
   if (table_offset < 1 || table_offset > 4) {
     cout << "\nInvalid input\n";
     return 1;
   }
   table_offset-;                  // Adjust offset to range
   (*add_table[table_offset]) (); // Access function using table
                                   // and offset entered by user

   return 0;
}


//****************************
//          functions
//****************************
void Action1(void) {
  cout << "\nAction 1 executed\n";
  return;
}
void Action2(void) {
  cout << "\nAction 2 executed\n";
  return;
}
void Action3(void) {
  cout << "\nAction 3 executed\n";
  return;
}
void Action4(void) {
  cout << "\nAction 4 executed\n";
  return;
}
```

6.9.2 Indexed Dispatch Table

The program SAM06-09.CPP, previously listed, shows the simplest possible way of implementing a dispatch table. The processing can be modified so as to display a menu of options, from which the user selects the one to be executed. The code then manipulates the user input so that it serves as the offset into the jump table. However, there are several objections to this simple mechanism. Perhaps the most important one is the that code assumes that the address of the various processing routines are stored in a single memory word. Therefore it uses an unsigned **int** as an index to the various entries. One possible risk of this approach is that it may be true in some memory models, machines, or compilers, but not in others.

A more elegant and rigorous solution, although slightly more complicated, is based on an *indexed dispatch table*. The indexed dispatch table approach allows ignoring the size of the stored addresses, since the correct one is found not by addition of an offset to a base, but by performing a table look-up operation. The table itself relates the input codes entered by the user (or other identification codes or strings) to the addresses of the various selectable functions. Program SAM06-10.CPP uses an indexed dispatch table to obtain the pointer to the corresponding function.

```cpp
//*******************************************************************
// C++ program to illustrate pointers to functions and the use
// of indexed dispatch tables
// Filename: SAM06-10.CPP
//*******************************************************************
#include <iostream.h>

// Prototypes
void Action1(void);
void Action2(void);
void Action3(void);
void Action4(void);
// Structure for creating an indexed dispatch table
struct index_cmd {
  int user_code;
  void (*function) (void);
};

//****************************
//          main()
//****************************
main() {
// Set up indexed dispatch table using the index_cmd structure
struct index_cmd add_table[] = {
  { 1,   Action1 },
  { 2,   Action2 },
  { 3,   Action3 },
  { 4,   Action4 }
};
// Create variable to store user input
int user_input = 0;
```

```cpp
// Prompt user for input
   cout << "\nEnter a number from 1 to 4: ";
   cin >> user_input;

// Test for invalid input
   if(user_input < 1 || user_input > 5){
      cout << "\nInvalid input\n" ;
      return 1;
   }

// Search lookup table for match
for (int i = 0; i < 5; i++) {
   if (user_input == add_table[i].user_code) {
      (*add_table[i].function) ();
      break;
      }
   }
   return 0;
}
//****************************
//         functions
//****************************
void Action1(void) {
   cout << "\nAction 1 executed\n";
   return;
}
void Action2(void) {
   cout << "\nAction 2 executed\n";
   return;
}
void Action3(void) {
   cout << "\nAction 3 executed\n";
   return;
}
void Action4(void) {
   cout << "\nAction 4 executed\n";
   return;
}
```

Program SAM06-10.CPP uses an integer value entered by the user to search into a structure that contains all four legal codes (1 to 4) matched with the addresses of the corresponding functions. The search is performed by comparing the value of the user input with the stored codes. Once the correct code is found, the function is called with the statement

```cpp
(*add_table[i].function) ();
```

An alternative approach, based on a string, can be implemented using **strcmp()** to perform the compare operation.

6.10 Compounding Indirection

C allows the creation of pointers to pointers, thus formulating a mechanism for compounding indirection. For example, first we create and initialize an integer variable:

```
in value1 = 10;
```

then we create and initialize a pointer to the variable **value1**:

```
int *int_ptr = &value1;
```

At this point we can create a pointer to the pointer variable **int_ptr** with the statement

```
int **ptr_ptr = &int_ptr;
```

Figure 6.3 is a representation of compounded indirection.

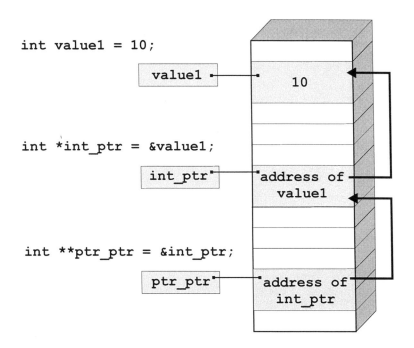

Figure 6.3 *Visualization of Compounded Indirection*

In Figure 6.3 the variable **ptr_ptr** points to the pointer **int_ptr**, which in turn points to the integer variable named **value1**. To access the variable value1 and change its value you can code:

```
value1 = 20;
```

or by simple indirection:

```
*int_ptr = 20;
```

also by compounded indirection:

```
**ptr_ptr = 20;
```

Programming mechanisms that use pointers to pointers are illustrated in Chapter 7 in the context of pointers to objects.

Chapter 7

C++ Object-Oriented Constructs

7.0 Implementation Issues

At the conclusion of the analysis and the design phases of program development we find ourselves with a set of diagrams and documents that attempt to define the system's structure and architecture in object-oriented terms. The coding phase consists of converting the analysis and design into lines of code that implement these rather formal and stereotypical concepts. Contrary to the opinion of some academics, coding is not trivial. To transform ideas, plans, and diagrams into routines and instructions in a programming language requires vision and imagination, as well as mastery of the environment. Many well-conceived, analyzed, and designed projects fail for lack of coding talents and skills.

Furthermore, object orientation was principally conceived to facilitate modeling the problem domain. Few claims have ever been made that coding in an object-oriented language is easier than in a procedural one. What is worse, C++ is a hybrid language. The object-oriented features were appended to an existing language structure, a process that sometimes required a forced fit. Although the result has been generally judged to be satisfactory, it is not without defects and shortcomings. Some object-oriented operations and constructs cannot be implemented in C++, while others are awkward or cumbersome. The C++ programmer often feels to be facing a monumental and intimidating task, especially at the beginning of the coding phase of a major application.

In this chapter we present an overview of some fundamental concepts of object-oriented programming in C++. We start with the fundamental idea of classes and objects and conclude with the notions of run-time polymorphism and templates. The material is not a review of C++, but a selection of topics that directly relate to the implementation of object orientation in the language, or that provide special programming powers.

7.1 The Fundamental Notions

Object-oriented programming languages must implement three core notions of the paradigm: encapsulation, inheritance, and polymorphism.

7.1.1 Encapsulation

Literally speaking, encapsulating means placing in a capsule. It is equivalent to the notion of hiding details by covering the substance with a protective shell. There is a double purpose to encapsulation: first, to prevent misuse; second, to hide details. In C++ encapsulation is achieved by means of objects. An object encapsulates data (attributes) and code (methods) that access and manipulate the data. Some of the attributes and methods are visible outside the encapsulated object, while others are hidden from view.

An object-oriented programmer considers an object as a variable of a user-defined data type. This notion may seem strange at first, since we do not associate the idea of a data type with code or processing operations. However, a data type by itself would be useless if there were no operations that could be performed on it. Why would we have integers if we were unable to do arithmetic with them? Of what use would be a stack if there were no push and pop operations? A data type exists in the context of a programming language because there are operations that can be performed on the data. An object exists in the context of a program because there are operations that can be performed on the object.

The discussion regarding which should be considered first, the object or the class, is of the same character as the one regarding the chicken and the egg. In nature objects exist by themselves. In object-oriented programming an object cannot exist without a class that defines it. Although, formally, the notion of an object is more elementary than that of a class, in coding practice we must define a class before we are able to instantiate an object. For this reason it is natural, in the context of a programming language, to discuss classification before discussing objects.

7.1.2 Polymorphism

Etymologically, *polymorphism* means "many forms." In object-oriented programming languages it relates to several methods that share the same interface. One way to implement polymorphism is by overloading functions or operators. Polymorphism can also be combined with inheritance by means of virtual functions. This mechanism allows the creation of extensible programs, helps prevent the propagation of program defects, and allows the effective construction of libraries, toolkits, and application frameworks.

Perhaps the most important feature of polymorphism is that it supports the definition of a common interface to a group of related actions. A classical example is that of a household thermostat, which allows the control of the temperature inside the house while hiding the details of how the heat or cold is generated or distributed. In this case the thermostat is the interface and the source of hot or cold air is the implementation. A programming analogy is a mathematical function that returns the absolute value of an operand independently of its data type. In this case the user of the function can disregard the fact that the operand is an integer or a real number since the correct result is returned in either case.

Polymorphism is a mechanism for reducing complexity by allowing the reuse of the interface element. In C++ the compiler is able to select the specific action that is required in each case. The final result is that the programmer can disregard more implementation details than in a non-object-oriented environment. C++ supports both compile time and run-time polymorphism.

C++ *static* (compile-time) *polymorphism* is achieved by means of object-to-class associations with or without virtual functions. In object-to-class associations the object type is used to select the corresponding method. Each object knows the class to which it belongs; therefore, execution can be directed to the corresponding method even though there are others with the same name. This type of polymorphism results in *early* or compile-time *binding*. A second mode of compile-time polymorphism is based on virtual function. Static polymorphism by virtual functions is also based on object-to-class associations or on explicit class selection by means of the scope resolution operator.

Dynamic or run-time *polymorphism* is based on either regular virtual functions or pure virtual functions. A pure virtual function is declared to be empty in the base class and implementations are provided exclusively in the derived classes. When a virtual function (either pure or not) is accessed by means of a pointer, the binding is deferred until run time. This type of late binding, or run-time polymorphism, is one of the most powerful features of C++.

7.1.3 Inheritance

Inheritance concepts originated in the field of knowledge representation. The basic notion refers to the inheritance of properties. It assumes a knowledge base organized into hierarchies, in which an individual inherits the properties of the class to which it belongs. For example, animals breathe, move, and reproduce. If bird belongs to the animal class, then we can infer that birds breathe, move, and reproduce since these properties are inherited from the base class.

Inheritance systems ensure the highest levels of abstraction. It also serves to reduce the size of the knowledge base by requiring that common properties be asserted only once. In addition, inheritance serves to maintain the consistency of the knowledge base and to simplify programming. C++ inheritance refers to the possibility of one class acquiring the public members of its parent class. Class inheritance promotes the highest level of abstraction, reduces code size, facilitates reuse, and simplifies programming. This allows the building of a class hierarchy, from the most general to the most specific. It also makes it possible for an object to be an instance of a class, which represents a more general case. There can be no object orientation without inheritance.

7.2 Classes

A C++ class is a conceptual construct that serves as a container for objects with similar properties. A class is a grouping for objects with analogous characteristics. Syntactically speaking, C++ classes are similar to structures, since the language defines a structure as a class type. In contrast with C, C++ structures can also include methods. The only difference between classes and structures is that by default all members of a structure are public while those in a class are private.

7.2.1 Class Declaration

A class is created by means of the **class** keyword, for example:

```
class Rectangle {
  private:
    float base;
    float side;
  public:
    float Area(float b, float s);
    float Perimeter(float b, float s);
};
```

This code fragment creates a class with the tag name **rectangle**. The class has two attributes named **base** and **side**, and two methods named **Area()** and **Perimeter()**. The methods will be implemented as functions. Both the attributes and the methods of a class are called its members. The attributes are the *data members* or *member variables*, and the methods are the *member functions*.

The keywords **private** and **public** are access specifiers. They refer to an entire member list within the class. In the case of the class **Rectangle private** refers to both attributes, base and side. The public specifier refers to both methods, **Area()** and **Perimeter()**. Private members are not visible outside the class. Public members are the class' interface since they can be freely accessed by other classes and by client code. By controlling access to certain class members we achieve encapsulation. A third access specifier, called *protected*, is discussed in the context of class inheritance, later in this chapter. Private access is the default; therefore, the use of the **private** keyword is optional. By the same token, public members must be explicitly declared. C++ allows the use of public attributes (variables) but most authors agree that access to attributes should be implemented through methods. The principles of encapsulation advise that data members be accessed only through class methods.

The general format for a class declaration is as follows:

```
class class-name {
[private:]
  // private attributes and methods
public:
  // public attributes and methods
} [object list];
```

Note that in the preceding example optional elements are enclosed in braces. Objects can be instantiated at the time the class is created, much the same way as with structure variables. More frequently objects are instantiated with a separate statement, for example:

```
Rectangle fig_1;
```

creates an object named **fig_1** that belongs to the Rectangle class. If we consider a class as a user-defined data type, then an object can be equated to a variable. The class name (**Rectangle**) becomes a new data type specifier and the object (**fig_1**) is a variable of this data type. This is also consistent with the notion of a variable being an instance of a data type.

C++ requires prototypes. If we refer to the class declaration for rectangle in Section 7.2.1 we can see the prototypes for its member functions:

```
float Area(float b, float s);
float Perimeter(float b, float s);
```

Member functions of a class are coded very much like regular functions, except that the code must declare the class to which they belong. In the case of the function area we could proceed as follows:

```
float Rectangle::Area(float x, float y) {
  return (x * y);
}
```

The :: symbol, called the *scope resolution operator*, tells the compiler to what class a method belongs. Another way to say it is that **Area()** is of rectangle's scope. When referring to a class member from code outside the class you must do so by means of an object instantiated from the class. The *dot operator* is used in this case to indicate the object and the method. For example:

```
Rectangle fig_1, fig_2; // declares two objects of class rectangle
fig_1.Area(8, 10);      // calls the area method of the rectangle
                        // class on the object fig_1.
```

Within the class the dot operator is not used. This means that a member function can call another member function or refer to an attribute directly. The dot operator is required when accessing member functions from code that is outside the class. The following sample program demonstrates classes and objects by means of a stack abstract data type.

```
//*******************************************************************
// C++ program to illustrate classes and objects by means of a
// stack abstract data type
// Filename: SAM07-01.CPP
//*******************************************************************
#include <iostream.h>
#define STACK_SIZE 80        // Constant establishes size of stack

//****************************
//        stack class
//****************************
class Stack {
  int stack_array[STACK_SIZE];   // Stack storage space
  int stack_top;                 // Stack top pointer
public:
  void Init_stack();             // Prototypes for methods
  void Push(int i);
  int Pop();
};

//****************************
//   methods implementation
//****************************
void stack::Init_stack() {
  stack_top = 0;
  return;
}

void stack::Push(int i) {
  if (stack_top == STACK_SIZE) {   // Check for stack overflow
    cout << "Stack overflow\n";
    return;
  }
  stack_array[stack_top] = i;
  stack_top++;
  return;
}

int stack::Pop() {
  if (stack_top == 0) {
    cout << "stack underflow\n";
    return 0;
  }
  stack_top-;
  return stack_array[stack_top];
}
```

```
//****************************
//           main()
//****************************
main() {
  Stack stack1, stack2;          // Two objects of type stack
  stack1.Init_stack();           // Both stacks are initialized
  stack2.Init_stack();
  stack1.Push(22);               // Data is stored in both stacks
  stack1.Push(33);
  stack2.Push(44);
  cout << stack1.Pop() << "\n";  // Stored data is displayed
  cout << stack1.Pop() << "\n";
  cout << stack2.Pop() << "\n";
  cout << stack1.Pop() << "\n";  // This stack is empty. Pop()
                                 // causes underflow error

  return 0;

}
```

7.3 Overloading Functions and Operators

C++ implements compile-time polymorphism (early binding) in three different ways: by function overloading, by operator overloading, and by inheritance. In this section we briefly discuss function and operator overloading. Inheritance is the topic of Section 7.4.

7.3.1 Function Overloading

Function overloading is based on C++ distinguishing between two functions with the same name as long as the number of parameters or their data types are different. An example often used in this context is the C function that returns the absolute value of a number: **abs()** when the argument is an **int**, **labs()** when it is a **long**, and **fabs()** when it is a **float**. In C++ it is possible to implement this operation by using three different functions with the name **abs()**, since the compiler is able to select the appropriate one by means of the argument.

Note that the return type of a function cannot be used in overloading, since this element may not be visible at call time. For example:

```
void fun1();          \\ ILLEGAL prototypes for two functions
int fun1();           \\ with the same name
  .
  .
cout << fun1();       \\ Compiler cannot resolve which function
                      \\ is referenced in the call
```

7.3.2 Operator Overloading

Compile time polymorphism is also achieved by means of operator overloading. In this case a standard C++ operator is given a functionality in addition to its conventional one. Every C++ programmer is familiar with the << and the >> operators used by the **cout** and **cin** functions of the **iostream** library. In this case the < and the > symbols retain their original meanings when used individually. In this same sense we sometimes fail to notice that some arithmetic operators (+, -, *, and /) work on various data types. Thus we use the same symbols for adding, subtracting, multiplying, and dividing integers or reals. In this case the language itself is overloading the operators.

What is unique about C++, relative to C, is that it allows the programmer to overload operators. When used judiciously this feature of C++ can make programs easier to use and more rational. When abused, it can cause a debugging nightmare.

7.4 C++ Implementation of Inheritance

In Chapters 3 and 6 we described inheritance as an element of object orientation. This notion, which originated in knowledge representation, has been adopted by many other fields of computer science. In object-oriented systems, inheritance structures ensure the highest levels of abstraction, reduce the size of the knowledge base by requiring that common properties be asserted only once, serve to maintain the consistency of the data, and simplify programming.

In C++ inheritance lets one class, called the **derived class**, incorporate members of another one, called the **base class**. This allows the programmer to build a hierarchy of classes that go from the more general to the more specific. A derived class inherits the public members of the base class, but is also able to add new functionalities or to replace existing ones.

In order to understand the inheritance mechanism of C++ we must start with *access specifiers*, namely: private, public, and protected. One of the difficulties in this respect is that the same keywords are used in two different contexts: to define access to members of the base class, and to control inheritance of the derived classes. In the following sections we discuss each function separately.

7.4.1 Access to Base Class Members

In Section 7.2.1 we saw that the access specifiers, private and public, control the visibility of class members: private members are not visible outside the class while public members can be freely accessed. A third access specifier, called *protected*, creates members that are private to the base class except that they can be inherited and accessed by derived classes. In other words, outside of derived classes protected members are private. Inside of derived classes protected members have public accessibility. Therefore, the protected specifier allows breaking encapsulation in order to support inheritance, but preserves it for noninherited code.

7.4.2 Derived Classes

A derived class is created by following the class name with the colon operator, an access specifier, and the name of the base class, as in the following template:

```
class derived-class-name : access-specifier base-class-name {
  // class body
}
```

In the case of a derived class the access specifer is used to determine the type of inheritance mechanism that applies. It can be the same or different from the access specifiers of the base class. Their functions are as follows:

1. *Public* causes all public or protected members of the base class to retain the same access specification in the derived class. In other words, public members in the base class are public in the derived class, and protected members in the base class are protected in the derived class. The access privileges of the base class are preserved in the derived class. Therefore, the private members of the base class cannot be accessed in the derived class. In this case inheritance does not break encapsulation.

2. *Private* causes all public and protected members of the base class to be private in the derived class. Therefore, the visibility of these members is restricted to the class code. Private access restricts visibility and breaks the inheritance path. This is the default access; if none is designated, private is assumed.

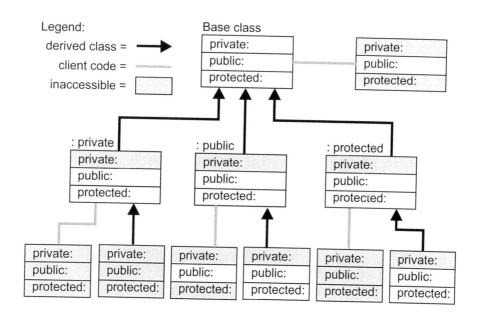

Figure 7.1 *Base Class Accessibility in Derived Classes and Client Code*

3. *Protected* causes all public and protected members of the base class to be protected members of the derived class. The result is that accessibility is restricted regarding inherited public members, which can no longer be accessed by client code; however, the inheritance path is maintained.

Figure 7.1 shows the effects of access specifiers in the derived class regarding the base class members and client code. Gray rectangles indicate that the member functions of the base class are not visible.

Note in Figure 7.1 that private members of the base class are not accessible by the client code or by derived classes at any level of inheritance. If C++ were to provide a mechanism for accessing private members of the base class, then encapsulation would be broken and the private attribute would be meaningless. Also observe that client code can sometimes access the public members of the base class, but never the private or protected members. When a derived class inherits with the **private** access specifier, then accessibility to both derived classes and client code is terminated. When a derived class inherits with the **public** access specifier, then public members remain accessible to client code, and both public and protected members can be further inherited. The same path is valid when a derived class inherits with the **protected** access specifier, but in this case client code is locked out of access to the parent class.

7.4.3 Access Declarations

In the preceding section we saw that a derived class that inherits with the private attribute makes public and protected members of the base class inaccessible to client code and to other derived classes. However, on some occasions we may want to preserve the public or protected accessibility of one or more members of the base class. The access declaration construct allows retaining the public or protected accessibility of some members of the base class even though it is inherited as private. The following template shows how this is achieved:

```
class Base1 {
    public:
        Method1();              // Method is public in base
        Method2();
    protected:
        Method3();              // Method is protected in base
        Method4();
    };

    class Derived1: private base1 {
      public:
        Base1::Method1();       // Public access declaration
      protected:
        Base1::Method3();       // Protected access declaration
    }
```

Hereafter **Method1()**, in the class **Base1**, retains public accessibility, while **Method3()** retains protected accessibility. Since the derived class is inherited with the private attribute, all other methods in the base class (such as **Method2()** and **Method4()**) are not accessible to client or inherited code beyond the class Derived1.

The actual syntax of the access declaration is as follows:

```
base-class-name::member-function-name;
```

Note that the access declaration is made in the corresponding access specifier field of the derived class. No data type is included.

Access declarations can be used to shield private or protected members of the base class from the inaccessibility that results from inheriting with a private access specifier. However, a private specification in the base class cannot be changed by means of an access declaration since this would break the encapsulation.

7.4.4 Multiple Inheritance

C++ supports class inheritance to any level. This means that a derived class can become the base class for another derived class, and so on indefinitely. However, multiple inheritance does not refer to the various levels of class derivation but to simultaneously inheriting from more than one base class. Figure 7.2 is a representation of multiple inheritance in which a derived class (**Derived1**) simultaneously inherits the public and protected methods of three base classes (**Base1**, **Base2**, and **Base3**).

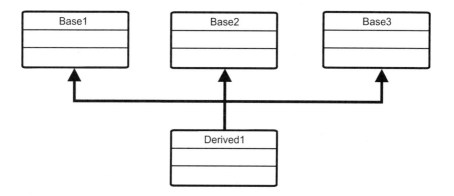

Figure 7.2 *Multiple Inheritance*

Multiple inheritance has detractors as well as defenders. The defenders claim that multiple inheritance mechanisms expand the usefulness and power of an object-oriented programming language. The detractors sustain that multiple inheritance is best avoided since it can give rise to many ambiguities and uncertainties. Most C++ programmers consider multiple inheritance as a powerful tool, when kept simple and used judiciously. Abuse can lead to undecipherable inheritance paths with often conflicting alternatives. It is interesting to note that Smalltalk, usually considered the founding language of object orientation, does not support multiple inheritance.

One common cause of ambiguity in multiple inheritance is when two or more base classes have methods with the same name, while there is no method of that name in the derived class. In this case objects of the derived class have no way of knowing which of the parent methods is to be executed. The scope resolution operator can be used to resolve the ambiguity, as in the following short program:

```
//*****************************************************************
// C++ program to illustrate ambiguity in multiple inheritance
// Filename: SAM07-02.CPP
//*****************************************************************

#include <iostream.h>

//***************************
//       base classes
//***************************
class Base1 {
public:
  void Display() { cout << "\nin class Base1"; }
};

class Base2 {
public:
  void Display() { cout << "\nin class Base2"; }
};

//***************************
//    derived class
//***************************
class Derived1 : public Base1, public Base2 {
};

//***************************
//         main()
//***************************

main() {
  Derived1 objA;                   // Object A of class Derived1

// Since both inherited methods have the same name, we cannot code:
// objA.Display();

// However, we can resolve the ambiguity as follows:

  objA.Base1::Display();           // Select Display() in Base1
  objA.Base2::Display();           // Select Display() in Base2

  return 0;

}
```

Virtual Base Classes

Another element of ambiguity in multiple inheritance arises when two or more derived classes inherit the same member from a common base class. If now another derived class inherits from these classes, two copies of the original member function could be inherited. Figure 7.3 shows one possible scenario that leads to inheritance of multiple copies.

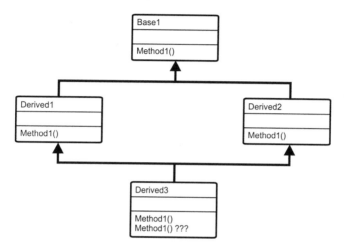

Figure 7.3 *Inheritance of Multiple Copies*

One possible solution to this duplicity is the use of the scope resolution operator, much the same way as we did in program SAM07-02.CPP. However, the scope resolution operator is a manual fix which is not always suitable, since it forces a compile-time binding that may be undesirable in some cases. Another solution is to declare the base classes to be virtual at the time they are inherited. In cases where multiple inheritance is possible, the conflicting method in the virtual base class is not inherited. The following short program shows the use of virtual base classes in multiple inheritance:

```
//*********************************************************************
// C++ program to illustrate virtual base classes in multiple
// inheritance
// Filename: SAM07-03.CPP
//*********************************************************************
#include <iostream.h>
//****************************
//   base and derived classes
//****************************
```

```
class Base1 {
public:
  int a;
};
// Derived classes use the virtual attribute
class Derived1 : virtual public Base1 {
public:
  int b;
};
class Derived2 : virtual public Base1 {
public:
  int c;
};

// Multiple inheritance takes place in class Derived3
class Derived3 : public Derived1, public Derived2 {
public:
  int sum;
};
//****************************
//         main()
//****************************
main() {
  Derived3 objA;          // objA is an object of Derived3
  objA.a = 22;            // Assign value to variable in Base1
  objA.b = 33;            // to a variable Derived1
  objA.c = 11;            // and to a variable in Derived2
// Access and add all three variables
  objA.sum = objA.a + objA.b +objA.c;
  cout << objA.sum;
  return 0;
}
```

One of the most common applications of multiple inheritance is to provide a mechanism whereby a new class is used to augment the functionality provided by an existing class, or to furnish an additional interface. Figure 7.4 is an inheritance diagram of such a structure. In Chapter 12 we discuss a class pattern based on multiple inheritance.

7.5 Friend Classes and Functions

In an effort to accommodate every possible programming eventuality, the designers of C++ provided us with a mechanism for breaking encapsulation and letting the private and protected members of a class be visible to other classes or to client code. The *friend* keyword is used for this purpose. Both classes and functions can be friends of a class.

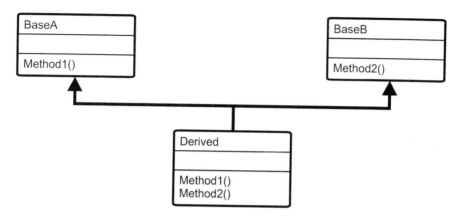

Figure 7.4 *A Practical Use of Multiple Inheritance*

The usefulness and appropriateness of friend classes and functions has been thoroughly discussed in the object-oriented literature. Many authors consider that these constructs are dangerous and unnecessary. In fact, friend classes are rarely used in practical C++ programming. Friend functions, on the other hand, are used rather frequently.

7.5.1 Friend Classes

When a class declares another one as its friend, the friend class acquires access to all the private and protected members of the first class. In the following discussion we will refer to the class that bestows the friend status as the *granting class* and the one that receives it as the *friend class*. Note that classes cannot grant themselves friend privileges with respect to other classes since this would permanently contaminate encapsulation. It is the granting class that assigns friend privileges to other classes.

The notion of friend classes is unrelated to inheritance. As shown in Figure 7.1, derived classes have access to the public and protected members of the base class and have no access to its private members. Client code can see the public members of any class but not those that are private or protected. A friend class, on the other hand, can see private, protected, and public members of the granting class. The various degrees of accessibility of friend classes, client code, and derived classes are shown in Figure 7.5.

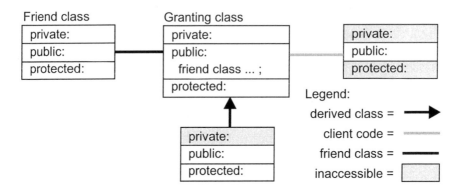

Figure 7.5 *Accessibility by a Friend Class*

7.5.2 Friend Functions

It is also possible to grant a nonmember function access to the private and protected members of a class by means of the **friend** keyword. The declaration of a friend function is actually a prototype preceded by the **friend** keyword, as in the following template:

```
friend return-type function-name(parameter-list);
```

Figure 7.6 shows accessibility of friend and non-friend functions.

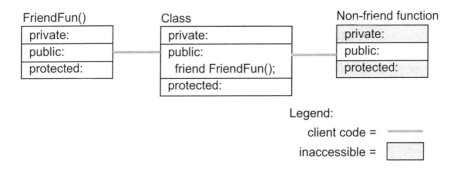

Figure 7.6 *Accessibility by Friend Functions*

Several programming situations suggest the use of friend functions. One of the most common ones is when several classes contain interrelated members. Suppose, for example, that error handlers in several classes can post a message to screen. In this case other program elements may need to know if an error message is currently displayed so that it is not erased before the user reads it. Code would have to check all functions that post error messages in order to ascertain if one is currently displayed. A more efficient solution would be to create a friend function to the classes that post error messages so that all error-posting classes could be checked in a single operation. Although this is sometimes considered a valid application of a friend function, an experienced programmer could probably think of several easier and simpler ways of accomplishing this. For instance, a *semaphore* could be set and reset by the error handlers. Code could then read the semaphore status to determine if a message is currently displayed.

The following short program shows how a friend class and a friend function gains access to a private member of the granting class.

```
//*********************************************************************
// C++ program to illustrate friend classes and functions
// Filename: SAM07-04.CPP
//*********************************************************************
#include <iostream.h>

//****************************
//    granting and friend
//         classes
//****************************
class Aclass {
  friend class AFriendClass;
  friend void AFriendFun(Aclass obj);
private:
  int a, b;
public:
  Aclass() { a = 3; b = 4; }         // Constructor
  void Show_ab();                    // Public member function
};
// Implementation of Show_ab method of Aclass
void Aclass::Show_ab() {
  cout << "\n\nVariables in Aclass are accessed through public
          method"
       << " Show_ab()\n";
  cout << "a = " << a << "  b = " << b;
};
// Declaration of AFriendClass
class AFriendClass {
public:
  void Afun();
```

```
};
// Implementation of Afun in AFriendClass
void AFriendClass::Afun() {
  Aclass obj;
  cout << "\nVariables in Aclass are accessed through friend
          class"
       << " AFriendClass\n";
  obj.a = 10;
  obj.b = 20;
  cout << "a now = " << obj.a << "  b now = " << obj.b << "\n";
}

//****************************
//          main()
//****************************
main() {
  Aclass objx;             // Object of Aclass
  AFriendClass objy;       // Object of AFriendClass
  objx.Show_ab();          // Access Aclass through its own method
  AFriendFun(objx);        // Access Aclass through AFriendFun
                           // passing to it an object of Aclass
  objy.Afun();             // Access Aclass through a method of
                           // AFriendClass

  return 0;
}

//****************************
//       friend function
//****************************
// Declaration and implementation of AFriendFun
void AFriendFun(Aclass anobj) {
  cout << "\nVariables in Aclass are accessed through friend
function"
          << " AFriendFun\n";
  anobj.a = 7;
  anobj.b = 8;
  cout << "a now = " << anobj.a << "  b now = " << anobj.b;
};
```

The statement declaring a friend class or function can appear any-where within the class declaration. Since friends violate encapsula-tion, perhaps the best coding style would be to list friend classes and functions prominently, preferably at the start of the class declaration.

Note that in the program SAM07-04.CPP the **constructor** and the **Show_ab** function of **Aclass** have direct access to the private vari-ables. However, nonmember functions and client code can only access the member functions of a class by means of an object. Therefore a friend function or class must access the members of the granting class through objects, as in SAM07-04.CPP.

A convenient mechanism for achieving this access is a function that receives an object as a parameter. In this case the standard call by value of C++ is applicable; therefore, the called function receives a copy of the passed object. To make this work the constructor function must not be called, otherwise the object could be changed by the constructor. The passed object exists while the function is executing. However, when it concludes, the object is destroyed and the allocated memory is freed. An example implementation of passing an object to a function can be seen in the program SAM07-04.CPP previously listed.

7.6 Objects

A C++ class is a grouping for objects of similar characteristics. Thus, a class is a conceptual entity while an object is a real program one. Object-oriented programming consists of creating, initializing, manipulating, and destroying objects. The whole set of object-related activities can be categorized as object handling operations.

7.6.1 The *this* Pointer

Elements of a class can be accessed directly by its own members. Derived classes, client code, even friend functions must access the members functions through objects. However, the class members need not reference the object, for example:

```
class Aclass {
private:
    int a_var;
public:
    Aclass() { a_var = 0 ;}
    void Show() { cout << "\nvalue of a_var: " << a_var; }
};
```

In **Aclass** the private variable **a_var** is accessed directly both by the constructor and by the **Show() member** function. In neither case is there an object reference. On the other hand, we know that a class exists as a program element in its instantiations only. If so, how can a member function operate independently of objects? The explanation to this apparent contradiction is that there is an implicit argument, automatically supplied to all nonstatic member functions: a pointer to the object that made the call. In C++ the pointer is called *this*. The following version of **Aclass** is identical to the preceding one, except that the *this* pointer is used to explicitly reference the address of the data.

```
class Aclass {
private:
    int a_var;
public:
    Aclass() { this-> a_var = 0 ;}
    void Show() { cout << "\nvalue of a_var: " << this-> a_var; }
};
```

Normally, there is nothing gained by explicitly coding the **this** pointer, although it is useful didactically since it explains the contradiction that results from class members accessing their data elements directly. In this sense the **this** pointer reminds us that the alternative syntax is simply a shorthand. One case in which the **this** pointer is required is when an object must pass its address to a function. Another one, perhaps more common, is when a function returns an object by reference, as is the case in some forms of operator overloading. The following short program illustrates the use of the **this** pointer in returning the address of an object:

```
//**************************************************************
// C++ program to illustrate the use of this pointer in
// returning the address of an object
// Filename: SAM07-05.CPP
//**************************************************************
#include <iostream.h>
//***************************
//           class
//***************************
class Oclass {
private:
    int a;
public:
    Oclass() { a = 25; }                      // Constructor (a = 25)
    void Showa() { cout << this-> a; }        // Display value of
                                              // variable a
    Oclass ObjAddress(Oclass an_obj) {        // Return object address
        return *this;
    }
};

//***************************
//           main()
//***************************
main() {
    Oclass x, y;             // Declare x and y, objects of Oclass
    cout << "\n\na in object x = " ;
    x.Showa();               // Display value of a in object x (25)
    y = x.ObjAddress(x); // Assign address of object x to object y
    cout << "\na in object y = " ;
    y.Showa();               // Display value of a in object y
```

```
                           // (will be the same as in object x)

    return 0;

}
```

7.6.2 Arrays of Objects

Since in C it is possible to create arrays of structures, it is reasonable to expect that in C++ we would be able to create arrays of objects. The syntax for creating an array of objects is the same as for any other array. The standard template is as follows:

```
class-name object-name[array-size];
```

The default constructor initializes each object in an array if it consists of a single parameter, as shown in the following code fragment.

```
class Xclass {
  private:
    int a;
  public:
    ...
};
main() {
  Xclass arr_ob1[4] = { 11, 22, 33, 44 };
  ...
}
```

After initialization, object **arr_ob1[0]** holds the value 11, **arr_ob1[1]** holds 22, and so on. Alternatively, a parameterized constructor can be used to initialize each object in the array. The number of data elements initialized determines the constructor's form. In the case of a constructor that takes a single parameter, we could also code as follows:

```
class Xclass {
  private:
    int a;
  public:
    Xclass( int x ) { a = x; }    // Parameterized constructor
    ...

};

main() {
  Xclass arr_ob1[3] = { 22, 33, 44 };
  ...
}
```

When each object of the array requires more than one argument, then a different initialization must be used, as shown in program SAM07-06.CPP:

```
//*****************************************************************
// C++ program to illustrate initialization of an array of
// objects by means of a parameterized constructor
// Filename: SAM07-06.CPP
//*****************************************************************
#include <iostream.h>

//****************************
//          class
//****************************
class Xclass {
private:
   int a;
   int b;
public:
   Xclass(int x, int y) { a = x; b = y;}   // Parameterized
                                           // constructor
   int Geta() { return a; }         // Read object variable a
   int Getb() { return b; }         // Read object variable b
 };
//****************************
//          main()
//****************************
main() {
   Xclass Ob_array[3] = {
     Xclass(1, 11),               // Initialize objects
     Xclass(2, 22),
     Xclass(3, 33)
   };
   // Display values of all objects
   for(int x = 0; x < 3; x++) {
      cout << "\nvalues of object " << x + 1 << ":";
      cout << " a = " << Ob_array[x].Geta() << "   "
           << " b = " << Ob_array[x].Getb();
      }
   return 0;
}
```

7.6.3 Pointers to Objects

C++ supports pointers to objects. In Section 6.4 we saw the use of the pointer-member operator (->) in the context of pointers to structures. This same operator is used to dereference pointers to objects. Pointers to objects are created and initialized much as pointers to structures, as shown in the following short program:

```
//*******************************************************************
// C++ program to illustrate a pointer to object
// Filename: SAM07-07.CPP
//*******************************************************************
#include <iostream.h>

//***************************
//          class
//***************************
class Xclass {
private:
   int a;
public:
   Xclass(int x) { a = x;}      // Parameterized constructor
   int Geta() { return a; }     // Read object variable a
};

//***************************
//          main()
//***************************
main() {
   Xclass obj1(22);             // Create an object of Xclass
   Xclass *obj_ptr;             // Create a pointer to object
   obj_ptr = &obj1;             // Initialize pointer to address
                                // of object

   cout << "\nvalue of a in obj1 is "
        << obj_ptr-> Geta();    // Dereference pointer

   return 0;
}
```

Pointer arithmetic also works on pointers to objects. Therefore incrementing a pointer to an array of objects bumps it to the next object in the array. The following short program shows how object pointers are used in dereferencing the corresponding elements of an object array:

```
//*******************************************************************
// C++ program to illustrate access to an array of objects by
// means of an object pointer
// Filename: SAM07-08.CPP
//*******************************************************************
#include <iostream.h>

//***************************
//          class
//***************************
class Xclass {
private:
   int a;
Public:
```

```
    Xclass(int x) { a = x;}              // Parameterized constructor
    int Geta() { return a; }             // Read object variable b
  };

//****************************
//          main()
//****************************

main() {
    Xclass Ob_array[3] = { 11, 22, 33 };  // Array of objects
    Xclass *obj_ptr;                      // Object pointer
    obj_ptr = Ob_array;                   // Pointer initialized
// Display values of all objects using pointer
    for(int x = 0; x < 3; x++) {
      cout << "\nvalues of object " << x + 1 << ":";
      cout << " a = " << obj_ptr-> Geta() << "  ";
      obj_ptr++;                          // Point to next object
    }

    return 0;

}
```

7.6.4 Pointers to Objects of Derived Classes

In Chapter 6 we stated that, with the exception of pointers to void, a pointer variable is related to a specific data type. Another exception is that a pointer to an object of a base class can also point to an object of any derived class. However, the opposite is not true: a pointer to an object of a derived class may not point to an object of the base class.

There are some restrictions to pointers to objects. When the pointer to an object of a base class is used in relation to a derived class, only the members of the derived class that were inherited from the base class can be accessed. Any member that appears in the derived class, but not in the base class, is not accessible through the pointer. The principal use of pointers that can simultaneously access members of the base class and the derived class is in implementing run-time polymorphism, discussed later in this chapter.

Note that classes are formal constructs, which have no tangible existence as a run-time program element. Since pointers are used to store addresses, we cannot have a pointer to a class. When we refer to a pointer to a base or a derived class we actually mean a pointer to *an object* of a base or derived class. The following short program shows how to access an object of the base class using a pointer to a derived class:

```
//********************************************************************
// C++ program to illustrate the use of a pointer to a base
// class in accessing an inherited method in a derived class
// Filename: SAM07-09.CPP
//********************************************************************
#include <iostream.h>
//****************************
//         classes
//****************************
// Base class
class BaseClass {
private:
   int a;
public:
   void Seta(int x) { a = x;}          // Set value of variable a
   int Geta() { return a; }            // Read object variable b
 };


  // Derived class
class DerClass: public BaseClass {
private:
   int b;
public:
   void Setb(int x) { b = x;}          // Set value of variable b
   int Getb() { return b; }            // Read object variable b
 };

//****************************
//          main()
//****************************
main() {
   BaseClass *base_ptr;     // Pointer to object of base class
   DerClass der_obj;        // Object of derived class
   base_ptr = &der_obj;     // Initialize pointer to derived object

// Access object of derived class using base class pointer
   base_ptr-> Seta(22);
   cout << "\nvalue of a in BaseClass is: "
        <<  base_ptr-> Geta()
        << "\n";

   return 0;
}
```

In the program SAM07-09.CPP the pointer to derived class **Der-Class** is used to access a method inherited from the base class, in this case the method is **Geta()**. However, this base class pointer could not be used to access a method in the derived class. For example, the statement:

```
   base_ptr-> Setb(44);              // ILLEGAL ACCESS
```

would be illegal since **Setb()** is a method defined in the derived class.

7.6.5 Arrays of Pointers to Pointers

Since we can have arrays of pointers to objects as well as pointers to pointers, it is a reasonable assumption that we can also have an array of pointers to pointers to objects. The result of a pointer to pointer construct was discussed in Chapter 6 in the context of compounded indirection (see Section 6.10 and Figure 6.3). Object access by means of arrays of pointers to pointers is particularly useful in the context of recursion with multiple objects, a topic discussed in Chapter 12. The following short program demonstrates the use of an array of pointers to pointers to objects.

```
//******************************************************************
// C++ program to illustrate multiple object indirection
// Filename: SAM07-10.CPP
//******************************************************************
#include <iostream.h>

//***************************
//        classes
//***************************
class BaseA {
public:
  virtual void ShowMsg() = 0;
};

class Der1 : public BaseA {
public:
  virtual void ShowMsg() { cout << "Der1 class\n"; }
};

class Der2 : public BaseA {
public:
  virtual void ShowMsg() { cout << "  Der2 class\n"; }
};
class Der3 : public BaseA {
public:
  virtual void ShowMsg() { cout << "    Der3 class\n"; }
};

//***************************
//          main()
//***************************
main() {
// Classes: BaseA, Der1, Der2, Der3
   BaseA*   ptr_ba;          // Base class pointer
   BaseA**  ptr_ptr;         // Base class pointer to pointer
```

```
    Der1      obj1;            // Objects of derived classes
    Der2      obj2;
    Der3      obj3;

// Array of pointers
    BaseA  *ptr_array1[10];     // An array of pointers
    BaseA  *ptr_array2[10];     // Another array of pointers
    BaseA  **ptr_ptr_array[10]; // Array of pointers to pointers

// Initialize 4 entries in first pointer array
    ptr_ba = &obj1;          // Base pointer to derived class object
    ptr_array1[0] = ptr_ba;// Base pointer entered in array
    ptr_ba = &obj2;
    ptr_array1[1] = ptr_ba;
    ptr_ba = &obj3;
    ptr_array1[2] = ptr_ba;
    ptr_ba = &obj1;
    ptr_array1[3] = ptr_ba;

// Set address of first pointer array in pointers-to-pointers
// array
    ptr_ptr_array[0] = ptr_array1;

// Initialize 3 entries in second pointer array
    ptr_ba = &obj2;          // Base pointer to derived class object
    ptr_array2[0] = ptr_ba;// Base pointer entered in array
    ptr_ba = &obj2;
    ptr_array2[1] = ptr_ba;
    ptr_ba = &obj2;
    ptr_array2[2] = ptr_ba;

// Set address of first second pointer array in
// pointers-to-pointers array
    ptr_ptr_array[1] = ptr_array2;
// Execute methods in both pointer arrays dereferencing the
// pointers-to-pointers array
cout << "\n\nExecuting polymorphic methods in first\n"
     << "pointer array\n";
    ptr_ptr = ptr_ptr_array[0];
for (int x = 0; x < 4; x++)
    ptr_ptr[x]->ShowMsg();
cout << "\n\nExecuting polymorphic methods in second\n"
     << "pointer array\n";
    ptr_ptr = ptr_ptr_array[1];
for (x = 0; x < 3; x++)
    ptr_ptr[x]->ShowMsg();
    return 0;
}
```

One point in program SAM07-10.CPP deserves a comment. Note that dereferencing the pointers to pointers array requires the use of an intermediate variable, in this case **ptr_ptr**, which is of type pointer to pointer to the class **BaseA**. The following program statements show how the intermediate variable is dereferenced and used.

```
ptr_ptr = ptr_ptr_array[0];
      for (int x = 0; x < 4; x++)

        ptr_ptr[x]->ShowMsg();
```

7.7 Run-time Polymorphism

Run-time polymorphism is also called late or dynamic binding. This topic is at the core of object-oriented programming since it provides a powerful mechanism for achieving two very desirable properties: reusability and isolation of program defects.

The fundamental notion of dynamic binding is that the method to be executed is determined when the program runs, not when it is compiled. Suppose a class hierarchy which includes a base class named **B** and several derived classes named **D1**, **D2**, and **D3** respectively. Also assume that there is a method named **M()** in the base class, which is inherited and perhaps modified in the derived classes. We now implement a pointer named **ptr** to the method in the base class. In C++ we can access this method by means of the statement:

```
ptr-> M();
```

However, in dynamic binding terms this does not imply that the method of the base class is forcefully executed. Instead, which method is used depends on the object referenced by the pointer variable. If **ptr** is currently pointing to method **M()** in class **D2**, then it is this implementation of **M()** that is executed, not the one in the base class.

In most modern object-oriented languages, methods are dynamically bound by default. This is not the case with C++, where methods are statically bound by default. In this section we describe how dynamic binding is implemented in C++, a subject not lacking in peculiarities. How to design and code programs that use C++ run-time polymorphism is the subject of Chapter 10.

7.7.1 Virtual Functions

Dynamic binding in C++ is accomplished by means of virtual functions. A virtual function is declared in the base class and redefined in one or more derived classes. This means that the function declared virtual in the base class defines a general type of methods and serves to specify the interface. Other functions with the same name and interface can be implemented in the derived classes to override the one in the base class. If the virtual function is accessed by means of its name, it behaves as any other function. However, when a function declared virtual in the base class is accessed via a pointer, then the one executed depends on the object which the pointer is referencing.

We saw in Section 7.6.4 that a pointer to an object in the base class can be set to point to an object in a derived class. It is this mechanism that allows implementation of dynamic binding in C++. The following short program shows how it is accomplished:

```cpp
//**********************************************************************
// C++ program to illustrate virtual functions and run-time
// polymorphism
// Filename: SAM07-11.CPP
//**********************************************************************
#include <iostream.h>

//***************************
//        classes
//***************************
// Base class
class BaseClass {
public:
    virtual void DisplayMsg() {
      cout << "Method in BaseClass executing\n" ;
    }
};
// A derived class
class DerClass1 : public BaseClass {
public:
    virtual void DisplayMsg() {
      cout << "Method in DerClass1 executing\n" ;
    }
};
// A second derived class
class DerClass2 : public BaseClass {
public:
    virtual void DisplayMsg() {
      cout << "Method in DerClass2 executing\n" ;
    }
};

//***************************
//          main()
//***************************
main() {
```

```
    BaseClass *base_ptr;        // Pointer to object of base class
    BaseClass base_obj;         // Object of BaseClass
    DerClass1 der_obj1;         // Object of DerClass1
    DerClass2 der_obj2;         // Object of DerClass2
// Access object of base class using base class pointer
    base_ptr = &base_obj;       // Pointer to base class object
    base_ptr-> DisplayMsg();
// Access object of first derived class using base class pointer
    base_ptr = &der_obj1;       // Pointer to derived class object
    base_ptr-> DisplayMsg();
// Access object of second derived class using base class pointer
    base_ptr = &der_obj2;       // Pointer to derived class object
    base_ptr-> DisplayMsg();
    return 0;
}
```

When SAM07-11.CPP executes, the display shows the following text messages:

```
Method in BaseClass executing
Method in DerClass1 executing
Method in DerClass2 executing
```

During program execution (run time) the base class pointer named **base_ptr** is first set to the base class and the base class method is executed. The coding is as follows:

```
base_ptr = &base_obj;
base_ptr-> DisplayMsg();
```

Next, the same pointer is reset to the first derived class and the execution statement is repeated:

```
base_ptr = &der_obj1;
base_ptr-> DisplayMsg();
```

The fact that the statement

```
base_ptr-> DisplayMsg();
```

executes different methods in each case proves that the decision regarding which method executes is made at run time, not at compile time, since two identical statements generate the same object code.

The program SAM07-12.CPP is a variation on the program SAM07-11.CPP that uses an array of pointers to the various functions.

```
//********************************************************************
// C++ program to illustrate virtual functions and run-time
// polymorphism by means of an array of pointers
```

```cpp
// Filename: SAM07-12.CPP
//*******************************************************************
#include <iostream.h>
//****************************
//        classes
//****************************
// Base class
class BaseClass {
public:
   virtual void DisplayMsg() {
     cout << "Method in BaseClass executing\n" ;
   }
};
// A derived class
class DerClass1 : public BaseClass {
public:
   virtual void DisplayMsg() {
     cout << "Method in DerClass1 executing\n" ;
   }
};
// A second derived class
class DerClass2 : public BaseClass {
public:
   virtual void DisplayMsg() {
     cout << "Method in DerClass2 executing\n" ;
   }
};
//****************************
//          main()
//****************************
main() {
   BaseClass* ptr_list[3];      // Array of 3 pointers
   BaseClass base_obj;          // Object of BaseClass
   DerClass1 der_obj1;          // Object of DerClass1
   DerClass2 der_obj2;          // Object of DerClass2
// Initialize pointer array with objects
   ptr_list[0] = &base_obj;
   ptr_list[1] = &der_obj1;
   ptr_list[2] = &der_obj2;
// Create variable to store user input
int user_input = 0;
// Prompt user for input
   cout << "\nEnter a number from 1 to 3: ";
   cin >> user_input;
// Test for invalid input
   if(user_input < 1 || user_input > 3){
     cout << "\ninvalid input\n" ;
     return 1;
   }
// Index into array of pointers using user input
   ptr_list[user_input - 1]-> DisplayMsg();
   return 0;
}
```

In the program SAM07-12.CPP selects the method to be executed using the user input as an offset into a pointer array, by means of the statement:

```
ptr_list[user_input - 1]-> DisplayMsg();
```

Characteristics of the Virtual Attribute

The preceding examples (programs SAM07-11.CPP and SAM07-12.CPP) both use pointers to access methods in the base and derived classes. In the first program (SAM07-11.CPP) a pointer to the base class is redirected to derived classes at run time, thus achieving dynamic binding. In the second example, three different pointers are stored in an array at compile time, with the statements:

```
ptr_list[0] = &base_obj;
ptr_list[1] = &der_obj1;
ptr_list[2] = &der_obj2;
```

The program then requests input from the user and scales this value to use it as an offset into the pointer array. The selection is done by means of the statement:

```
ptr_list[user_input - 1]-> DisplayMsg();
```

In this case, although the pointer to be used is not known until program execution, the selection is not based on redirecting a base class pointer at run time; therefore, it is not a true example of dynamic binding. However, if we eliminate the **virtual** keyword from the code, then every valid user input brings about the execution of the base version of the **DisplayMsg()** method. This leads to the conclusion that the **virtual** keyword is doing something in the code, although it is not producing dynamic binding.

Virtual functions, by themselves, do not guarantee dynamic binding since a virtual function can be accessed by means of the **dot** operator. For example, if **der_obj1** is an object of the class **Der1Class**, then the statement:

```
der_obj1.DisplayMsg();
```

executes the corresponding method in this class. However, in this case the virtual attribute is not necessary since the class is bound directly by its object.

The mechanism for selecting among two or more functions of the same name by means of the virtual attribute is called *overriding*. It is different from the notion of *overloaded* functions (discussed in Section 7.3) since overloaded functions must differ in their data types or number of parameters. Overridden functions, on the contrary, must have an identical interface. The prototypes of virtual functions must be identical in the base and in the derived classes. If a function with the same name is defined with a different prototype, then the compiler reverts to overloading and the function is bound statically.

The **virtual** keyword is not necessary in the derived classes, since the virtual attribute is inherited. For this reason the class definition for **DerClass1** in SAM07-11.CPP and SAM07-12.CPP could have read as follows:

```
// A derived class
class DerClass1 : public BaseClass {
public:
    void DisplayMsg() {
       cout << "Method in DerClass1 executing\n" ;
    }
};
```

The implicit virtual attribute is inherited; consequently, we may have to trace through the entire inheritance tree in order to determine if a method is virtual or not. For this reason we prefer to explicitly state the virtual attribute since it should not be necessary to refer to the base class to determine the virtual or nonvirtual nature of a method.

Virtual functions exist in a class hierarchy that follows the order of derivation. This concept is important since overriding a method in a base class is optional. If a derived class does not contain a polymorphic method, then the next one in reverse order of derivation is used.

7.7.2 Pure Virtual Functions

Virtual functions are implemented in the base class and possibly redefined in the derived classes. However, what would happen if a polymorphic method were not implemented in the base class? For instance, suppose that the class named **BaseClass** in the program SAM07-11.CPP were recoded as follows:

```
class BaseClass {
public:
```

```
    virtual void DisplayMsg();
};
```

In a DOS based C++ compiler if the method **DisplayMsg()** was not implemented in the base class, the program would compile correctly but would generate a linker error. That happens because there is no address for the method **DisplayMsg()** in the base class since the method does not exist. Therefore, the statement:

```
    base_ptr-> DisplayMsg();
```

cannot be resolved by the linker. However, there are occasions in which there is no meaningful definition for a method in the base class; for example, the class structure shown in Figure 7.7.

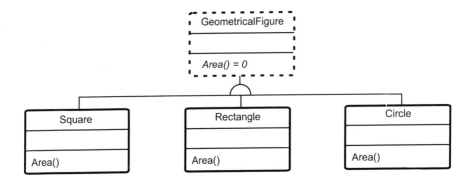

Figure 7.7 *Abstract Class Structure*

In the case of Figure 7.7 there is no possible implementation of the method **Area()** in the base class **GeometricalFigure**. Not until we define a specific geometrical figure can a formula for calculating the area be applied. The **Area()** method in the base class serves to define the class name and the interface, but the implementation is left for the derived class or classes.

In C++ a pure virtual function is declared in the following general form:

```
    virtual return-type function-name(parameter-list) = 0;
```

When a function is declared in the preceding manner, implementation must be provided by all derived classes. A compiler error occurs if any derived class fails to provide an implementation for a pure virtual function. Note that the case of the pure virtual function is quite differ-ent from that of nonvirtual functions, in which a missing implementa-tion is automatically replaced by the closest one in reverse order of derivation.

Pure virtual functions have two effects that could be desirable. The first one is that the base class serves to define a general interface that sets a model that all derived classes must follow. The second one is that implementation in the derived classes is automatically assured since the code does not compile otherwise.

Abstract Classes

C++ pure virtual functions furnish a mechanism whereby a base class is used to define an interface by declaring the method's parame-ters and return type, while one or more derived classes define imple-mentations for the specific cases. A class that contains a pure virtual function is designated an abstract class. The abstract class model sat-isfies the "one interface, multiple methods" approach that is a core notion of object orientation. The programmer is able to create a class hierarchy that goes from the most general to the more specific; from conceptual abstraction to implementation details. The following short program shows a possible use of abstract classes.

```cpp
//****************************************************************
// C++ program to illustrate pure virtual functions
// Filename: SAM07-13.CPP
//****************************************************************
#include <iostream.h>

//***************************
//        classes
//***************************
// Abstract base class

class GeoFigure {
private:
    float dim1;              // First dimension
    float dim2;              // Second dimension
public:
    virtual float Area(float, float) = 0;
// Pure virtual function
};
// derived class
class Rectangle : public GeoFigure {
public:
    virtual float Area(float x, float y) {
```

```
        return (x * y);
        }
};
class Triangle : public GeoFigure {
public:
    virtual float Area(float x, float y) {
    return (x * y)/2;
    }
};
class Circle : public GeoFigure {
public:
    virtual float Area(float x, float y) {
    return (x * x)* 3.1415;
    }
};

//***************************
//          main()
//***************************
main() {
    GeoFigure *base_ptr;     // Pointer to the base class
    Rectangle obj1;          // Declare objects of derived classes
    Triangle obj2;
    Circle obj3;
// Polymorphically access methods in derived classes
    base_ptr = &obj1;        // Set base class pointer to Rectangle
    cout << "\nRectangle area: " << base_ptr-> Area(5.1, 10);
    base_ptr = &obj2;        // Set base class pointer to Triangle
    cout << "\nTriangle area: " << base_ptr-> Area(3.7, 11.22);
    base_ptr = &obj3;        // Set base class pointer to Circle
    cout << "\nCircle area: " << base_ptr-> Area(3.22, 0);
    return 0;
}
```

In the program SAM07-13.CPP we note that the pure virtual function in the base class defines the interface, which must be adhered to by all implementations in the derived classes. In this manner the **Area()** method in the class **Circle** must preserve the interface, which passes two parameters, although a single one suffices for calculating the area in the circle case.

In C++ it is not possible to declare an object of an abstract class, even if the class contains other methods that are not virtual. For example, we modify the class **GeoFigure** in the program SAM07-13.CPP as follows:

```
class GeoFigure {
private:
    float dim1;            // First dimension
    float dim2;            // Second dimension
public:
```

```
    float GetDim1() { return dim1; }
    virtual float Area(float, float) = 0; // Pure virtual function
};
```

The class now includes a nonvirtual function named **GetDim1()**. However, we still cannot instantiate an object of class **GeoFigure**; therefore the statement:

```
GeoFigure objx;              // ILLEGAL STATEMENT
```

would be rejected by the compiler. However, any method implemented in the base class can be accessed by means of a pointer to an object of a derived class; in which case the C++ rules for inheritance are followed. If a method has a unique name in the base class, then it is executed independently of the object referenced. If the classes constitute a simple inheritance hierarchy, then the selection is based on the rules for overloading. If the classes contain nonpure virtual functions, overriding takes place. If the class is an abstract class, then the derived classes must provide implementations of the method declared to be pure virtual.

The following short program contains a base class that includes two nonvirtual methods, a parameterized constructor, a virtual function, and a pure virtual function. The pure virtual function makes the base class an abstract class. The derived classes override the parameterized constructor and contain implementations of the pure and nonpure virtual functions. The nonvirtual methods of the base class are accessed through pointers to the derived classes.

```
//*****************************************************************
// C++ program to illustrate an abstract class with nonvirtual
// functions and a parameterized constructor
// Filename: SAM07-14.CPP
//*****************************************************************
#include <iostream.h>
//***************************
//        classes
//***************************
// Abstract base class has pure virtual functions, parameterized
// constructor, and nonvirtual functions
class GeoFigure {
protected:
// Protected status makes data visible to derived classes
    float dim1;              // First dimension
    float dim2;              // Second dimension
public:
// Constructor
    GeoFigure(float w, float z) { dim1 = w, dim2 = z;}
// Nonvirtual functions
```

```cpp
   float GetDim1() { return dim1; }
   float GetDim2() { return dim2; }
// Virtual function
   void virtual ShowClass() { cout << "\nin base class"; }
// Pure virtual function
   virtual float Area() = 0;
};

// derived class
class Rectangle : public GeoFigure {
public:
   Rectangle(float w, float z) : GeoFigure(w, z) {  }
   virtual float Area() {
   return (dim1 * dim2);
   }
   void virtual ShowClass() { cout << "\nin Rectangle class\n"; }
};

class Triangle : public GeoFigure {
public:
   Triangle(float w, float z) : GeoFigure(w, z) {  }
   virtual float Area() {
   return (dim1 * dim2)/2;
   }
   void virtual ShowClass() { cout << "\nin Triangle class\n"; }};

class Circle : public GeoFigure {
public:
   Circle(float w, float z) : GeoFigure(w, z) {  }
   virtual float Area() {
   return (dim1 * dim1)* 3.1415;
   }
   void virtual ShowClass() { cout << "\nin Circle class\n"; }
};

//****************************
//           main()
//****************************
main() {
   GeoFigure *base_ptr;     // Pointer to the base class
   Rectangle obj1(3, 4);    // Declare objects of derived classes
   Triangle obj2(4, 5);     // and initialize
   Circle obj3(6, 0);

// Polymorphically access methods in derived classes
   base_ptr = &obj1;        // Set base class pointer to Rectangle
   cout << "\n\nRectangle area: " << base_ptr-> Area();
   cout << "  dim1 = " << base_ptr-> GetDim1();
   cout << "  dim2 = " << base_ptr-> GetDim2();
   base_ptr-> ShowClass();
   base_ptr = &obj2;        // Set base class pointer to Triangle
   cout << "\nTriangle area: " << base_ptr-> Area();
   cout << "  dim1 = " << base_ptr-> GetDim1();
```

```
    cout << "   dim2 = " << base_ptr-> GetDim2();
    base_ptr-> ShowClass();
    base_ptr = &obj3;           // Set base class pointer to Circle
    cout << "\nCircle area: " << base_ptr-> Area();
    cout << "   dim1 = " << base_ptr-> GetDim1();
    cout << "   dim2 = " << base_ptr-> GetDim2();
    base_ptr-> ShowClass();
    return 0;
}
```

C++ supports several types of inheritance, most of which can coexist in the same class structure. This makes it possible for a programmer or program designer to conceive an over-complicated inheritance structure that mixes abstract classes, virtual functions, compile-time polymorphism, and dynamic binding. The result could easily turn into an undecipherable smorgasbord of unnecessary complications. It is good programming design sense to avoid these extremes.

Modeling Complex Inheritance

In the program SAM07-14.CPP we note that several inheritance paths have been combined in the same class structure. C++ code allows this combination of inheritance paths in the same classes. To model a complex inheritance pattern that could include abstract and concrete classes, as well as early and late binding, it is usually preferable to concentrate on the inheritance structures rather than on coding mechanics. Figure 7.8 attempts to model the inheritance structures in program SAM07-14.CPP.

Although the class structures shown in Figure 7.8 can serve as an approximate model, there are some basic weaknesses in the representation. One of them is that in C++ the presence of pure virtual functions makes the class an abstract class. This means that no object of the class can be instantiated and that methods in the base class can be accessed only through a pointer to the derived classes. This fact is not evident in Figure 7.8. Another characteristic of the code that is not clear in the class diagram is the mechanism whereby the constructors of the derived classes pass parameters to the one in the base class. In conclusion, although class diagrams are a useful modeling tool during the analysis and design phases, sometimes they are not an accurate model of the actual inheritance mechanisms as they are implemented in code. In Chapter 8 we supplement the Coad and Yourdon notation with other symbols that serve to improve the modeling accuracy.

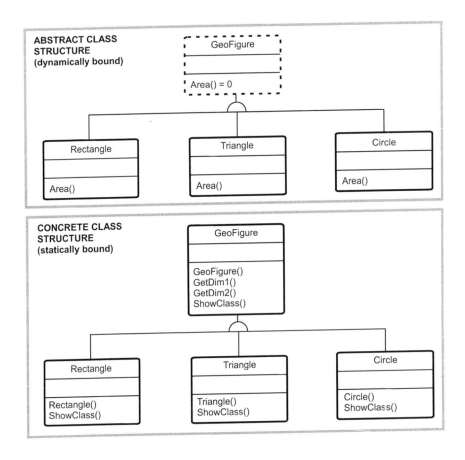

Figure 7.8 *Modeling a Complex Inheritance Structure*

7.8 Templates

The notion of a C++ template is associated with generic functions and classes that operate with several data types. This feature was added to the C++ specification in 1990 and later incorporated in the ANSI standard. Although templates are not central to the notion of object-oriented programming they are a useful tool in constructing robust C++ programs and in avoiding the propagation of errors. Templates are implemented in the context of both functions and classes.

7.8.1 Template Functions

Because template functions allow us to abstract the data type some authors refer to them as *generic functions*. The idea is to create a source code mold (template) that describes the processing operations in abstract. This mold is used by the C++ compiler to generate instructions that will accommodate any of the legal data types. In other words, the programmer defines the fundamentals of the algorithm and the compiler plugs in the necessary instructions. For example, in Section 7.3.1 we mentioned the three functions that are used in the traditional C libraries to obtain the absolute value of an operand. These are **abs()**, **labs()**, and **fabs()** for integer, long, and float operands respectively. In C++ we can use overloading to create three different functions with the same name, and let the compiler select the pertinent one by observing the operand's data type. However, in overloading a function we have to produce code for each possible implementation. Not only is this time consuming, but also the possibility for a coding mistake increases proportionally to the number of instances that must be coded.

In C++ we can use a function template to create a single, generic definition of the algorithm and let the compiler produce as many implementations as necessary. The general format for a function template is as follows:

```
template <class Atype>
return-type function-name(parameter-list) {
  // function body
}
```

The following short program shows an implementation of the **abs()** function by means of a function template:

```
//*****************************************************************
// C++ program to illustrate the use of a C++ template function
// Filename: SAM07-15.CPP
//*****************************************************************
#include <iostream.h>

//***************************
//         template
//***************************
// Function template
template <class AnyType>
AnyType abs (AnyType a_number) {
  if (a_number < 0)
    return -a_number;
```

```
  else
      return a_number;
}

//****************************
//           main()
//****************************
main() {
// Variables of different types
   int a = -10;
   long b = -567890;
   float c = -33.44;
   cout << "\ndemonstrating template function abs()\n";
// Passing constants
   cout << abs(-22.3) << "\n";
   cout << abs(-3) << "\n";
   cout << abs(334556) << "\n";
// Passing variables
   cout << abs(a) << "\n";
   cout << abs(b) << "\n";
   cout << abs(c) << "\n";
   return 0;
}
```

Note the function template definition in SAM07-15.CPP:

```
template <class AnyType>
AnyType abs (AnyType a_number) {
   if (a_number < 0)
      return -a_number;
   else
      return a_number;
}
```

The word *class* enclosed in angle brackets actually means a data type. It should not be equated with the object-oriented meaning of this term as a class of objects. The generic data type is represented by an arbitrary identifier. In this case we chose the name **AnyType**. **AnyType** is used as a placeholder for whatever variable type is referenced in the code. In the actual function header we again use the generic type as a placeholder for both the return type and the parameter list. Therefore we are saying that this implementation of **abs()** can return a variable of any valid type and receive any valid type as an argument.

A template function can receive more than one generic type in the parameter list. In this case the generic types are separated by commas. The following code fragment shows the implementation of a generic function that displays two variables of whatever type using the **cout** object:

```
#include <iostream.h>
template <class OneType, class AnotherType>
void Display(OneType x, AnotherType y) {
  cout << x << " " << y << "\n";
}
```

In execution the variables **x** and **y** can be any valid data type.

Although templates and overloaded functions sometimes seem to achieve the same purpose, they have distinct applications. Overloaded functions can implement different algorithms. In this case the processing operations are coded separately and share no common base. Function templates, on the other hand, can only differ in the data types. The processing operation is defined once, in the template, and must be applicable to all possible implementations generated by the compiler. An interesting point is that a conventional function can override the template for a particular data type. This adds a special functionality when there is a particular case which must be handled separately.

7.8.2 Template Classes

C++ supports generic classes. The underlying notions for generic classes are the same as for generic functions: a program element that defines a general algorithm without committing to any specific data type. There are many programming situations in which the processing logic can be generalized in a template class. For example, generic classes to maintain queues, linked lists, or stacks can be defined independently of data types that are manipulated. As with template functions, the compiler generates the necessary code for each implementation of a template class.

The general form for a generic class is as follows:

```
template<class Atype>
class class-name {
  // class code
};
```

The following program shows the implementation of a generic stack by means of a template class. Once created, stacks for various data types can be implemented and the methods produce the expected results.

```cpp
//*****************************************************************
// C++ program to illustrate abstract classes by means of a
// generic stack
// Filename: SAM07-16.CPP
//*****************************************************************

#include <iostream.h>
#define STACK_SIZE 100         // Constant establishes size of stack

//***************************
// template for stack class
//***************************
template <class AnyType>
class stack {
  AnyType stack_array[STACK_SIZE];    // Stack storage space
  AnyType stack_top;                  // Stack top pointer
public:
  void Init_stack();                  // Prototypes for methods
  void Push(AnyType i);
  AnyType Pop();
};

//***************************
//    stack class methods
//***************************
// Initialize stack
template <class AnyType>
void stack<AnyType>::Init_stack() {
  stack_top = 0;
  return;
}

// Push
template <class AnyType>
void stack<AnyType>::Push(AnyType i) {
  if (stack_top == STACK_SIZE) {    // Check for stack overflow
    cout << "Stack overflow\n";
    return;
  }
  stack_array[stack_top] = i;
  stack_top++;
  return;
}

// Pop
template <class AnyType>
AnyType stack<AnyType>::Pop() {
  if (stack_top == 0) {
    cout << "stack underflow\n";
    return 0;
```

```
    }
    stack_top--;
    return stack_array[stack_top];
}
//****************************
//          main()
//****************************
main() {

    cout << "\nDemonstration of template class stack\n";
// Stacks are created
    stack <int> stack1;            // Stack of int type
    stack <double> stack2;         // Stack of double
    stack <char> stack3;           // Stack of char
// Stacks are initialized
    stack1.Init_stack();
    stack2.Init_stack();
    stack3.Init_stack();
// Data is pushed on the stacks
    stack1.Push(22);
    stack2.Push(33.44);
    stack3.Push('a');
// Data on the stacks is popped and displayed
    cout << stack1.Pop() << "\n";
    cout << stack2.Pop() << "\n";
    cout << stack3.Pop() << "\n";
    cout << stack1.Pop() << "\n";    // This stack is empty. Pop()
                                     // displays underflow error

    return 0;
}
```

Note that the member functions of a generic class are automatically generic. Therefore, in the example of program SAM07-16.CPP, the methods named **Init_stack()**, **Push()**, and **Pop()** operate with any of the data types, as would be expected. Observe that in the declarations of the individual stacks the corresponding types are placed inside angle brackets, as follows:

```
    stack <int> stack1;
    stack <double> stack2;
    stack <char> stack3;
```

In this case the programmer must keep track of the types of the individual stacks so as not to mix them. However, it is possible to use the methods of the generic stack in regards to user-defined data types. For instance, we could define a structure and then generate a stack to store objects of this type.

Chapter 8

Reusability

8.0 Reusability Modes

Several methods and techniques have been devised to improve productivity in program analysis, design, coding, and testing by reusing components. In general, reusability refers to two types of program elements: design and code.

8.1 Reusing Code

Reusable code is not a new idea. For high-level programmers, who enjoy the luxury of a friendly environment, reusing code is an option, but not a necessity. Low-level programmers, on the other hand, cannot prosper without reusing code. This explains why code cookbooks proliferate in the low-level languages but are much less common at the higher programming levels. Listings of routines and libraries, purchased or developed, are a low-level programmer's equity. For this reason, low-level programmers are usually more aware of the importance of code reusability than their high-level counterparts. At the low-level the maxim is *reuse or perish*; high-level practitioners may have something to learn regarding code reusability from their low-level colleagues. Figure 8.1 graphically represents the advantages of code reuse in high- and low-level code.

8.1.1 Methods of Code Reuse

The success of object-oriented languages, at least in some measure, is related to the fact that they provide additional mechanisms for reusing code. Inheritance, abstraction, extensibility, class couplings, templates, and object structures are C++ characteristics that facilitate reuse. There can be no doubt that reusing code shortens the development cycle and reduces the maintenance cost of a software project. Most programming languages provide internal mechanisms for code reuse. These mechanisms, generically called *subprograms*, are the subroutines, procedures, or functions of the various languages. In the context of this section, we are mainly concerned with interproject reusability; in other words, in recycling blocks of code from one application to another one.

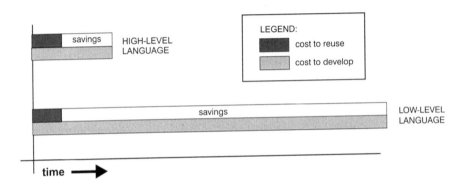

Figure 8.1 *Code Reuse in High- and Low-level Languages*

Scavenging

Salvaging code from other projects is the most primitive form of reuse. The usual mechanism is to locate the pertinent block of code and then cut-and-paste it into the current project. Although scavenging is a common practice, there are some associated problems:

1. The scavenger needs to understand the code. Therefore scavenging is usually limited to our own code or to that with which we are intimately familiar.

2. Modifications are often required on the scavenged code. Interaction of the scavenged code with other parts of the program may make this difficult. For example, names in the scavenged code may conflict with names in the new environment, or the code may make assumptions that are not valid.

3. There is little assurance that the scavenged code will work correctly in the new environment.

The result is that writing code from scratch is often easier than scavenging, even when one know where to find the pertinent code. Here again, the development environment is a determining factor on the feasibility of scavenging code. If the cost of development is very high, as is the case in low-level programming, scavenging may be an attractive option, even considering the mentioned drawbacks.

Properties of Reusable Code

The following are the minimal characteristics that will make a code fragment reusable:

1. Easy to locate

2. Easy to understand and modify

3. Reasonable assurance of correctness

4. Requires minimal surgery from other code

The passion of the defenders of reusable code has given rise to a few myths. Perhaps the most notable one is the assumption that reusable code will solve the software crisis. It is true that as reusability increases, coding tasks become simpler and programming problems less complicated. However, the software crisis originated in many elaborate circumstances, of which programmer productivity is but one.

Another falsehood is that all code should be reusable. In reality, designing and coding reusable code adds cost to the development process. If it is unlikely that the code will be reused, there is little justification for paying this price.

A third myth related to reusability is that it is always better to reuse than to code from scratch. Although this statement could be almost true for low-level languages, it is certainly not at higher programming levels. For example, a C++ program to calculate the volume of a cube is probably easier to code from scratch than to reuse. In this sense, we can speak of a *law of diminishing reuse returns* in relation to the ease of development in a particular environment. As the ease of development increases, the benefits from reusing code decrease. The extreme cases are development environments so difficult that virtually every form of reuse is justified. At the other extreme is an environment in which development is so easy that reusability would always be unjustified. Figure 8.2 graphs reuse benefits and development ease.

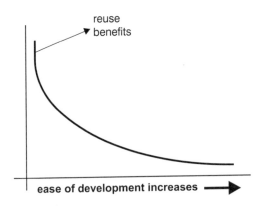

Figure 8.2 *Development Ease and Reuse Benefits*

Finally, there is a myth that object-oriented languages make it easy to reuse code. While it is true that object-oriented development facilitates reuse, it does not make reuse effortless. Even in an object-oriented environment, code reuse presupposes knowledge, experience, and hard work.

Obstacles to Reuse

There are major obstacles to reusing code. One of them is that the context in which the code executes may be different from the one for which it was originally developed. The following are related factors:

1. Lack of knowledge regarding the context in which the code is to be reused

2. User requirements are different from those for the original code

3. To provide for all possible requirements would require a body of code that would be too difficult and expensive to produce

4. The context in which the code is used is likely to change in time

However, the greatest obstacles to systematic code reuse are not of a technical nature. In the first place, programming in a way that creates reusable code takes time and effort. Many programmers are not willing to make the additional investment that is required to create reusable code. Software development companies must also sponsor reusability. This often mandates looking beyond the needs of the current project, since it is less expedient to produce reusable code. A corporate attitude that promotes reusability can be summarized as follows:

1. The creator of reusable code must be suitably rewarded and the higher expense in time and effort for creating reusable code must be taken into account.

2. Provisions must be made for maintaining reusable code.

3. Potential users of reusable code must be aware of its availability.

4. Potential users must be able to obtain the code to be reused, as well as the support products associated with the code.

5. There must be no legal obstacles to reusing code. Those reusing code must be assured of the legality of their actions.

6. Code reusers must also be rewarded.

In today's commercial development environment the support of reusability is more the exception than the rule. Most analysts and project managers are unwilling to sacrifice current performance for the sake of future and uncertain benefits. This attitude often mirrors that of superiors at higher management levels who are not aware of the advantages of reusability and do not support it. The implementation of development practices that support code reuse requires a change of attitude along all levels of the corporate structure.

8.1.2 Code Reusability and Programming Style

In addition to the specific reusability structures, discussed later in this chapter, there are elements of programming style that promote code reusability. Most of these are related to good programming practices, namely:

1. Modular program composition

2. Careful source code formatting through indentation, labeling, and the judicious use of comments and comment blocks

Modularization

We have established that modularization, as an organizational element, is as important in an object-oriented environment as it is in traditional structured programming, perhaps even more so. The subdivision of a program into modules was originally based on creating page-sized units. This style of modularization is called *coincidental cohesion* by Pressman. A more modern notion of modularization is based on functional or logical units of processing, rather than on physical ones. The module is defined as a logical or functional grouping of program elements associated with a particular module name. However, the module itself may not be a directly addressable program component. In other words, the module should not be equated with a unit of execution such as a procedure or subroutine. In this respect Ghezzi, Jazayeri & Mandrioli have stated:

> "*It is quite common to equate modules and routines, but this view of a module is too narrow. A module is a software fragment that corresponds to more than just a routine. It may be a collection of routines, a collection of data, a collection of type definitions, or a mixture of all of these. In general, we may view a module as a provider of computational resources or services.*"

Beginning programmers often modularize according to development stages. In this manner, a new program is divided into sequential units in the order in which the code is created. This primitive form of modularization, although slightly better than using page-size units, is of little service for reusability. However, we must recognize that any kind of program division serves a useful purpose, since it makes a large project more manageable. This is true even when modularization is based on less than ideal factors.

A more sophisticated and effective ground for modularization is based on functional elements. Functionally, we divide a program into modules that represent units of execution. For example, a program based on a menu-driven interface could contain one or more modules for each menu item. An additional refinement of the functional model may include an initialization module, as well as one or more modules to hold general support primitives that are used with a given frequency by the other elements of the program. The support module holds the code that has the highest potential for reuse.

A further refinement consists of dividing the program into logical units of processing, rather than on functional ones. Logical decomposition promotes reusability since units of code are reused in relation to their processing responsibilities, rather than to their functional tasks in the context of a particular application. Note that functional and logical modularization models are often complementary. A program can be decomposed into functional units of code while some or all of the functional elements are further divided into logical sections and subsections. Alternatively, the primary classification could be based on logical elements and the secondary one on functional considerations.

Pressman mentions that the problem of effective modular design can be addressed in terms of the functional independence of the modules. Independence is achieved by designing modular units that correspond to a single and well defined function, or a group of functions, and by minimizing interaction between modules. The notions of *cohesion* and *coupling* are used in this sense: cohesion serves to measure the module's functional strength, and coupling its relative interdependence from other modules. Modular cohesion increases the possibility of reuse by fostering a logical structuring of the program's functionalities. This, in turn, facilitates locating and isolating a piece of potentially reusable code. Loose coupling between modules also serves reusability since it makes a piece of code independent from its neighbors.

Libraries and Toolkits

The most used mechanism for code reusability is the library. In fact, a library or toolkit can be defined as a packaged collection of reusable routines. The actual implementation of libraries is system-dependent. In C++ a library can include any of the following components:

1. Header files

2. Source files

3. Object files

4. Template files

A library designed to be used from a particular language does not necessarily imply that it was coded in that language. For example, a C++ library for interfacing with a particular device may be, and often is, coded in assembly language.

Everyone that has used a PC-based C or C++ compiler is aware of the existence of selectable libraries. The math libraries are a typical example. If the programmer intends to generate code that will be used exclusively in machines equipped with a mathematical coprocessor functionality (Intel's x87), then a so-called real math library is selected at link time. On the other hand, if the code is to execute in machines which may not be equipped with the coprocessor, then an emulated library is used. A third option may be a BCD math library that offers higher precision than the coprocessor based or emulated libraries at a substantial loss in performance. Figure 8.3 shows a mechanical analogy of selectable libraries in which a sliding component determines which of three possible library modules is linked with the user's code.

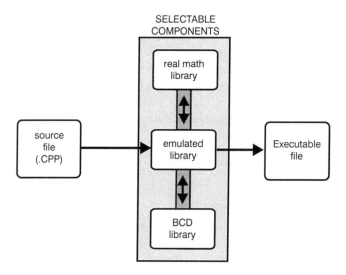

Figure 8.3 *Selectable Libraries*

One way to implement selectable libraries is by polymorphism. For example, if the functions to perform basic arithmetic operations are represented by the operators +, -, *, and /, in all three libraries, then the source code can be developed transparently of which library is selected at link time. This simple mechanism is used in many programming toolkits. For example, a library of graphics functions can provide a device driver that furnishes the most elementary operations. A minimal functionality could be achieved as shown in Table 8.1.

Table 8.1 *Design of a Polymorphic Graphics Library*

FUNCTION	DESCRIPTION
PARAMS	Return viewport parameters, namely: vertical and horizontal definition and color range
SET_PIXEL	Set a screen pixel at a specified location to requested attributes
READ_PIXEL	Read the pixel attributes at a specified screen location
SHOW_CHAR	Display a text character at a specified screen location

Graphics primitives can now be developed based on these services. The set of primitives can include drawing screen points, lines, and geometrical figures, filling enclosed areas, and displaying strings of text characters. The code containing the primitives would be portable to different graphics devices by replacing the polymorphic library that contains the elementary device driver. The PARAMS service would be used to accommodate output to different viewports. The result is code that can be reused under different environments by replacing the low-level component that acts as a device driver. Figure 8.4 shows the design of a polymorphic graphics toolkit.

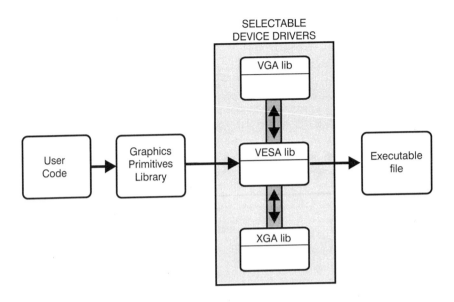

Figure 8.4 *Structure of a Polymorphic Graphics Toolkit*

In the PC's C++ environment a library is a set of one or more object files which have been integrated into a unit by means of a library management utility. All C++ compilers on the market for the PC include library management utilities. A library is composed of individual elements which correspond to the source files fed into the library manager. The public elements in the individual source files remain visible in the library file. Figure 8.5 shows the construction of an object file library.

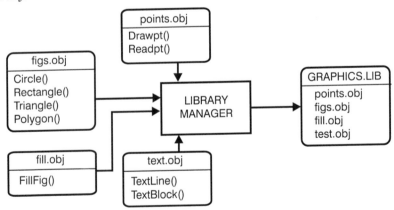

Figure 8.5 *Construction of an Object File Library*

8.1.3 Code Reusability and Interface Design

The *one interface multiple methods* philosophy lies at the heart of object-oriented programming. In C++ a base class defines the nature of the interface, and the derived classes implement specific operations related to the type of data referenced in the derived type. The actual construct for achieving one interface and multiple methods in C++ are virtual functions, abstract classes, and run-time polymorphism. Using these features the programmer can create a class hierarchy that goes from the base to the derived classes. The common features and the interface are defined in the base class. If actions can be implemented only by derived classes then the virtual function mechanism is used. If not, the base class takes care of the general case, and the derived classes fill in the details.

Code reuse by means of class libraries is an important application of abstract classes and virtual functions. One programmer creates an extensible class library which defines an interface and implements a function subset. Other programmers are able to extend the library's functionality by inheriting from its base classes and adding new functions. This flexibility of C++ class libraries facilitates reuse since the original code need not meet the exact requirements of the user, who has the potential of modifying the library as required. In other words, the library operations are not cast in stone. An interesting feature is that this flexibility is achieved without giving the user access to the library's source code. This means that code that has been already tested is not modified, and the original developer retains control of the source.

The following are three variations allowed by the class inheritance mechanisms of C++:

1. The user wants to inherit the interface of a base class but not its implementation. This is achieved by virtual functions and abstract classes.

2. The user wants to inherit the implementation but not the interface. This is accomplished by private derivation.

3. The user wants to inherit both the interface and the implementation. This is achieved by public derivation.

Reusability is fostered by a common or standard interface. This is true when reusing code and when reusing design elements. In the case of selectable libraries we must provide a common interface for all library modules. This standardization of the interface makes it possible to interchange the library components. The problem set related to the design of a common interface can best be seen in an example case. Suppose that we were to design and code an DOS graphics library to provide support for the VESA true color modes. These graphics modes have in common that they execute in 16.7 million colors. Most systems implement the true color modes by mapping 8 bits of video to each of the primary colors (red, green, and blue). The total of 24 bits, 8 bits per color, allows 16,777,215 combinations. Figure 8.6 depicts a true color graphics mode.

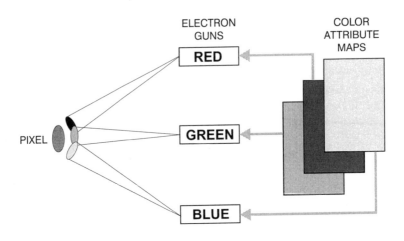

Figure 8.6 *Visualization of a True Color Graphics Mode*

In Figure 8.6 three memory areas are mapped to three electron guns, one for each of the primary colors. In a 24-bit color mode, one byte encodes the color value in each map. Therefore the red, green, and blue values are all in the range 0 to 255, which also determines the intensity of the corresponding electron beam. If a screen pixel is mapped to red, green, and blue attributes of value 0-200-0 respectively, then it is displayed as bright green. If a pixel is mapped to values 255-255-255 it is the brightest possible white. In each case the red-green-blue triplet determines the pixel color.

The color attribute maps are actually regions of video memory. We can assume a simple linear mapping in which the first byte in the attributes map corresponds to the pixel at the screen's top left corner. Successive map bytes correspond to pixels along the screen pixel rows. Simple arithmetic lets us determine how much video memory storage is necessary for a particular definition. For example, a mode that contains 640 pixels per row and 480 rows requires 640 x 480 x 3 bytes of video memory, in this case 921,600 bytes. Table 8.2 shows the definition and video memory requirements of the VESA true color modes.

Table 8.2 *Video Memory and Definition for VESA True Color Modes*

VESA MODE	RESOLUTION	MEMORY	ADAPTER
112H	640-by-480	921,600	1Mb
115H	800-by-600	1,440,000	2Mb
118H	1024-by-768	2,359,296	4Mb
11BH	1280-by-1024	3,932,160	4Mb

Each of the four VESA true color modes in Table 8.2 requires a certain amount of video memory. Thus, a video adapter with 1Mb video RAM is capable of supporting mode 112H, but not the other ones. By the same token, an adapter equipped with 4Mb video memory is capable of supporting all four VESA true color modes. Note that these memory requirements do not mean that a video system necessarily supports all modes for which it has sufficient memory, although this assumption is valid in most cases.

Interface Design Example

The choice of an implementation affects the library's class design and inheritance structures. However, the fundamental rule at the starting point is to concentrate on the library's interface rather than on details of its eventual implementation. We start by listing the primitive services that must be made available by a bare bones graphics library. Operations to set a pixel, read a pixel, display text, set a video mode, and read the attributes associated with a video mode cover the fundamental processing operations. More sophisticated functions, such as drawing geometrical figures or performing BitBlits, can be developed in terms of the core primitives. The following descriptions refer to the individual methods in detail:

1. A *ReadModeData()* method receives the VESA mode number as a pa-

rameter (112H, 115H, 118H, or 11BH) and returns a data structure loaded with the attributes associated with the selected mode. The attribute list typically includes vertical and horizontal resolution, window granularity, number of scan lines, character size, bank size, and other information necessary to the programmer. The method is usually designed so that it returns a boolean argument which is true if the mode is supported by the hardware and false otherwise.

2. A *SetVesaMode()* method receives the desired true color mode as a parameter. Returns true if the mode was set and false otherwise.

3. A *SetPixel()* method receives the screen pixel's address and its red, green, and blue color values. It sets the corresponding pixel to the attribute passed by the caller.

4. A *ReadPixel()* method receives a pixel address and returns the corresponding color triple.

5. A *TextLine()* method receives a pointer to a string which is displayed on the screen, at the corresponding location, with the attributes passed by the caller.

One viable approach for the library's class design is in terms of replaceable modules, one for each VESA graphics mode. An abstract class can be used to describe the general interface, while each of the mode-specific modules provides the particular implementation. The resulting class structure is shown in Figure 8.7.

Note that the class structure in Figure 8.7 is one of many possible design options. An early bound class inheritance design could have been based on a concrete base class instead of an abstract class.

Implementation Options

The class structure in Figure 8.7 leaves open several possibilities of implementation. The first implementation option, and perhaps the simplest one, is to reproduce the abstract class for each of the mode-dependent modules and thus create four independent libraries, one for each VESA true color mode. Since the four libraries have identical interfaces, client code would be compatible with any of them.

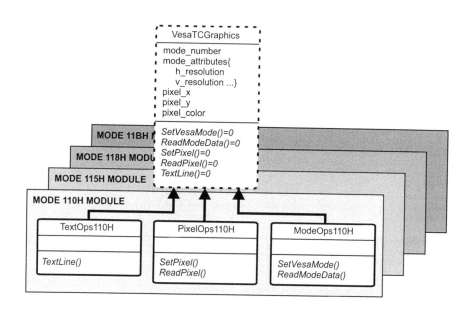

Figure 8.7 *Class Diagram for a VESA True Color Library*

A second possible implementation of the VESA library could be to separate the base class, in this case called VesaTGGraphics, from the library by placing its interface in a header file accessible to the user. The libraries would then be reduced to four modules, one for each VESA true color mode. Except for the fact that the interface is now in a header file, this implementation variation is almost identical to the first one described.

A third implementation option, which is more complicated to code, is to provide a method in the interface which automatically couples to a particular VESA mode. The mode can be either selected by the user or automatically determined by testing which one with the highest resolution is supported by the hardware. Once a valid mode is available, the code sets the corresponding run-time pointers to the methods in the corresponding module. This type of processing assumes that the programmer would make the necessary adjustment to accommodate the varying resolution of the individual VESA modes.

The choice of implementation determines the degree of user control and ease with which the library can be applied. Often these elements are in contradiction: the higher the degree of control the lesser the ease of use, and vice versa. Another factor that often depends on the choice of implementation is whether the binding with client code takes place at compile time, link time, or run time. Some form of implementation allows a single type of binding while another one supports all three.

8.2 Mechanisms for Code Reuse

In Section 8.1.3 we saw how a programmer's library can be implemented in several different ways, each associated with a set of advantages and drawbacks. Since implementation should be a consequence of analysis and design, a particular implementation implies a specific pattern of classes, interfaces, and inheritance hierarchies. In object-oriented systems there are three general mechanisms for achieving reusability: the first one is based on simple class inheritance, the second one on virtual functions and run-time polymorphism, and the third one on parameterized types. In this section we discuss the characteristics, advantages, and disadvantages of each one.

8.2.1 Reuse by Simple Inheritance

We now concern ourselves with what can be called *simple* inheritance; specifically, to class structures supported by object-oriented languages in which one class, sometimes called the derived class, is able to access members of another class, usually called the base class. Another form of simple inheritance is by means of compile-time polymorphism. However, in C++ terms, simple inheritance does not include function and operator overloading or templates. Neither does simple inheritance refer to inheritance structures based on virtual functions and abstract classes, which are mechanisms used in implementing run-time polymorphism.

In C++, one class, called the derived class, incorporates the public members of one or more base classes. This mechanism allows the programmer to build a hierarchy of classes in which a derived class inherits the base class, and can pass these members on to its descendants. At the same time, the derived class is able to add new functionalities or to replace existing ones. Several C++ constructs add flexibility to class inheritance mechanics.

The access specifiers, private, public, and protected, determine the type of inheritance that applies. They can be used in base or in derived classes. In the base class, the access specifiers control the visibility of the class members. In the derived classes the access specifiers define how the visibility attributes of the base class are passed along the inheritance line. In the case of a derived class the public access specifier causes all public or protected members of the base class to retain the same accessibility. **Private** causes all public and protected members of the base class to be private in the derived class. **Protected** causes all public and protected members of the base class to be protected members of the derived class. Figure 7.1 shows the results of combining base and derived class access specifiers.

Multiple inheritance allows a derived class to inherit simultaneously from more than one base class. Although the benefits of this construct have been extensively debated, it is well supported in C++. Additionally, friend classes and friend functions let the private and protected members of a class be visible to other classes or to client code. The friend mechanism provides a useful way for breaking encapsulation.

Simple Inheritance

We can fashion an example of class inheritance by extending the functionality of the VESA true color library shown in Figure 8.7. Suppose that the library were to include primitives for drawing geometrical elements and figures (such as lines, ellipses, and parallelograms), for displaying ASCII characters and text strings, and for copying and transferring bitmaps from one memory area to another one (BitBlts). All of these higher-level functions are performed by means of the two low-level operations of setting a single screen pixel, and reading a pixel's attributes. In the language of low-level programming these fundamental operations are sometimes associated with a program element called a *device driver*, while the higher-level operations are called *drawing primitives*. Figure 8.8 shows a possible inheritance structure that allows the three categories of primitive functions to inherit and reuse the device driver operations.

Note that in the diagram of Figure 8.8 we have not linked the classes by means of Gen-Spec or Part-Whole structures (see Section 4.2). Rather, the inheritance diagram uses *Directed Acyclic Graph* (DAG) notation to show that the three primitive classes inherit the methods in the device driver base class. Although inheritance often takes place across Gen-Spec and Whole-Part structures, a structure relationship is not strictly necessary. In fact, simple inheritance should be regarded as nothing more than an effective, object-oriented mechanism for code reuse. Also observe in Figure 8.8 that the base class is a concrete class and that polymorphism is not present. Abstract classes and polymorphism are used in implementing inheritance by virtual functions, discussed in the following section.

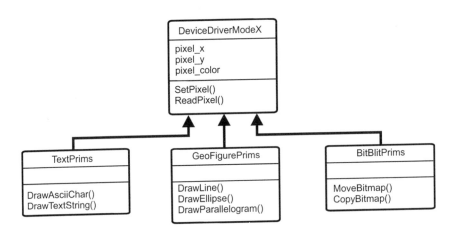

Figure 8.8 *Class Diagram for Simple Inheritance*

Several benefits result from casting simple inheritance structures into object-oriented code. The following list includes some of the most important ones:

1. Functionalities are located in a single place in the code structure. There is a single routine, function, or method that performs a particular program operation. This feature reduces the coding effort and facilitates locating and fixing program defects.

2. Derived classes can reuse with a high degree of confidence code which was carefully crafted and tested in the base class. Therefore, new defects will not be introduced in processing operations that have been already found to perform correctly.

3. Simple inheritance is based on a straightforward design and is easy to

code. Selection takes place at compile time, resulting in code that is tight, efficient, and easy to understand.

The main disadvantages of simple inheritance is that the derived classes obtain at least some of their functionality from the base class. This breaks encapsulation by exposing implementation details. Therefore any change in the implementation of the base class is likely to force other changes in the derived classes. Suppose that we needed to provide a new functionality in the toolkit shown in Figure 8.8 by adding a new class called **FillPrims**. This new class would perform graphic fill operations on closed figures. Furthermore suppose that the **SetPixel()** and **ReadPixel()** methods of the base class had to be modified to accommodate the new operations to be performed by the **FillPrims** class. In this case, it is likely that the modifications of the methods in the base class would contaminate the previously existing classes, namely **TextPrims**, **GeoFigurePrims**, and **BitBlitPrims**, and their corresponding methods.

Compile-time Polymorphism

Another form of inheritance is based on polymorphism. Polymorphism is considered a mechanism for reducing complexity by allowing the reuse of the interface element. The principal advantage of polymorphism is that the programmer can disregard more implementation details than in a non-object-oriented environment. C++ supports both compile-time and run-time polymorphism. In object-oriented programming languages, simple or compile-time polymorphism relates to methods that share the same interface. One way to implement polymorphism is by overloading functions or operators.

In Chapter 7, Section 7.1.2, we saw that C++ polymorphism is achieved by means of virtual functions. The fundamental notion is that an object knows the class to which it belongs; therefore, execution can be directed to the corresponding method even though there are others with the same name.

We can illustrate inheritance through compile-time polymorphism by means of a variation of the VESA true color graphics library mentioned in previous examples. Figure 8.7 shows a possible class structure based on selectable modules. In Figure 8.9 we have refined and adapted the model to represent compile-time polymorphic inheritance.

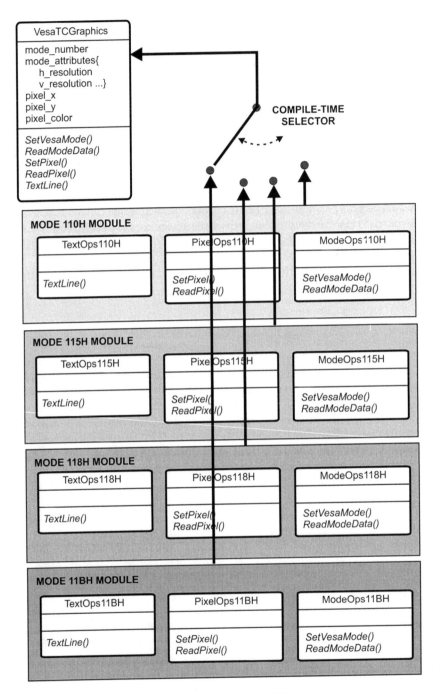

Figure 8.9 *Simple Inheritance by Polymorphism*

Note in Figure 8.9 that the methods in the various module classes have the same corresponding names. Since each object knows the class to which it belongs, execution can be directed to the corresponding method even though there are others with the same name. This type of polymorphism results in early or compile-time binding. Typically, code would access the corresponding function by means of the **dot** operator. For example, if **m118H_obj1** is an object of the class **PixelOps118H**, then the statement:

```
m118H_obj1.SetPixel();
```

executes the method **SetPixel()** in the class **PixelOps118H**. This operation corresponds to the compile-time selector in Figure 8.9. Note that in this case the virtual attribute is not necessary since the class is bound directly by its object.

8.2.2 Reuse by Virtual Functions

C++ provides mechanisms for achieving run-time polymorphism, which often has advantages over compile-time selection. C++ dynamic binding is achieved by means of virtual functions. A virtual function is declared in the base class and redefined in one or more derived classes. Usually, the function declared virtual in the base class defines a general type of method and specifies the interface. Other polymorphic functions can be implemented in the derived classes to override the one in the base class. If the virtual function is accessed by means of its name, it behaves as any other one. However, when accessed via a pointer, the method executed depends on the object which the pointer is referencing.

The virtual function's construct assumes that the polymorphic function is implemented in the base class. Otherwise a linker error results, since no address is assigned to a method that performs no processing operations (see Section 7.7.2). However, there are many occasions in which there is no meaningful definition for a method in the base class. For example, in reference to the class diagram of Figure 8.9 we see that for the methods **SetPixel()**, **ReadPixel()**, and **TextLine()**, there is no useful processing possible in the base class **VesaTCGraphics**. These methods require that a particular VESA mode be previously selected, since it is meaningless to set a pixel otherwise. Therefore, in order for this class structure to work in code, we have to provide a dummy method in the base class, and then make sure that this method is not called during actual execution.

Pure Virtual Functions

In C++ a pure virtual function is equated to zero in the base class. This peculiar mechanism ensures that implementation must be provided in all derived classes, since a compiler error results otherwise. Regarding reusability, the pure virtual function construct has several effects that are often desirable:

1. The base class serves to define a general interface that sets a model that all derived classes must follow.

2. Implementation in the derived classes is automatically assured since the code will not compile otherwise.

3. Encapsulation is preserved since objects are accessed through a common interface. Implementation dependencies are reduced.

4. Run-time substitutions are made possible by the fact that all objects must have the same type.

There are also several disadvantages to the use of pure virtual functions.

1. Software constructs based on pointers and references are harder to understand and apply than those based on class hierarchies.

2. Run-time selection is less efficient than compile-time selection.

In general, most authors agree that we should prefer run-time polymorphism over compile-time method selection. Dynamic polymorphism based on abstract classes usually provides a more powerful and flexible mechanism. However, there is a small processing overhead required to achieve run-time polymorphism. Code that uses compile-time selection has slightly better performance than its run-time counterpart. In a few occasions this small performance differential may favor the compile-time option. Additionally, because run-time constructs are more elaborate and difficult to code, we must make sure that the problems they solve are worth the complications.

Figure 8.10 shows a representation of run-time polymorphism for the VESA true color graphics library of Figure 8.7 and Figure 8.9.

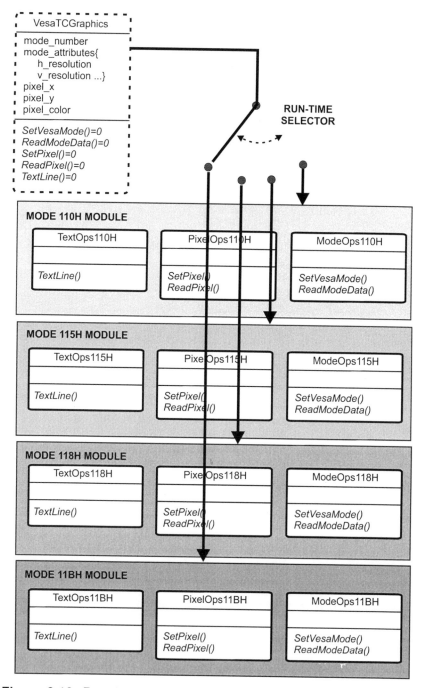

Figure 8.10 *Run-time Polymorphism*

Note in Figure 8.10 that there are some differences in relation to the compile-time polymorphism shown in Figure 8.9. The first one is that the base class is an abstract class. The polymorphic methods are equated to zero in the base class, following the C++ convention for pure virtual functions. Also, note that the arrows are now pointing toward the derived classes, since they represent references held in the base class, not the flow of inheritance. Finally, note that the selection takes place at run time rather than at compile time.

8.2.3 Reuse by Parameterized Types

In addition to simple inheritance and virtual functions there is a third mechanism for code reuse, based on parameterized types. Parameterized types are implemented by the **template** construct in C++. Although parameterized types are not strongly related to object orientation, occasionally they do provide a powerful reuse option.

A C++ template is a generic construct that operates with several data types. C++ templates are implemented in the context of both functions and classes. The idea behind template functions is to create a source code mold that describes the processing operations in abstract. This mold is used by the C++ compiler to generate instructions that can accommodate any of the legal data types. Thus, the programmer defines the fundamentals of the algorithm and the compiler plugs in the necessary instructions. Template functions were discussed in Section 7.8.1.

The notion of a *generic class* is similar to that of a generic function: a program element that defines a general algorithm without committing to any specific data type. Many programming problems can be expressed in terms of a generalized processing logic that can be represented in a template class. Template classes were discussed in Section 7.8.2.

8.2.4 Selecting the Reuse Mechanism

Selecting a reuse mechanism is often a complicated and transcendental decision. Virtual functions make possible dynamic binding, which favors certain forms of reusability, but dynamic binding requires pointers, indirection, and often complicated program structures that are difficult to understand and code. Also, there is a performance penalty for run-time selection. Inheritance and parameterized types are simple and straightforward, have optimal performance, but do not allow selection at run time. Although, in general, dynamic binding is a more powerful and sophisticated mechanism, the practical analyst and programmer find many occasions in which the simpler, static binding should be preferred.

8.2.5 The Client's View

A factor that often decides in favor of a particular approach is the client's view of the reusable components. A first look at the class structures of Figure 8.9, representing simple inheritance, and Figure 8.10, representing run-time polymorphism, may lead us to believe that both approaches are quite similar regarding complexity. Both models consist of a base class and four sets of derived classes. A selection mechanism determines which of the polymorphic methods is used in each case. However, from the client's viewpoint, this is not the case.

A client using the simple inheritance structures depicted in Figure 8.9 would have to see the entire class hierarchy. This is necessary since in simple inheritance selection is made at compile time by means of objects that belong to the corresponding class. Therefore, client code would address the method **SetPixel()** in the mode 118H module by first declaring an object of the class **PixelOps118H**, and then selecting the desired method. For example:

```
PixelOps118H obj1;     // Create object of class PixelOps118H

obj1.SetPixel();       // Set pixel using class method
```

By exposing the entire class mechanism to the client code we make the interface vulnerable and break encapsulation. On the other hand, run-time polymorphism is implemented through objects that are manipulated through their interface to one or more abstract classes. In this case client code sees only the interface provided by the abstract class. The mechanics of how the different functionalities are achieved is not visible to the client. Neither do the clients see the class structure that supports this functionality. In this case, the whole implementation mechanism is transparent, as long as the client adheres to the interface. Figure 8.11 represents the client's view of the run-time structure in Figure 8.10.

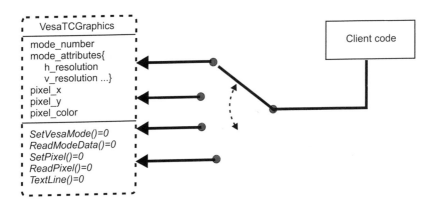

Figure 8.11 *Client's View of Run-time Polymorphism*

8.3 Design Reuse

Software development is a multiphase process of which coding is but one component. In most projects more time and effort is spent in program design activities than in actual coding. Therefore, reusing design components entails substantial rewards.

The first notions regarding the reuse of design components date back only to the beginning of the 1990s. It is not surprising that shortly after modeling methods for class and object structures were developed, it became evident that, under similar circumstances, some of these patterns could be reused.

The rationale for reusing design elements is based on the observation that experienced program designers often reutilize solutions developed for other projects. If we observe object-oriented systems we see many recurring instances of class and object patterns. By recording these patterns we are able to capture a design experience so that it can be effectively transmitted and reapplied. The goal of those who propose design reuse is that new developers will be able to consult catalogs of patterns and object models in order to locate and apply those that refer to their particular problem domain. The result should be a better program, based on components that have been tested in practice, and a designing phase that takes less effort and expense.

There is little doubt that these fundamental notions of design reuse are reasonable and well founded. However, one element that is often omitted is that the design patterns and models of object structures that are appealing for reuse are not the simple, straightforward ones. The uncomplicated class and object structures can be easily designed from scratch. The ones in which there is greater reuse benefit are those patterns and models that are most sophisticated, elaborate, and difficult to grasp. The trivial ones can usually be ignored. The fact that only the most complicated designs are considered as patterns presupposes that the potential user has considerable knowledge of system analysis and design, as well as rather thorough coding skills. Here again, persons with this knowledge and skill level are not the ones most likely to reuse design components. So there seems to be an inherent contradiction in the practicality of reusing design components: the patterns that are most difficult to understand and apply are the most likely candidates for reuse; however, the programmers and designers with less knowledge and skills are the ones most in need of reusing design components.

For this reason, we have adopted a didactical approach to the topic of design patterns and object models. We start by making a distinction between simple combinations of classes and objects and the more complex ones. We call the simple ones "class constructs" and reserve the word "patterns" for those class configurations and composition of object that address a particular design problem and that are sufficiently complex to have practical reapplications. We devote three chapters to class constructs: Chapter 9 is related to constructs used in simple inheritance, Chapter 10 with those used in dynamic binding, and Chapter 11 with constructs of object composition. The topic of class patterns is found in Chapter 12.

Beyond the fact that program design components can be reused, there is little agreement among authors in this new field. Two terms are often almost indistinguishable: object models and design patterns. Design patterns seems to be the more comprehensive one. In the forthcoming discussions we use both designations, although we prefer the term design patterns when referring to static class structures, and the term object models when referring to the run-time image of interrelated objects.

Chapter 9

Static Inheritance Constructs

9.0 Inheritance in Object Orientation

In the last few years, a new notion has emerged in the software development and object-oriented programming communities which proposes that patterns of inheritance structures and models of object compositions can be reused during application design. In Chapter 8 we mentioned that the terms *object models* and *design patterns* have been employed with little differentiation in this context. The original idea of design patterns is said to have originated in the use of models for designing buildings by manipulating standard components such as windows and doors. A classic book in this field, titled *A Pattern Language*, by Christopher Alexander and others, appears to have inspired authors in the fields of software patterns and models.

The possibility of using inheritance patterns and models of object-oriented structures to simplify and facilitate the design of software products is certainly an appealing one. However, design patterns and object models are not a magic elixir that will make a novice into a master designer. In fact, beginners sometimes have a difficult time understanding the fundamentals of the various patterns. Design patterns and object models are no panacea, nor can they be grasped intuitively or applied effortlessly.

In Section 8.3 we mentioned that, in this book, we have adopted a didactical approach to the topic of design patterns and object models. We start by making a distinction between simple combinations of classes and objects, which we call class constructs, and the more complex ones, which are the true class patterns and object models. This chapter deals with constructs that use static inheritance. We exclude from the chapter cases of inheritance based on dynamic binding, which are found in Chapter 10, as well as those based on object composition, which are the topic of Chapter 11.

The reusability value of these static inheritance constructs is rather limited. In most cases these class configurations are so simple, and the results are so apparent, that any moderately competent programmer or designer would hardly need to refer to a model in order to apply them. However, these simple constructs are useful as a gradual introduction to the more complex ones. Their purpose is mainly instructional.

9.1 Inheritance Revisited

Inheritance is a powerful mechanism for code reuse. The core notion is that a useful construct is often a variant of another one. Instead of producing the same code for each variation, a derived class inherits the functionality of a base class. The derived class can then be modified by adding new members, by changing existing functions, or by altering access privileges. The idea of a taxonomy that can be used to summarize a large body of knowledge is central to all science. For example: once we have learned that mammals are warm-blooded, higher vertebrates, that nourish their young by means of milk-producing glands, we have acquired knowledge that can be reapplied to any member of the mammal class. Therefore, this knowledge is automatically extensible to any mammal, whether it be a mouse, a lion, or an elephant. In this context we say that the class lion is derived from the base class mammal, which is derived from the base class animal, which is derived from living being.

In an object-oriented system we say that a lion is a mammal, is an animal, is a living being, and therefore has the properties and characteristics of all mammals, animals, and living beings. We establish a class inheritance relationship and define an inheritance path. The derived class (lion) inherits the public and protected members of the base classes (animal, mammal, and living being). At the same time, a derived class can add new members that are not in the base class. Or it may substitute an implementation for another one. The great advantage of inheritance is that code can be effectively reused since the derived class uses existing, tested, program elements that appear in the base class.

9.1.1 Inheritance and Class Structures

In object-oriented terms, inheritance is not necessarily linked to class structures. The notions of a class being in a-part-of (Gen-Spec) or a-kind-of (Whole-Part) relationship to another class imply inheritance, but inheritance is not limited to these two class associations. The notion of class structures is related to modeling of the problem domain; the associations correspond to those often found in real world objects. Programs, on the other hand, often contain elements that are unrelated to the real world. For example, a software product that consists of a library of graphics functions has elements that are pure software components. One example is the VESA true color graphics toolkit mentioned in Chapter 8. In this case, as in most software products, there are classes that represent pure software objects. These classes of software objects often have inheritance relations with other classes with which they do not form a part-of or a kind-of association. Figure 9.1 is an example of class inheritance that does not imply a structure relation.

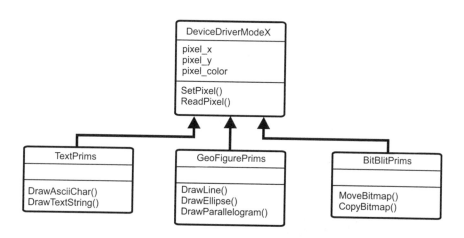

Figure 9.1 *Inheritance without Class Structures*

Note in Figure 9.1 that the derived class **TextPrims** cannot be said to be a part-of the base class **DeviceDriverModeX**; neither can it be said to be in a kind-of the base class.

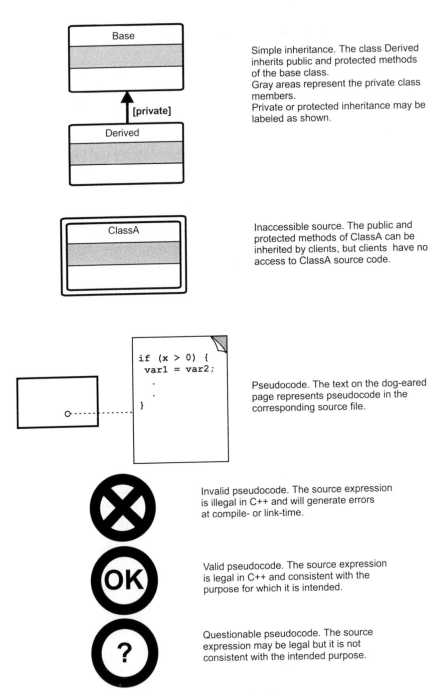

Simple inheritance. The class Derived inherits public and protected methods of the base class.
Gray areas represent the private class members.
Private or protected inheritance may be labeled as shown.

Inaccessible source. The public and protected methods of ClassA can be inherited by clients, but clients have no access to ClassA source code.

Pseudocode. The text on the dog-eared page represents pseudocode in the corresponding source file.

Invalid pseudocode. The source expression is illegal in C++ and will generate errors at compile- or link-time.

Valid pseudocode. The source expression is legal in C++ and consistent with the purpose for which it is intended.

Questionable pseudocode. The source expression may be legal but it is not consistent with the intended purpose.

Figure 9.2 *Symbols for Patterns and Models*

9.1.2 A Notation for Inheritance

In Chapter 8 we informally introduced Directed Acyclic Graph notation to depict inheritance without implying structure relations between the participating classes. For modeling inheritance and object structures we will need a few more symbols. The round-cornered rectangle is still used for depicting classes. The solid border indicates a concrete class and the dashed border an abstract class. Figure 9.2 shows the symbol set that is used in the graphic depiction of patterns and object models.

9.2 Fundamental Constructs

In this section, we describe some common constructs based on simple inheritance. Object-oriented languages support a mechanism whereby one class can inherit the public methods of another one. In C++ there are several programming constructs that support simple inheritance. For this discussion, the term inheritance refers only to compile-time operations. Dynamic binding and run-time polymorphism are discussed in Chapter 10.

9.2.1 Nonpolymorphic Inheritance

In C++ one class, called the derived class, incorporates the public and protected members of one or more base classes. This mechanism allows the programmer to build a hierarchy of classes in which a derived class inherits the base class. The inheriting class can choose to pass or not pass these members to its descendants. Therefore, it can control the inheritance path.

The access specifiers private, public, and protected determine the type of inheritance that applies. The same specifiers are used in relation to both the base and derived classes. In the base class, access specifiers control the visibility of the class members. In derived classes the same access specifier keywords define how the visibility attributes of the base class are passed along the inheritance line. Thus, in the case of a derived class, the public access specifier causes all public or protected members of the base class to retain the same accessibility. Private access specifier causes all public and protected members of the base class to be private in the derived class; while protected ones cause all public and protected members of the base class to be protected members of the derived class. Figure 7.1 shows the results of combining base and derived class access specifiers. Figure 9.3 shows inheritance of a method by a derived class.

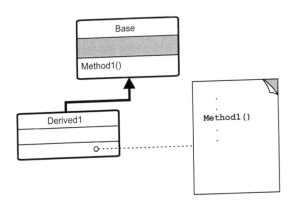

Figure 9.3 *Nonpolymorphic Inheritance of a Method*

The pseudocode in Figure 9.3 shows that the derived class can access the inherited method as if it were its own, that is, without instantiating an object of the base class. The fact that **Method1()** is a public member makes it visible outside the class. Other classes and client code can freely access **Method1()**, but in order to do so outside of an inheritance structure they have to first declare an object of the base class.

9.2.2 Multiple Inheritance

Multiple inheritance allows a derived class to inherit from more than one base class. Although the need for multiple inheritance has been extensively debated, it is supported by C++. Figure 9.4 is a diagram of the fundamentals of multiple inheritance.

The inheritance construct in Figure 9.4 is sometimes referred to as a mix-in construct. In this case a new class is used to augment the functionality provided by an existing class or to provide an additional interface. In this sense, we could say that class **BaseB** in Figure 9.4 is a mix-in class.

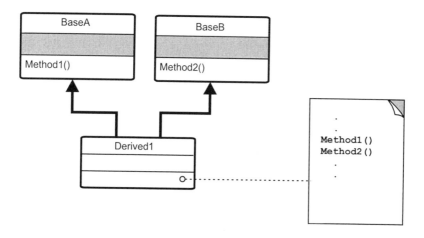

Figure 9.4 *Multiple Inheritance*

The defenders of multiple inheritance claim that it expands the usefulness and power of an object-oriented programming language. The detractors sustain that multiple inheritance is best avoided since it can give rise to many ambiguities and uncertainties. It is true that multiple inheritance can be a powerful tool, especially if kept simple and used carefully. But it is also true that it can lead to undecipherable inheritance paths with often conflicting alternatives. Smalltalk does not support multiple inheritance. Another interesting fact is that the designers of Microsoft's *Foundation Class Library* decided to do without multiple inheritance.

One common cause of ambiguity is when two or more base classes have methods with the same name. In this case an object's reference to the method can be to any one of them. The scope resolution operator can be used to resolve the ambiguity. Figure 9.5 shows ambiguity in multiple inheritance.

9.2.3 Static, Polymorphic Inheritance

Another case of inheritance takes place when a method of the same name and type is defined in the base class and then redefined in a derived class. Figure 9.6 shows the corresponding class structure for this case.

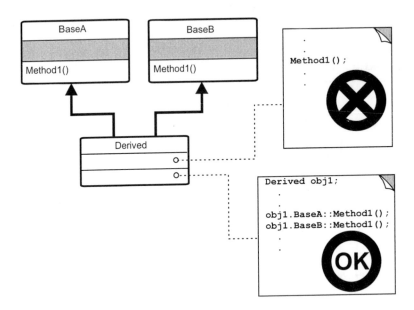

Figure 9.5 *Ambiguity in Multiple Inheritance*

Inheritance is not reversible. For this reason, in Figure 9.6, the class named **Derived** inherits and can access **Method1()** in the class named BaseA, but not vice versa. The methods of the base class and the derived class can be accessed by means of objects of either class. This case is signaled with a question mark because it does not require inheritance. The following short program is a demonstration of static, polymorphic inheritance.

```
//***************************************************************
// C++ program to illustrate static, polymorphic inheritance
// Filename: SAM09-01.CPP
//***************************************************************
#include <iostream.h>

//***************************
//        classes
//***************************
// Base class
class BaseA {
public:
    void DisplayMsg() {
      cout << "\nMethod in BaseA class executing\n" ;
    }
};
// A derived class
class Derived : public BaseA {
```

```
public:
   void DisplayMsg() {
     cout << "Method in Derived class executing\n" ;
   }
};

//****************************
//          main()
//****************************
main() {
   Derived obj1;          // Object of Derived class
// Accessing method DisplayMsg() in classes BaseA and Derived
   obj1.BaseA::DisplayMsg();
   obj1.Derived::DisplayMsg();

   return 0;
}
```

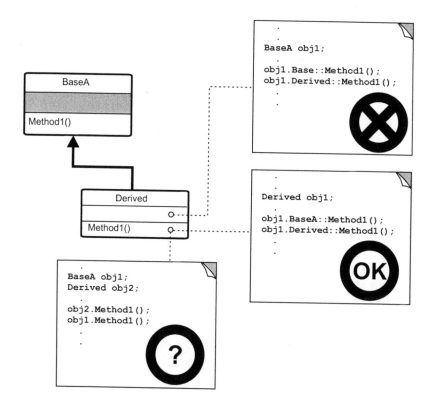

Figure 9.6 *Static, Polymorphic Inheritance*

9.3 Applied Inheritance Constructs

In Section 9.2 we saw the three fundamental mechanisms of simple inheritance:

1. Simple, nonpolymorphic inheritance. In this case a derived class gains access to the public and protected members of the base class as if they were their own.

2. Multiple inheritance. A derived class obtains access to the members of more than one base class.

3. Static, polymorphic inheritance. A derived class gains access to a method of the same name and type defined in a base class.

These mechanisms can be put to work in several programming situations in order to implement a particular design and to foster reusability. Note that the problems solved with simple inheritance can often also be solved by means of dynamic binding and run-time polymorphism. The discussions that follow do not suggest that static solutions are to be preferred over dynamic ones. In Section 8.2 we discussed under what circumstances simple inheritance is considered a viable alternative. The programmer should refer to this discussion, as well as to Chapter 10, when deciding among various possible alternatives.

9.3.1 Interface Accommodation

Sometimes a class performs a desired functionality but does not conform to the application's interface. For example, a program that calculates the areas of geometrical figures contains a class with methods that apply to rectangles and triangles. The methods assume two parameters corresponding to the two sides of a rectangle, and the base and height of a triangle. Another class is available that contains a method to calculate the area of a circle, but this method takes a single parameter since the radius is the only dimension that is necessary to calculate the area. In order to use a class with a different interface we may be forced to make substantial adjustments in client code or have access to the source. An alternative solution is the creation of a new class that adapts the interface of the incompatible class so that it conforms to a standard. Figure 9.7 is a class diagram showing one form of interface accommodation.

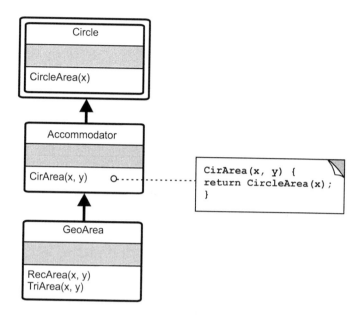

Figure 9.7 *Interface Accommodation through Simple Inheritance*

The following program shows the implementation of interface accommodation through simple inheritance.

```cpp
//*****************************************************************
// C++ program to illustrate interface accommodation through
// simple inheritance
// Filename: SAM09-02.CPP
//*****************************************************************
#include <iostream.h>
//***************************
//          classes
//***************************
// Class with different interface
class Circle {
public:
    float CircleArea(float x) {
    return (x * x)* 3.1415;
    }
};
// Class to accommodate interface
class Accommodator :  private Circle {
public:
```

```
    float CirArea(float x, float y) {
    return CircleArea(x);
    }
};
// Original class that inherits from Adapter class
class GeoArea : public Accommodator {
public:
    float RecArea(float x, float y) {
    return (x * y);
    }
    float TriArea(float x, float y) {
    return (x * y)/2;
    }
};
//****************************
//          main()
//****************************
main() {
    GeoArea obj1;          // Object of class GeoArea
    float dim1 = 4.0;   // Dimension variables
    float dim2 = 3.0;
// Display areas calling methods visible to GeoArea class
    cout << "\nRectArea() in class GeoArea - Rectangle area = "
      << obj1.RecArea(dim1, dim2)
      << "\n";
    cout << "TriArea() in class GeoArea - Triangle area = "
      << obj1.TriArea(dim1, dim2)
      << "\n";
    cout << "CirArea() visible to class GeoArea - Circle area = "
      << obj1.CirArea(dim1, dim2)
      << "\n";
    return 0;

}
```

9.3.2 Hiding Implementation

Sometimes we wish to create a class that provides a simpler interface to one or more other classes. This is accomplished by hiding implementation details that need not concern the user. For example,
three classes contain methods for setting and reading pixels in VESA
true color modes 112H, 115H, and 118H. The programmer wants to
hide these details from the user of the toolkit, who sees a single, mode-
independent pixel read and pixel set method. This can be achieved by
creating a class that inherits privately from the device driver classes.
The new class serves as an interface to the device drivers and hides
many implementation details from the user. Multiple inheritance can
be used to accomplish this simplification of the interface, as shown in
Figure 9.8.

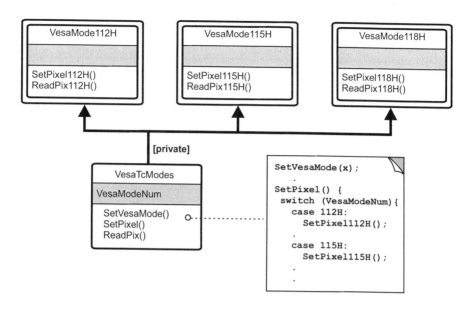

Figure 9.8 *Interface Hiding*

A graphics programmer would object to the functionality offered by the example in Figure 9.8 on the grounds that the selection mechanism would have to execute in every iteration of a pixel-setting or pixel-reading loop, thus considerably affecting performance. In later chapters we address this issue and offer solutions that eliminate the contingency code contained in the **switch** construct.

9.3.3 Connecting to an Implementation

A common programming problem consists of selecting one among several possible implementations. In this case the actual inheritance construct is very similar to the one shown in Figure 9.8; it is the intention that is different. For example, several device drivers provide software support for spooling three different printer devices, but only one can be active at a given time. In this case a connector class can privately inherit from the three device drivers and present a single interface to the user. Figure 9.9 shows this case.

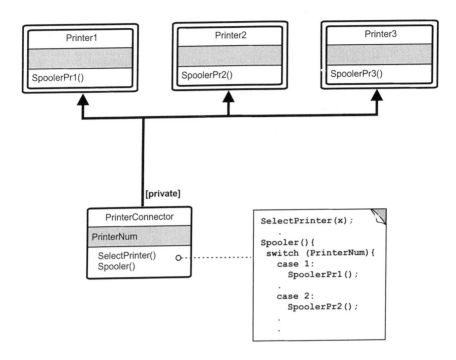

Figure 9.9 *Connecting to One of Several Implementations*

9.3.4 Providing a Unified or Default Interface

In our efforts to improve reusability we often create smaller and smaller classes so that functionalities are individualized. The same happens when we attempt to increase flexibility and controllability by providing the user with access to implementation details. For example, a windowing toolkit may contain one or more classes that implement scroll bar definition and operation. In order to make the scroll bars adaptable to many different requirements, the code allows the individual control of vertical and horizontal scroll bars, as well as defining the scrolling unit in screen pixels, the initial position of the thumb and its size, the page size, and perhaps other fine-grain controls. However, it is reasonable to assume that some users would be satisfied with a standard set of scroll bars, based on default settings, and would rather not get involved in the finer operational details. For this case we can use simple inheritance to add a default interface to the scroll bar control classes, as shown in Figure 9.10.

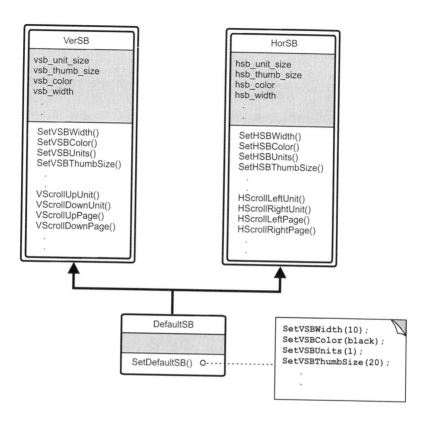

Figure 9.10 *Providing a Default Interface*

Note that in the case of Figure 9.10 we have inherited publicly from the base classes. Therefore, the visibility of the public and protected methods of the base classes is not impaired. The result is that a client of the class **DefaultSB** can access the public and protected members of the base classes (**HorSB** and **VerSB**) as well as the member function **SetDefaultSB()** in the derived class. Comparing this case to the ones in Figure 9.8, we observe that here we have complemented the interface, rather than hiding or simplifying it.

9.3.5 Controlling Accessibility

Compile-time polymorphism provides a mechanism whereby we can control, to a considerable degree, the accessibility of methods in a base class. Suppose that we have access to a class that contains several public methods and that we wish to hide some of these methods from client code. In this case we may create a derived class that inherits privately from the base class. The derived class then provides public interface to those methods that we wish to make visible, but not to those that we wish to hide. C++ allows us to control accessibility by means of a simple mechanism based on the scope resolution operator. Note that granting access to the public methods of a base class is not a form of true polymorphism, since there is actually a single method defined in code, and also that the derived class inherits privately; therefore, the methods in the base class that are not specifically granted access in the derived class are not be visible to client code. Figure 9.11 shows the class structure for achieving static accessibility control.

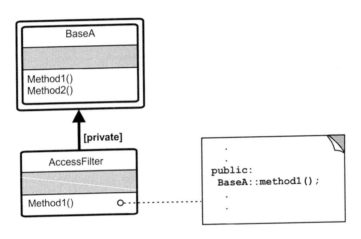

Figure 9.11 *Static Accessibility Control*

The following short program contains the code details for implementing the inheritance construct shown in Figure 9.11:

```
//************************************************************
// C++ program to control accessibility through compile-time
// polymorphism
// Filename: SAM09-03.CPP
//************************************************************
#include <iostream.h>
//****************************
//        classes
//****************************
// Class with several public methods. Example assumes
// that this class is not directly visible to client
// code
```

```
class BaseA {
public:
   void method1(void) {
   cout << "\nMethod1() in class BaseA\n";
   }
   void method2(void) {
   cout << "\nMethod2() in class BaseA\n";
   }
};
// Derived class preserves visibility of method1()
// in the base class by granting access to it,
// but hides method2().
class AccessFilter : private BaseA {
public:
   BaseA::method1;     // method1() in BaseA is granted
                       // public accessibility
};
//***************************
//          main()
//***************************
main() {
   AccessFilter obj1;       // Object of the derived class
// An object of the derived class can access method1() of the
// base class (indirectly), but not method2()
   obj1.method1();          // Valid access
// obj1.BaseA::method2();   // ILLEGAL ACCESS
// obj1.method2();          // ALSO ILLEGAL
   return 0;
}
```

Note that accessibility control as shown in this example assumes that the client has no information regarding the base class, its interface, or its definition files. In this case, we presuppose that the base class is physically located in a separate file or library. If a client has knowledge of the existence of a class, and information regarding the interface of a public method, access cannot be prevented. For example, in the program SAM07-03.CPP listed previously we could access the base class method2() as follows:

```
BaseA obj2;        // Object of the base class

obj2.method2();    // Valid access to "hidden" method
```

9.3.6 Restricting Functionality

One possible use for accessibility control is to create program units that offer a subset of the functionalities contained in another one. For example, a graphics library provides support for all four VESA true color modes and we wish to make available a version of the library that supports a single one of these modes. Another example can be a refinement of the case shown in Figure 9.10. Suppose that we wished to provide a default interface to the scroll bar configuration functions so that the lower-level controls in the base class are invisible to the client. At the same time we wish to preserve accessibility to the scroll bar control methods in the base classes so that the client can still operate the scroll bars. Therefore, our task in this case is to selectively control accessibility to the methods of several base classes in order to provide a specific functionality. Figure 9.12 shows the creation of a class that makes available a subset of the public and protected methods of its parent classes.

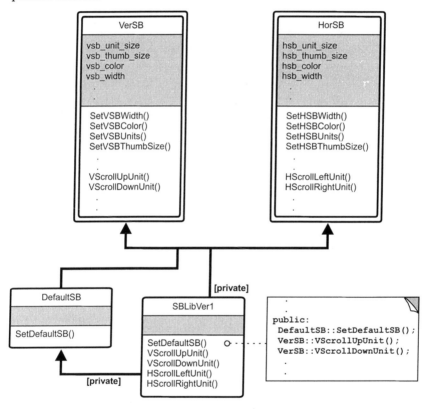

Figure 9.12 *Versions and Subsets through Static Inheritance*

Note in Figure 9.12 that the class **SBLibVer1** inherits privately from three parent classes and then filters out the methods in the parent classes that are to be granted public visibility. This is accomplished through the simple access granting mechanism of C++ previously mentioned. Although the class **DefaultSB** inherits publicly from **VerSB** and **HorSB**, this accessibility is intercepted by the class **SBLibVer1**, which inherits privately from **DefaultSB**. In summary, the process consists of using private accessibility to break the inheritance line and then selectively restoring it by granting access to some of the methods in the parent classes.

9.3.7 Polymorphism by Object-to-Class Binding

In Figure 9.6 we can see how static polymorphism can be achieved by using the C++ scope resolution operator to select among several methods of the same name and type. Another option for implementing static polymorphism is based on selecting the corresponding method by addressing an object of the desired class. This form of method selection is based on the fact that an object is bound to the class to which it belongs; therefore, execution is directed to the desired method even though there are others with the same name. Note that this type of method selection can take place among classes that are linked by inheritance as well as among those that are not. We use the term *object-to-class binding* to indicate that method selection is based on objects; the fact that an object must belong to a class, and only to one class, defines the polymorphic method to be used. Figure 9.13 shows static, polymorphic binding by means of object-to-class binding.

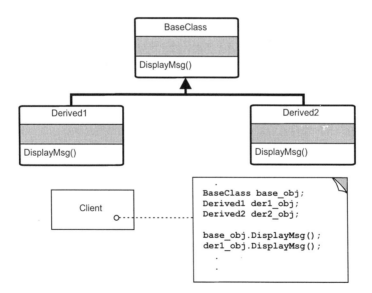

Figure 9.13 *Polymorphic Selection by Object-to-Class Binding*

The following short program shows the code details:

```cpp
//*********************************************************************
// C++ program to illustrate static polymorphism by means of
// object-to-class binding
// Filename: SAM09-04.CPP
//*********************************************************************

#include <iostream.h>

//***************************
//         classes
//***************************
// Base class
class BaseClass {
public:
   void DisplayMsg() {
     cout << "\nMethod in BaseClass executing\n" ;
   }
};

// A derived class
class Derived1 : public BaseClass {
public:
   void DisplayMsg() {
     cout << "Method in Derived1 class executing\n" ;
   }
};

// A second derived class
class Derived2 : public BaseClass {
public:
   void DisplayMsg() {
     cout << "Method in Derived2 class executing\n" ;
   }
};

//***************************
//         main()
//***************************
main() {
   BaseClass base_obj;       // Object of BaseClass
   Derived1 der1_obj;        // Object of Derived1 class
   Derived2 der2_obj;        // Object of Derived2 class

// Accessing method DisplayMsg() by means of object-to-class
// binding
   base_obj.DisplayMsg();    // Method in BaseClass
   der1_obj.DisplayMsg();    // Method in Derived1 class
   der2_obj.DisplayMsg();    // Method in Derived2 class
   return 0;
}
```

9.3.8 Decoupling Interface and Implementation

One of the core concepts of object orientation is the notion of one interface and multiple methods. The term polymorphism is often used in this context since the method that contains the interface and the method or methods that contain the implementation can have (and often do have) the same name. Decoupling interface and implementation can be achieved statically by the simple mechanism of defining a method that performs no meaningful processing operations. For example:

```
class BaseA {
  public:
    void method1() { };
};
```

For lack of a better term we can say that an *empty method* or *function* is one that does not provide a meaningful implementation. Alternatively, an empty method can be made to include a return statement. For example:

```
class BaseA {
  public:
    void method1() { return; };
};
```

Empty methods should not be confused with virtual functions and pure virtual functions, which are special constructs used extensively in run-time polymorphism. If we assume that the method named **DisplayMsg()** in the **BaseClass** of Figure 9.13 is an empty method, then the illustration can be stretched to represent a decoupling between interface and implementation at compile time. The major limitation of this mechanism is that the only way of statically accessing polymorphic methods of the same type is either by explicit object-to-class references or by scope resolution. In either case, the method has to be explicitly defined in the code; therefore, most of the advantages of interface/implementation decoupling are lost.

If C++ did not support dynamic binding then the use of empty methods and the compile-time selection by means of object-to-class binding or scope resolution would be the only way of approximating the one-interface, multiple-methods paradigm. Fortunately, this is not the case. C++ supports dynamic binding by means of virtual functions and pure virtual functions and by method selection through pointers to objects. This mechanism is so powerful and flexible that it leaves little justification for putting up with the limitations and restrictions of static binding. Chapter 10 is entirely devoted to dynamic polymorphism and in it we consider in detail the applications and complications of run-time method selection.

Chapter 10

Dynamic Binding Constructs

10.0 Dynamic Binding Revisited

C++ provides mechanisms for achieving run-time polymorphism, which is accomplished by means of pure and nonpure virtual functions. Nonpure virtual functions are declared and implemented in the base class and redefined in one or more derived classes. Pure virtual functions have no implementation in the base class. Therefore, in the case of pure virtual functions the base class defines the interface and the derived classes the implementation. When a virtual function, nonpure or pure, is accessed by means of a pointer, the method executed depends on the object which the pointer is referencing. Since the pointer is resolved as the program executes, the method selection does not take place until then. This explains the terms dynamic binding and run-time polymorphism.

The nonpure virtual function mechanism assumes that there is implementation in the function defined in the base class. Otherwise a linker error occurs, since no address is assigned to a method that performs no processing operations. However, there are cases in which there can be no meaningful implementation in the base class. Using virtual functions, we would have to provide a dummy method in order for this class structure to work in code. Furthermore, we would have to make sure that this method is not called during actual execution. The C++ pure virtual function provides a solution to this problem. In C++ a pure virtual function is equated to zero in the base class. Upon detecting a pure virtual function, the language ensures that implementation must be provided in all derived classes; otherwise, a compiler error is generated.

The pure virtual function construct has several effects that could sometimes be desirable:

1. The base class serves to define a general interface that sets a model that the derived classes must follow.

2. Implementation in the derived classes is guaranteed since the code does not compile otherwise.

3. Encapsulation is preserved since objects are accessed through a common interface. Therefore, implementation dependencies are reduced.

4. Run-time substitutions are made possible by the fact that all objects must have the same type.

There are also disadvantages to the use of dynamic binding through object composition:

1. Software constructs based on pointers or reference variables are harder to understand and apply than those based on class hierarchies.

2. Run-time selection is less efficient than compile time.

In spite of these shortcomings, most authors agree that we should prefer run-time over compile-time polymorphism. The reason is that dynamic binding is usually a more powerful and flexible mechanism.

10.0.1 Object Model Notation

For representing object composition and C++ run-time polymorphism we need to create some additional symbols and to refine some of the ones we have been using in the preceding chapters. A round-cornered rectangle with a dashed border represents an abstract class. In C++ an abstract class is one that has at least one pure virtual function. However, an abstract class can also have nonpure virtual functions and nonvirtual functions. We use italic typeface for virtual functions and equate pure virtual functions to zero.

Several new symbols are used to depict class and object associations. A continuous line between classes or between client code and a clss denotes that the program element at the arrow's start instantiates an object of the class at the arrow's head. A dashed line between a program element (class or client code) and a class denotes that the program element maintains a pointer to an object of the class at the arrow's head. A thick, gray arrow indicates that a class contains an object of another class. This is accomplished by means of a member object, which can be declared in the public, private, or protected section of the class and has the corresponding visibility.

Figure 10.1 shows the symbol set that is used in the graphic depiction of dynamic binding (this chapter) and object composition (Chapter 11).

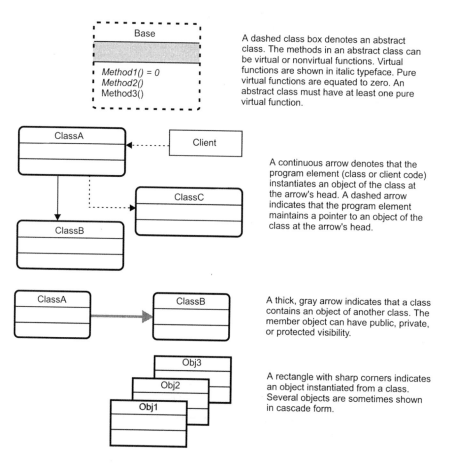

A dashed class box denotes an abstract class. The methods in an abstract class can be virtual or nonvirtual functions. Virtual functions are shown in italic typeface. Pure virtual functions are equated to zero. An abstract class must have at least one pure virtual function.

A continuous arrow denotes that the program element (class or client code) instantiates an object of the class at the arrow's head. A dashed arrow indicates that the program element maintains a pointer to an object of the class at the arrow's head.

A thick, gray arrow indicates that a class contains an object of another class. The member object can have public, private, or protected visibility.

A rectangle with sharp corners indicates an object instantiated from a class. Several objects are sometimes shown in cascade form.

Figure 10.1 *Symbols for Object Models and Dynamic Binding*

Note that the new symbols in Figure 10.1 are not identical to the ones used in *Object Modeling Technique* (OMT) or the ones adopted by Gamma et al. Since this book relates specifically to C++, we have adopted symbols that correspond to the programming constructs specifically supported by the language.

10.1 Modeling Dynamic Binding

Using the new symbols introduced in Figure 10.1 as well as the ones used in modeling inheritance structures (depicted in Figure 9.2) we can now use class diagrams and object models to show the fundamental constructs of dynamic, polymorphic inheritance in C++. Note that in the models of this chapter we are avoiding all the variations that do not lead to dynamic polymorphism.

10.1.1 Polymorphism by Virtual Functions

The simplest case is a class that inherits polymorphic methods from a base class. This case is shown in Figure 10.2.

Figure 10.2 shows a class named **BaseA**, which contains a virtual function named **Method1()**. Two classes named **Derived1** and **Derived2**, which inherit the public and protected members of the base class, also contain methods of the same name. The fact that **Method1()** is declared virtual in the base class makes possible the selection of any one of the three polymorphic methods by means of a pointer. Since the pointer is not instantiated until runtime, the selection takes place during program execution. The following short program shows the code to implement the class structure of Figure 10.2:

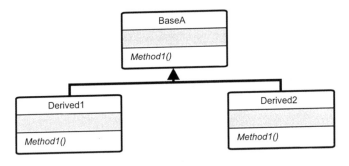

Figure 10.2 *Virtual Function and Class Inheritance*

```
//*********************************************************************
// C++ program to illustrate a virtual function and
// run-time polymorphism
// Filename: SAM10-01.CPP
//*********************************************************************
#include <iostream.h>

//***************************
//        classes
//***************************
// Base class contains a virtual function
class BaseA {
private:
public:
    virtual void ShowMsg() {
      cout << "\nBaseA class method executing\n" ;
    }
};
// Derived classes
class Derived1 : public BaseA {
public:
    void ShowMsg() {
      cout << "\nDerived1 class method executing\n" ;
    }
};
class Derived2 : public BaseA {
public:
    void ShowMsg() {
      cout << "\nDerived2 class method executing\n" ;
    }
};

//***************************
//         main()
//***************************
main() {
    BaseA *base_ptr;              // Pointer to base class object
    BaseA base_obj;               // Object of BaseA class
    Derived1 der_obj1;            // Objects of derived classes
    Derived2 der_obj2;
// Prompt user for input
int user_input = 0;
    cout << "\n   Menu of class methods:  \n"
      << "1. Method in BaseA class\n"
      << "2. Method in Derived1 class\n"
      << "3. Method in Derived2 class\n"
      << "   Enter the desired number: ";
      cin >> user_input;
// Use user input to set base class pointer to the
// corresponding object
  switch (user_input) {
    case (1):
      base_ptr = &base_obj;
```

```
      break;
    case (2):
      base_ptr = &der_obj1;
      break;
    case (3):
      base_ptr = &der_obj2;
      break;
    default:
      cout << "\ninvalid input\n" ;
      return 1;
}
// Use pointer to access the desired method
    base_ptr-> ShowMsg();
    return 0;
}
```

In program SAM10-01.CPP, the method is selected by means of a switch construct based on a numeric value input by the user. The fact that the user selects the input value at run time makes it clear that the code construct conforms with the requirements of run-time polymorphism. Note that this form of dynamic method selection is based on using the virtual attribute for the method defined in the base class. If we modified program SAM10-07.CPP so that the function in the base class was not virtual, then the base class method always executes, independently of the user's input. Also, if the classes containing the polymorphic methods were not derived from the base class, a compile error would be produced since the assignment statements to an object of the derived classes could not be resolved. In summary, in C++, the recipe for run-time polymorphism requires the following ingredients:

1. The polymorphic method must be declared virtual in the base class.

2. Access to the polymorphic method must be by means of a pointer to an object of the base class.

3. The polymorphic methods must be associated by class inheritance.

Adding Model Details

Figure 10.2 shows the fundamentals of class associations based on virtual functions; however, it does not show how client code accesses the class construct or if the result is dynamic or static polymorphism. In this case we can add details to the model by showing how a client can access the class structure, as shown in Figure 10.3.

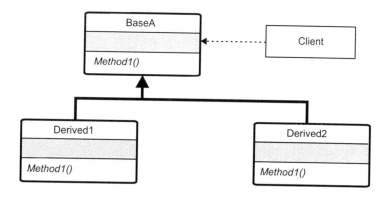

Figure 10.3 *Virtual Function and Dynamic Polymorphism*

By adding information about the client interface to the class inheritance construct we show that method selection is by means of a pointer to the base class, and, consequently, that the result is run-time polymorphism. However, if we look at the code listing in SAM10-01.CPP we see that the client instantiates objects of all three classes. Therefore, we may consider adding continuous-line arrows from the client to each of the classes. Although this addition is not incorrect, it is superfluous. In C++ clients must access class methods by means of objects; there is no other alternative. Therefore, the fact that the polymorphic methods are accessed by the client implies that objects of each of the classes must be instantiated. In this case, adding the three continuous-line arrows from the client to the classes would make the graphic more difficult to read while adding little to its modeling value.

10.1.2 Inheriting Virtual Functions

We note in program SAM10-01.CPP that the methods in the derived classes are not declared virtual. However, it would not be an error to include the **virtual** keyword; for example, we could have coded:

```
class Derived1 : public BaseA {
public:
    virtual void ShowMsg() {
      cout << "\nDerived1 class method executing\n" ;
    }
};
```

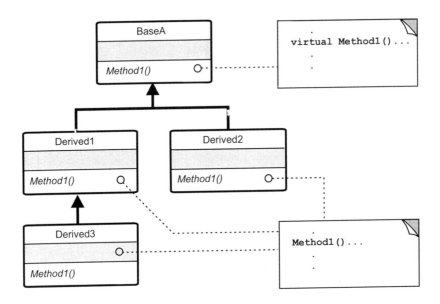

Figure 10.4 *Inheriting the Virtual Attribute*

The reason why the virtual keyword can be omitted is that the virtual attribute is inherited. When a virtual function is inherited by a subclass it remains virtual, no matter how many times it is inherited. Therefore, once a function is made virtual in the base class there is no need to explicitly restate its virtual character in the derived classes. Figure 10.4 shows another example of inheritance of virtual functions.

The following short program implements the inheritance structure shown in Figure 10.4:

```
//*********************************************************************
// C++ program to illustrate inheriting the virtual attribute
// and run-time polymorphism
// Filename: SAM10-02.CPP
//*********************************************************************
#include <iostream.h>

//***************************
//          classes
//***************************
// Base class
class BaseA {
private:
public:
```

```
      virtual void ShowMsg() {
        cout << "\nBaseA class method executing\n" ;
    }
  };


  // Derived classes
  class Derived1 : public BaseA {
  public:
      void ShowMsg() {
        cout << "\nDerived1 class method executing\n" ;
      }
  };
  class Derived2 : public BaseA {
  public:
      void ShowMsg() {
        cout << "\nDerived2 class method executing\n" ;
      }
  };
  // Derived3 inherits from Derived1
  class Derived3 : public Derived1 {
  public:
      void ShowMsg() {
        cout << "\nDerived3 class method executing\n" ;
      }
  };


  //***************************
  //            main()
  //***************************
  main() {
     BaseA *base_ptr;              // Pointer to base class object
     BaseA base_obj;               // Object of BaseA class
     Derived1 der_obj1;            // Objects of derived classes
     Derived2 der_obj2;
     Derived3 der_obj3;

  // Prompt user for input
  int user_input = 0;
     cout << "\n   Menu of class methods:  \n"
       << "1. Method in BaseA class\n"
       << "2. Method in Derived1 class\n"
       << "3. Method in Derived2 class\n"
       << "4. Method in Derived3 class\n"
       << "   Enter the desired number: ";
     cin >> user_input;

  // Use user input to set base class pointer to the
  // corresponding object
    switch (user_input) {
      case (1):
        base_ptr = &base_obj;
        break;
      case (2):
```

```
      base_ptr = &der_obj1;
      break;
    case (3):
      base_ptr = &der_obj2;
      break;
    case (4):
      base_ptr = &der_obj3;
      break;
    default:
     cout << "\ninvalid input\n" ;
     return 1;
}
// Use pointer to access the desired method
   base_ptr-> ShowMsg();
   return 0;
}
```

10.1.3 Virtual Function Hierarchies

In an inheritance structure based on virtual functions the methods in the derived classes hierarchically override the ones in the base classes. If one of the derived classes does not define a virtual function, then the first redefinition in reverse order of derivation is used. Figure 10.5 shows a class structure of virtual functions in which one class (Derived1) does not define the polymorphic function.

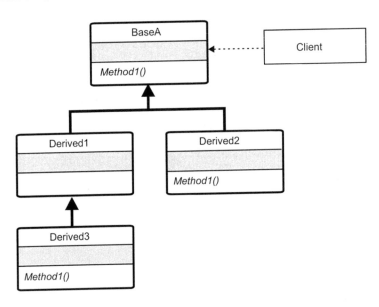

Figure 10.5 *Overriding a Virtual Function*

In the case of Figure 10.5 if **Method1()** is accessed in reference to an object of the class **Derived1**, in which the method is not implemented, the first one in reverse order of derivation is used, which in this case is **Method1()** of the class **BaseA**. The following short program illustrates virtual function hierarchies and overriding of a method not implemented in a derived class:

```
//****************************************************************
// C++ program to illustrate overriding a virtual function
// Filename: SAM10-03.CPP
//****************************************************************
#include <iostream.h>

//***************************
//        classes
//***************************
// Base class
class BaseA {
private:
public:
   virtual void ShowMsg() {
     cout << "\nBaseA class method executing\n" ;
   }
};

// Derived classes
class Derived1 : public BaseA {
public:
};
class Derived2 : public BaseA {
public:
   void ShowMsg() {
     cout << "\nDerived2 class method executing\n" ;
   }
};

// Derived3 inherits from Derived1
class Derived3 : public Derived1 {
public:
   void ShowMsg() {
     cout << "\nDerived3 class method executing\n" ;
   }
};

//***************************
//         main()
//***************************
main() {
   BaseA *base_ptr;          // Pointer to base class object
   BaseA base_obj;           // Object of BaseA class
   Derived1 der_obj1;        // Objects of derived classes
   Derived2 der_obj2;
```

```
    Derived3 der_obj3;

// Prompt user for input
int user_input = 0;
    cout << "\n   Menu of class methods:  \n"
      << "1. Method in BaseA class\n"
      << "2. Method in Derived1 class (NOT IMPLEMENTED)\n"
      << "3. Method in Derived2 class\n"
      << "4. Method in Derived3 class\n"
      << "   Enter the desired number: ";
      cin >> user_input;

// Use user input to set base class pointer to the
// corresponding object
  switch (user_input) {
    case (1):
      base_ptr = &base_obj;
      break;
    case (2):
      base_ptr = &der_obj1;
      break;
    case (3):
      base_ptr = &der_obj2;
      break;
    case (4):
      base_ptr = &der_obj3;
      break;
    default:
      cout << "\ninvalid input\n" ;
      return 1;
}
// Use pointer to access the desired method
    base_ptr-> ShowMsg();
    return 0;
}
```

In program SAM10-03.CPP, when we use a pointer to the class **Derived1**, in which **Method1()** is not implemented, the implementation in the class **BaseA** executes in its place.

10.1.4 Combining Virtual and Nonvirtual Functions

C++ allows us to combine virtual and nonvirtual functions in the same class. Therefore, we can create a class structure that includes polymorphic and nonpolymorphic components. The polymorphic methods are usually accessed as previously described, while the nonvirtual methods can be accessed using any valid addressing form. Figure 10.6 shows a base class that contains a virtual and a nonvirtual function.

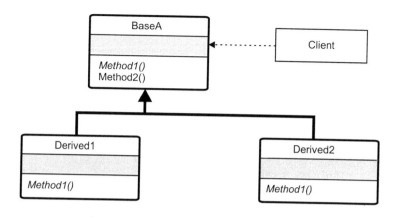

Figure 10.6 *Combining Virtual and Nonvirtual Functions*

The following program shows access to virtual and nonvirtual functions using the same pointer variable:

```cpp
//*******************************************************************
// C++ program to illustrate combining virtual and nonvirtual
// functions in the same base class
// Filename: SAM10-04.CPP
//*******************************************************************
#include <iostream.h>
//****************************
//          classes
//****************************
// Base class has virtual and nonvirtual functions
class BaseA {
public:
    virtual void ShowMsg() {
      cout << "\nBaseA class virtual method executing\n" ;
    }
    void ShowMsgNV() {
      cout << "\nBaseA class nonvirtual method executing\n" ;
    }};
// Derived classes
class Derived1 : public BaseA {
public:
    virtual void ShowMsg() {
      cout << "\nDerived1 class method executing\n" ;
    }
};
class Derived2 : public BaseA {
public:
    virtual void ShowMsg() {
      cout << "\nDerived2 class method executing\n" ;
    }
};
```

```
//****************************
//              main()
//****************************

main() {
    BaseA *base_ptr;          // Pointer to base class object
    BaseA base_obj;           // Object of BaseA class
    Derived1 der_obj1;        // Objects of derived classes
    Derived2 der_obj2;

// Prompt user for input
int user_input = 0;
    cout << "\n   Menu of class methods:   \n"
         << "1. Virtual function in BaseA class\n"
         << "2. Virtual function in Derived1 class\n"
         << "3. Virtual function in Derived2 class\n"
         << "4. Nonvirtual function in BaseA class\n"
         << "   Enter the desired number: ";
    cin >> user_input;
// Use user input to set base class pointer to the
// corresponding object
    switch (user_input) {
      case (1):
        base_ptr = &base_obj;
        break;
      case (2):
        base_ptr = &der_obj1;
        break;
      case (3):
        base_ptr = &der_obj2;
        break;
      case (4):
// In this case the base pointer must be reset to the
// nonvirtual function ShowMsgNV()
        base_ptr-> ShowMsgNV();
        return 0;
      default:
        cout << "\ninvalid input\n" ;
        return 1;
    }
// Use pointer to access the desired method
    base_ptr-> ShowMsg();

    return 0;
}
```

10.1.5 Polymorphism by Pure Virtual Functions

What would happen if a polymorphic method were not implemented in the base class? For instance, suppose that the class named **BaseA** in the program SAM10-03.CPP were recoded as follows:

```
class BaseA {
public:
   virtual void ShowMsg();
};
```

In a DOS-based C++ compiler the program compiles correctly but generates a linker error, because there is no address for the nonexistent method **ShowMsg()** in the base class. Therefore, the statement

```
base_ptr-> ShowMsg();
```

cannot be resolved by the linker.

Programming situations abound in which there is no meaningful definition for a method in the base class. The class structure in Figure 10.7 is an example. In this case, the formula for calculating the area of an undefined geometrical figure is meaningless. Not until we decide if the figure is a square, a rectangle, or a circle can we apply a specific formula and determine the area. The **Area()** method in the base class serves to define the interface, but the implementation is left for the derived class or classes.

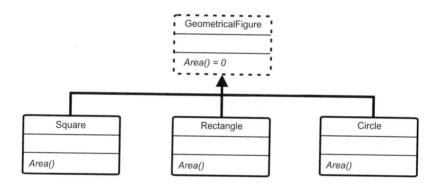

Figure 10.7 *Inheriting from an Abstract Class*

In the case of a pure virtual function, implementation must be provided by all derived classes. A compiler error occurs if any derived class fails to provide an implementation for a pure virtual function. The case of the pure virtual function is different from that of nonvirtual functions, in which a missing implementation is automatically replaced by the closest one in reverse order of derivation.

The two most notable effects of pure virtual functions are:

1. The base class serves to define a general interface that sets a model that all derived classes must follow.

2. Implementation in the derived classes is automatically assured since the code does not compile otherwise.

This mechanism allows code to use a base class to define an interface by declaring the method's parameters and return type: the implementation is left to one or more derived classes. Therefore, the abstract class model satisfies the "one interface, multiple methods" approach that is a core notion of object orientation.

10.1.6 Combining Methods in an Abstract Class

In C++, the actual implementation of run-time polymorphism by means of an abstract class has certain unique characteristics. C++ does not allow the instantiation of an object of an abstract class. Once a class contains a pure virtual function it cannot be instantiated, even if it also contains other functions that are virtual and nonvirtual. Therefore, a diagram such as the one in the lower part of Figure 10.8 is invalid under any circumstances.

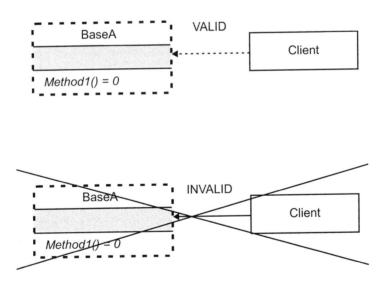

Figure 10.8 *An Abstract Class Cannot be Instantiated*

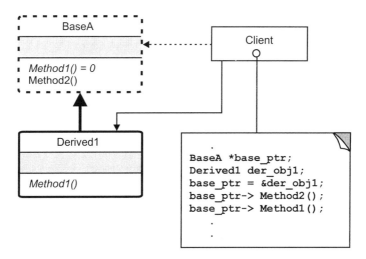

Figure 10.9 *Accessing Methods in an Abstract Class*

The fact that client code cannot create an object of an abstract class determines that if an abstract class contains virtual or nonvirtual functions these cannot be accessed directly. Therefore, we must use a roundabout way of getting to the methods in the abstract class. One alternative is to create a class that inherits from the abstract base class. Since the derived class is not an abstract class we can instantiate objects of it. Furthermore, since the derived class inherits the methods of the abstract class we now have a way for accessing these otherwise invisible methods. Figure 10.9 shows the class diagram that includes an abstract class with a nonvirtual function and how this function can be accessed through a derived class.

The following program shows the code necessary to implement the inheritance diagram in Figure 10.9:

```
//******************************************************************
// C++ program to illustrate access to methods in an abstract
// base class
// Filename: SAM10-05.CPP
//******************************************************************
#include <iostream.h>
//***************************
//         classes
//***************************
// Abstract base class has a nonvirtual function
class BaseA {
public:
   virtual void Method1() = 0;
```

```
    void Method2() {
      cout << "\nBaseA class nonvirtual Method2() executing\n" ;
    }
};
// Derived class
class Derived1 : public BaseA {
public:
    void Method1() {
      cout << "\nDerived1 class Method1() executing\n" ;
    }
};
//****************************
//          main()
//****************************
main() {
   BaseA *base_ptr;              // Pointer to base class object
   Derived1 der_obj1;            // Object of derived class
   base_ptr = &der_obj1;         // Pointer set to derived class
object
   base_ptr-> Method2();         // Access to base class nonvirtual
                                 // function
   base_ptr-> Method1();         // Method1() can also be accessed in
                                 // the derived class

   return 0;

}
```

10.2 Applying Inheritance

Object composition and class inheritance are the two major design
alternatives. In this section we present a real-world programming
problem which we attempt to solve using dynamic, polymorphic inheritance. In Chapter 12 we present an alternative solution based on
object composition. We have eliminated many of the complications in
order to make the solution more focused and easier to follow. The example is based on a hypothetical VESA true color graphics library that
we have used in previous chapters. The problem can be stated as follows:

The Video Electronics Standards Association has implemented
four modes to support true color graphics. These modes are numbered
112H, 115H, 118H, and 11BH. All of them have in common that they
execute in 16.7 million colors. Most systems implement the true color
modes by mapping 8 bits of video to each of the primary colors (red,
green, and blue). The total of 24 bits, 8 bits per color, allows
16,777,215 combinations. Figure 8.6 depicts a true color graphics
mode. Table 10.1 shows the definition and video memory requirements of the VESA true color modes.

Table 10.1 *Specifications of VESA True Color Modes*

VESA MODE	RESOLUTION	MEMORY	ADAPTER Mb.
112H	640-by-480	921,600	1Mb
115H	800-by-600	1,440,000	2Mb
118H	1024-by-768	2,359,296	4Mb
11BH	1280-by-1024	3,932,160	4mb

To a programmer the only difference between the various true color modes is the size of the viewport, which is determined directly by the mode's resolution.

In this case we assume that the design problem consists of providing the client with the following minimal functionality:

1. A way of setting the desired VESA true color mode

2. A way of obtaining the current VESA mode as well as the vertical and horizontal resolution

3. A way of drawing a screen pixel defined in terms of its screen x and y coordinates and color attribute

4. A way of reading the color attribute of a screen pixel located at given screen coordinates

10.2.1 An Inheritance Solution

The fundamental idea of our VESA true color graphics library is to give the client a way of performing all four functions listed in the preceding section. Figure 10.10 represents a model of the problem domain in terms of a Gen-Spec class structure.

The diagram in Figure 10.10 gives us some information about the class relations in the VESA true color graphics library. At this point we have defined that the base class would be an abstract class that contains two pure virtual functions (**DrawPixel()** and **ReadPixel()**) as well as three nonvirtual functions (**SetVesaMode()**, **GetVRes()**, and **GetHRes()**). The four mode-specific classes contain the implementation for drawing and reading a screen pixel in each of the supported modes. In Figure 10.11 we have replaced the Gen-Spec structure graphics with inheritance lines and included the client.

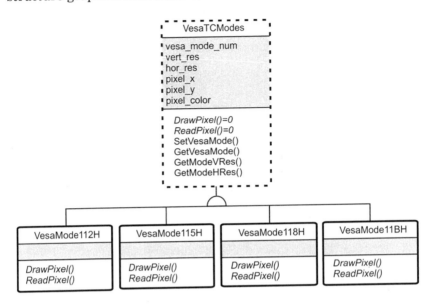

Figure 10.10 *Class Structure for a VESA True Color Graphics Library*

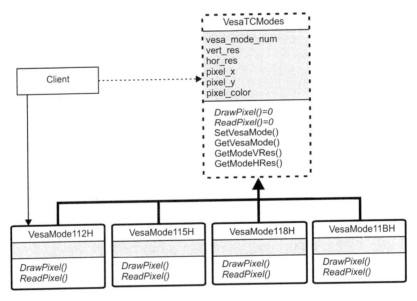

Figure 10.11 *Inheritance and Client Interface Diagram*

As defined in Figure 10.11, the VESA true color graphics library implements all of the specified functionality. Note that there is a solid line from the client to the class VesaMode112H. This is necessary in order to gain access to the nonvirtual functions defined in the base class, as discussed in Section 10.1.6. Also, the client keeps a pointer to the base class since this mechanism is necessary to produce dynamic binding. The following program contains the schematic implementation of the class and inheritance structure in Figure 10.11:

```
//*******************************************************************
// C++ program to illustrate the processing necessary for
// implementing a VESA true color graphics library by means
// of class inheritance
// Filename: SAMP10-06.CPP
//*******************************************************************
#include <iostream.h>

//*******************************************************************
//                           classes
//*******************************************************************
// Abstract base class
class VesaTCModes {
private:
    int vesa_mode_num;              // First dimension
    int vert_res;
    int hor_res;
public:
// Pure virtual functions
    virtual void DrawPixel(int row, int column, int color) = 0;
    virtual unsigned long ReadPixel(int row, int column) = 0;
// Nonvirtual functions
    int SetVesaMode(char a_mode);
    int GetVesaMode();
    int GetModeVRes();
    int GetModeHRes();
};

//******************************
// Methods for class VesaTCModes
//******************************
int VesaTCModes::SetVesaMode(char vesa_mode) {
// The SetMode() method checks for a valid ASCII
// code (a through d). If so, the corresponding
// mode is set, the resolution is installed in
// the corresponding structure variables, and 1
// is returned. If not, mode 0 is set and 0 is
// returned to the caller.
    int ret_code = 1;
    switch (vesa_mode) {
    case 'a':
        vesa_mode_num = 0x112;
```

```
      hor_res = 640;
      vert_res = 480;
      break;
  case 'b':
      vesa_mode_num = 0x115;
      hor_res = 800;
      vert_res = 600;
      break;
  case 'c':
      vesa_mode_num = 0x118;
      hor_res = 1024;
      vert_res = 768;
      break;
case 'd':
      vesa_mode_num = 0x11b;
      hor_res = 1280;
      vert_res = 1024;
      break;
default:
      vesa_mode_num = 0x0;
      hor_res = 0;
      vert_res = 0;
      ret_code = 0;
}
   return ret_code;
}

// Methods that return the mode information
int VesaTCModes::GetVesaMode() {
  return vesa_mode_num;
}
int VesaTCModes::GetModeVRes() {
  return vert_res;
}
int VesaTCModes::GetModeHRes() {
  return hor_res;
}

//*****************************
//    Polymorphic classes
//*****************************
// Note: methods have stub implementations in this demo
//       program
class VesaMode112H : public VesaTCModes  {
public:
   virtual void DrawPixel(int row, int column, int color) {
   cout << "Setting pixel in Mode 112H\n";
   return;
   }
   virtual unsigned long ReadPixel(int row, int column) {
   cout << "Reading pixel in Mode 112H\n" ;
   return 0;
   }
```

```
};
class VesaMode115H : public VesaTCModes  {
public:
   virtual void DrawPixel(int row, int column, int color) {
   cout << "Setting pixel in Mode 115H\n";
   return;
   }
   virtual unsigned long ReadPixel(int row, int column) {
   cout << "Reading pixel in Mode 115H\n" ;
   return 0;
   }
};
class VesaMode118H : public VesaTCModes  {
public:
   virtual void DrawPixel(int row, int column, int color) {
   cout << "Mode 118H methods not implemented\n";
   return;
   }
   virtual unsigned long ReadPixel(int row, int column) {
   cout << "Mode 118H methods not implemented\n";
   return 0;
   }
};
class VesaMode11BH : public VesaTCModes  {
public:
   virtual void DrawPixel(int row, int column, int color) {
   cout << "Mode 11BH methods not implemented\n";
   return;
   }
   virtual unsigned long ReadPixel(int row, int column) {
   cout << "Mode 11BH methods not implemented\n";
   return 0;
   }
};
//*********************************************************************
//                           client code
//*********************************************************************
main() {
// Objects and pointers to objects
VesaTCModes *base_ptr;         // Pointer to base class object
VesaMode112H obj_112H;      // Objects of derived classes
VesaMode115H obj_115H;
VesaMode118H obj_118H;
VesaMode11BH obj_11bH;
// User selects VESA mode from menu
   char user_mode;
   int valid_code, current_mode;
   cout << "\n\n    VESA true color modes: \n"
     << " a. Mode 112H\n"
     << " b. Mode 115H\n"
     << " c. Mode 118H\n"
     << " d. Mode 11BH\n"
     << "    type a, b, c, or d: ";
```

```
     cin >> user_mode;
// Set VESA mode using method in class VesaTCModes
     valid_code = obj_112H.SetVesaMode(user_mode);
     if (valid_code == 0 ) {
        cout << "\nINVALID MODE SELECTED\n";
        return 1;
        }
// Display VESA mode resolution
     cout << "\nVESA mode: "
        << hex << obj_112H.GetVesaMode()
        << "H\n";
     cout << "Vertical resolution: "
        << dec << obj_112H.GetModeVRes()
        << "\n";
    cout << "Horizontal resolution: "
        << obj_112H.GetModeHRes()
        << "\n";
// Set pointer to selected mode
    current_mode = obj_112H.GetVesaMode();
    switch (current_mode) {
    case 0x112:
      base_ptr = &obj_112H;
      break;
    case 0x115:
      base_ptr = &obj_115H;
      break;
    case 0x118:
      base_ptr = &obj_118H;
      break;
    case 0x11b:
      base_ptr = &obj_11bH;
      break;
}
// Use base pointer to select SetPixel() method
    base_ptr -> DrawPixel(24, 122, 0xff00b0);
    base_ptr -> ReadPixel(12, 144);
    return 0;
}
```

Chapter 11

Object Composition Constructs

11.0 Fundamental Notions

In some cases object composition can be an alternative to inheritance. However, programmers and designers seem to favor the use of inheritance more than they do object composition. It is not surprising. Many programming books entirely ignore the subject of object composition. The ones that do mention it as a reuse methodology usually describe it as being difficult to understand and apply.

As the term implies, object composition is based on achieving new functionalities by assembling objects and object references. It is based on the following basic facts of C++ programming:

1. A class can access the public members of another class.

2. An object can be a member of a class.

3. An object of one class can instantiate an object of another class.

4. A class can maintain pointers to objects of other classes and to other class members.

Object composition requires a unique view of the problem domain. It demands thinking in terms of a class *containing* another class rather than of a class being a kind-of another class. The container relation is compatible with the is-a-part-of modeling concept that derives from Whole-Part structures discussed in earlier chapters. However, in many cases, both views are simultaneously possible. We can often visualize the same class relationship in terms of is-a-kind-of or is-a-part-of associations.

A classic example relates to the calculation of the area of a class window in relation to a class rectangle. In this sense we can say that a class window is a kind-of class rectangle since it has width and height. Therefore, window inherits the method to calculate the area from the class rectangle. Alternatively we can imagine that a window has a or uses a rectangle class to calculate its area. Both models are shown in Figure 11.1.

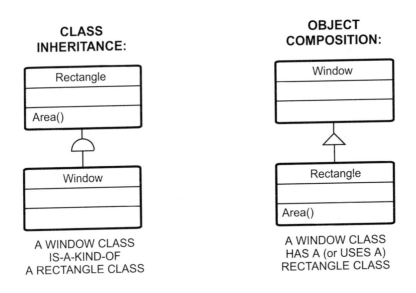

Figure 11.1 *Alternative Modeling of Window and Rectangle Classes*

The model on the left-hand side of Figure 11.1 is normally implemented through class inheritance. The one on the right-hand side is implemented through object composition. The inheritance implementation has already been described in detail. The implementation through object composition is based on the class **window** instantiating an object of the class **rectangle**, which calculates and returns the area parameter. Figure 11.2 is a class diagram for this case.

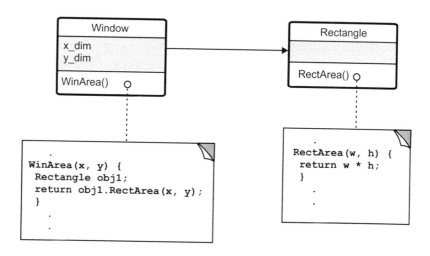

Figure 11.2 *Implementation through Object Composition*

The short program that follows shows the implementation of the case in Figure 11.2:

```cpp
//*********************************************************************
// C++ program to illustrate object composition
// Filename: SAM11-01.CPP
//*********************************************************************
#include <iostream.h>
//***************************
//         classes
//***************************
class Rectangle {
public:
    int RectArea(int height, int width) {
    return height * width;
    }
};
class Window {
private:
    int x_dim;                          // Window dimensions
    int y_dim;
public:
    Window (int dim1, int dim2) {  // Parameterized constructor
    x_dim = dim1; y_dim = dim2;
    }
    int WinArea() {                     // Area() method
    Rectangle obj1;
    return obj1.RectArea(x_dim, y_dim);
    }
};
```

```
//****************************
//          main()
//****************************
main() {
    Window objw1(12, 2);          // Constructing object of class
Window
    cout << "\nCalculating area of Window object: "
      << objw1.WinArea()
      << "\n";
    return 0;
}
```

Note that the class diagram in Figure 11.2 does not use inheritance, since class **rectangle** is not a derived class. The **Window** class gains access to the method **RectArea()** in **Rectangle** class by instantiating and keeping a **Rectangle** object. In cases such as this one we often speak of a class *delegating its behavior* to another class, since it is the rectangle class that determines how the area of the window is calculated. To calculate the window area by a different method we could replace the rectangle instance at run time.

11.0.1 Object Relationships

The object composition model refers to two kinds of relationships: the first one corresponds to the notion of a class that *has* another one, and the second one to a class that *uses* another one. In the first case, corresponding to a class that *has* or *is-a-part-of* another class, there is an aggregation relationship. In the second case, in which a class *uses* another class, there is an acquaintance relationship. We can, somewhat arbitrarily, associate acquaintance with pointers, and aggregation with member objects or object references. We can also state that acquaintance binds looser than aggregation, or that aggregation implies a tight association between classes and acquaintance a looser one. Aggregation and acquaintance relationships are discussed separately in the following sections.

11.1 Aggregation Constructs

The example in Figure 11.2, implemented in the program SAM11-01.CPP, is one of class aggregation. The fact that the class **Window** instantiates an object of the class **Rectangle** binds both classes permanently at compile time. In this case nothing can happen at run time to change the association between the class **Rectangle** and the class

Window. Incidentally, examining whether a class association can be changed at run time provides a good test for determining if a class relationship is one of aggregation or of acquaintance. A relationship that can vary at run time is one of acquaintance; otherwise, the relationship is a class aggregation.

11.1.1 Member Objects

In addition to instantiating an object of another class, we can also achieve aggregation by means of a class that *contains* an object of another class. In this case we speak of a class having a *member object*. In this sense, we can say that the class that has the object is the containing class, and the other one the contained class. In Figure 10.1 we introduced a thick, gray arrow symbol to depict the member object relation. A simple example is a class called **PersonInfo** that has a member object of a class named **Date** that serves to preserve the birthdate of every object of **PersonInfo** class. Therefore, the class **PersonInfo** is the containing class and the class **Date** is the contained class. Figure 11.3 depicts a class aggregation relationship by means of a member object.

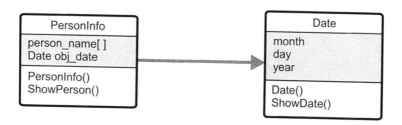

Figure 11.3 *Class Aggregation by a Member Object*

The following program implements the class aggregation relationship shown in Figure 11.3:

```
//*******************************************************************
// C++ program to illustrate aggregation by means of a member
// object of a class
// Filename: SAM11-02.CPP
//*******************************************************************
```

```cpp
#include <iostream.h>
#include <string.h>

//****************************
//          classes
//****************************
class Date {
private:
    int month;
    int day;
    int year;
public:
    Date (int m, int d, int y);        // Constructor
    void ShowDate();                   // A method
};
// Implementation of parameterized constructor
Date::Date(int m, int d, int y) {
    month = m;
    day = d;
    year = y;
}
// Method to display date
void Date::ShowDate() {
    cout << month << "   " << day << "   " << year;
}
class PersonInfo {
private:
    char person_name[30];              // Storage for name array
    Date obj_date;                     // A member object declared
public:
    PersonInfo (char *name, int mo, int da, int yr);  // Constructor
    void ShowPerson();                               // A method
};

// Implementation of parameterized constructor must also
// initialize member object
PersonInfo::PersonInfo (char *name, int da, int mo, int yr)
        : obj_date (mo, da, yr) {      // Member object constructor
    strncpy( person_name, name, 30);   // Copy name to variable
}
// ShowPerson method displays name and calls method ShowDate()
// in the Date class
void PersonInfo::ShowPerson() {
    cout << "\n" << person_name;
    cout << " birth date: ";
    obj_date.ShowDate();
}

//****************************
//          main()
//****************************
main() {
// Declare objects of PersonInfo class
```

```
    PersonInfo person1("John Smith", 12, 11, 1962);
    PersonInfo person2("Mary Riley", 3, 9, 1856);
    cout << "\n\n";
//  Access method ShowPerson in PersonInfo class
    person1.ShowPerson();
    person2.ShowPerson();
    return 0;
}
```

11.1.2 Member Object Constructors

Certain requirements must be met in the implementation of a class that contains an object of another class. The constructors for the containing and the contained classes are a major concern. For a valid initialization of both classes one of the following conditions must be met:

1. The contained class requires no constructor.

2. The contained class has a default constructor available to the containing class.

3. The containing class constructor explicitly initializes the object of the contained class.

The constructor of the contained class is not called until the containing class is created. The constructor of the member object must be called explicitly. A colon symbol is placed after the parameter list of the containing class' constructor. In program SAM11-02.CPP the initialization is performed as follows:

```
PersonInfo::PersonInfo (char *name, int da, int mo, int yr)
        : obj_date (mo, da, yr) {        // Member object constructor
        strncpy( person_name, name, 30);  // Copy name to variable
}
```

When correctly implemented, the client class creates an object of the containing class, while the contained object is created transparently. Thus, the client code in the program SAM11-02.CPP instantiates objects of the class **PersonInfo**, which, in turn, has a member object of the class **Date**. **Date** handles the date element of the information. Because the date object is explicitly initialized for each **PersonInfo** object, the signature of **Date** for that object matches the corresponding object of the PersonInfo class. During program execution the birthdate for each object of the class **PersonInfo** is correctly maintained.

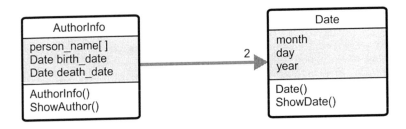

Figure 11.4 *Multiple Member Objects*

11.1.3 Multiple Member Objects

Another case of object composition is a containing class that holds several objects of a contained class. For example, suppose an **Author-Info** class that must maintain two date elements, one for the birth-date and another one for the death date, of each author. In this case the containing class can have two member objects of the contained class, as shown in Figure 11.4.

Note that in Figure 11.4 we have used the digit 2 above the member object arrow to indicate that two objects are instantiated. The following short program shows the implementation of multiple member objects:

```
//******************************************************************
// C++ program to illustrate aggregation by means of multiple
// member objects
// Filename: SAM11-03.CPP
//******************************************************************
#include <iostream.h>
#include <string.h>

//****************************
//         classes
//****************************
class Date {
private:
    int month;
    int day;
    int year;
public:
    Date (int m, int d, int y);      // Constructor
    void ShowDate ();                // A method
};
```

```
// Implementation of parameterized constructor
Date::Date(int m, int d, int y) {
    month = m;

    day = d;
    year = y;
}

// Method to display date
void Date::ShowDate() {
    cout << month << "  " << day << "  " << year;
}
class AuthorInfo {
private:
    char author_name[30];      // Storage for name array
    Date birth_date;           // Two member objects declared
    Date death_date;
public:
    AuthorInfo(char *name, int bmo, int bda, int byr,
            int dmo, int dda, int dyr);  // Constructor
    void ShowAuthor();              // A method
};

// Implementation of parameterized constructor must also
// initialize member object
AuthorInfo::AuthorInfo (char *name, int bda, int bmo, int byr,
                    int dda, int dmo, int dyr)
        : birth_date (bmo, bda, byr),
        death_date (dmo, dda, dyr) {    // Member objects
constructors
        strncpy( author_name, name, 30);   // Copy name to variable
}

// ShowAuthor method displays name and calls method ShowDate()
// in the Date class
void AuthorInfo::ShowAuthor() {
    cout << "\n" << author_name;
    cout << "  birth date: ";
    birth_date.ShowDate();
    cout << "  death date: ";
    death_date.ShowDate();
}

//****************************
//          main()
//****************************
main() {
// Declare objects of PersonInfo class
  AuthorInfo author1("John Jones", 12, 11, 1862, 11, 1, 1904);
  AuthorInfo author2("Mary Riley", 3, 9, 1856, 12, 1, 1900);
  cout << "\n\n";

// Access method ShowAuthor in AuthorInfo class
  author1.ShowAuthor();
```

```
author2.ShowAuthor();
return 0;
}
```

Member objects are generated at run time, while class associations are defined at compile time. In this sample program, client code can determine the number of objects and attributes of the containing class, but not which objects are associated with the containing class. It is this feature which allows us to classify the relationship as one of aggregation, not one of acquaintance.

11.1.4 Aggregation by Instantiated Objects

In the preceding sections we saw how a class can contain a member object, and how code instantiates a copy of the member object for each object of the containing class. Thus, in the sample program SAM11-02.CPP there is a date object instantiated for the individual named John Smith, and another one for the individual named Mary Riley. The code automatically keeps track of the object associations since the member object constructor is called by the constructor of the containing class. This determines that the date object created for John Smith is always associated with the John Smith object and will never be confused with the date object of another individual. Furthermore, the program SAM11-03.CPP shows how we can instantiate multiple objects of the same base class and how code keeps track of the object-to-object associations. Both options provide a powerful and versatile mechanism for associating objects and, therefore, classes.

On the other hand, SAM11-01.CPP shows the instantiation of an object of another class within a class member function. Note that this case is different from that of a member object. In SAM11-01.CPP the same object is created for every object of the containing class. Although this mechanism provides a simple and sometimes attractive alternative to object aggregation, it has limitations and restrictions. Figure 11.5 represents the object associations in each case:

Note that in Figure 11.5 the member object method creates a separate **Date** object for each instance of the **PersonInfo** class. Instantiation within the class code reuses the same object of the contained class for each object of the containing one. The following program implements a class named **Copyright** which prints the same copyright notice for every object of another class named **project**:

MULTIPLE INSTANTIATION OF MEMBER OBJECTS

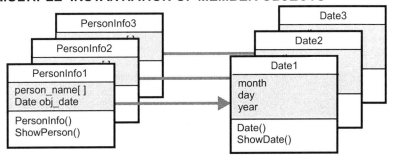

MULTIPLE USE OF THE SAME OBJECT

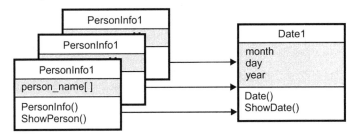

Figure 11.5 *Comparing Member Objects and Object Instantiation*

```
//*******************************************************************
// C++ program to illustrate aggregation by means of multiple
// instantiated objects
// Filename: SAM11-04.CPP
//*******************************************************************
#include <iostream.h>
#include <string.h>

//****************************
//          classes
//****************************
class Copyright{
public:
    void ShowNotice();                  // A method
};
// Implementation of ShowNotice() method
void Copyright::ShowNotice() {
    cout << " - Copyright 1997 by Skipanon Software\n";
}

class Project{
private:
```

```
   char project_name[30];          // Storage for name array
public:
   Project (char *name);           // Constructor
   void ShowProject();             // A method
};

// Implementation of parameterized constructor
Project::Project (char *name) {
     strncpy( project_name, name, 30);   // Copy name to variable
}

// ShowProject method instantiates an object of the class
// Copyright
void Project::ShowProject() {
   Copyright an_obj;
   cout << "\n" << project_name;
   an_obj.ShowNotice();
}

//****************************
//           main()
//****************************
main() {
// Declare objects of PersonInfo class
  Project software1("SAT Program");
  Project software2("Editor Program");
  cout << "\n\n";
// Access method ShowProject() in Project class
  software1.ShowProject();
  software2.ShowProject();
  return 0;
}
```

Which implementation variation is adequate depends on the case at hand. If we need a single copy of the same object, then multiple instantiation by means of member objects would be wasteful, even if we could make it execute the desired operation. On the other hand, if we need to create objects with different attributes for each object of the containing class, then we can use the member object construct.

11.1.5 Aggregation by Pointers

We can also access the contained class by means of a pointer. For example, we could modify the **ShowProject** method of the program SAM11-04.CPP in order to create and initialize a pointer to an object of the class **Copyright** and then access the **ShowNotice** method by means of this pointer, as shown in the following code fragment:

```
void Project::ShowProject() {
    Copyright an_obj;            // An object of class copyright
    Copyright *obj_ptr;          // A pointer to class
    obj_ptr = &an_obj;           // Pointer is set to object
    cout << "\n" << project_name;
    obj_ptr->ShowNotice();       // Access method through pointer
}
```

The use of pointer variables is often indicated in implementing acquaintance relationships, although it is possible to construe circumstances that may advise their use in cases of aggregation. Class pointers and dynamic method selection is discussed later in the chapter.

11.2 Acquaintance Constructs

Acquaintance implies a dynamic class association. In the case of acquaintance a class *knows of* other classes but is not directly bound to any particular one. For example, suppose that a class **Window** could be rectangular, triangular, or circular in shape. Figure 11.6 shows a possible object composition in this case.

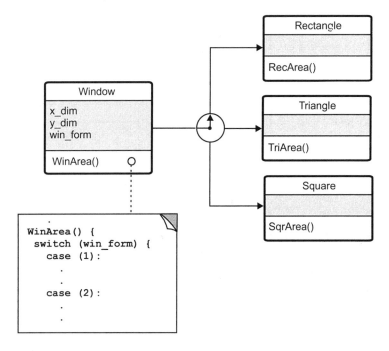

Figure 11.6 *Model of a Class Acquaintance Association*

In Figure 11.6 there is a data member of the **Window** class named **win_form**. The **win_form** attribute encodes if the window is rectangular, triangular, or circular. The clock-like diagram component, which intercepts the instantiation line, indicates that a pointer is resolved either to the class **Rectangle**, **Triangle**, or **Circle**.

11.2.1 Acquaintance by Member Objects

The notion of an acquaintance association can be implemented in several ways. One option is to use member objects, with one selected at run time. Figure 11.7 is a variation of Figure 11.6 in which the class **Window** contains member objects of the classes **Rectangle**, **Triangle**, and **Square**.

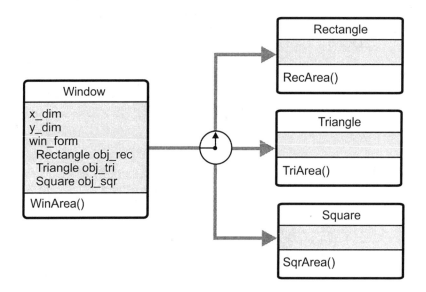

Figure 11.7 *Example of Class Acquaintance by Member Objects*

The following program shows this form of implementing acquaintance as modeled in Figure 11.7:

```
//********************************************************************
// C++ program to illustrate acquaintance by means of dynamic
// selection of a member object
// Filename: SAM11-05.CPP
//********************************************************************
```

```
#include <iostream.h>
//***************************
//        classes
//***************************
class Rectangle {
public:
   int RecArea(int height, int width) {
   return height * width;
   }
};
class Triangle {
public:
   int TriArea(int height, int width) {
   return ((height * width) /2);
   }
};

class Square {
public:
   int SqrArea(int side) {
   return side * side;
   }
};

class Window {
private:
   int x_dim;                     // Window dimensions
   int y_dim;
   int win_form;                  // Window form code:
                        // 1 = rectangle, 2 = triangle
                        // 3 = circle
   Rectangle  obj_rect;           // Member objects
   Triangle   obj_tria;
   Square     obj_sqr;
public:
   Window (int, int, int);        // Constructor declaration
   int WinArea();                 // Area method declaration
};

// Implementation of parameterized constructor
Window :: Window (int dim1, int dim2, int form ) {
   x_dim = dim1; y_dim = dim2, win_form = form;
   }

// Implementation of method to calculate window area
int Window :: WinArea() {
int area;

// Contingency code to select an area calculation object
switch (win_form) {
  case (1):
    area = obj_rect.RecArea(x_dim, y_dim);
    break;
```

```
  case (2):
    area =obj_tria.TriArea(x_dim, y_dim);
    break;
  case (3):
    area = obj_sqr.SqrArea(x_dim);
    break;
  }
  return area;
}
//****************************
//          main()
//****************************
main() {
  Window obj1(2, 4, 1);       // A rectangular window
  Window obj2(3, 5, 2);       // A triangular window
  Window obj3(4, 0, 3);       // A square window
//                  -  -  -
//                  |  |  |_____ window form code:
//                  |  |         1 = rectangular, 2 = triangular
//                  |  |         3 = circular
//                  |  |_____ second window dimension
//                  |_____ first window dimension
// Calculating and displaying area of Window-type objects
  cout << "\n\nArea of obj1: ";
  cout << obj1.WinArea();
  cout << "\nArea of obj2: ";
  cout << obj2.WinArea();
  cout << "\nArea of obj3: ";
  cout << obj3.WinArea();
  return 0;

}
```

11.2.2 Acquaintance by Object Instantiation

The program SAM11-05.CPP can be modified so that instead of maintaining three member objects, the required objects are instantiated inside the **WinArea()** method. In this case there is little difference between both methods of achieving an acquaintance relationship. The following code fragment shows the modification to the **Win-Area()** method:

```
// Implementation of method to calculate window area
int Window :: WinArea() {
  int area;
  Rectangle   obj_rect;    // Objects instantiated
  Triangle    obj_tria;
  Square      obj_sqr;
// Contingency code to select an area calculation object
switch (win_form) {
  case (1):
```

```
    area = obj_rect.RecArea(x_dim, y_dim);
    break;
  case (2):
    area =obj_tria.TriArea(x_dim, y_dim);
    break;
  case (3):
    area = obj_sqr.SqrArea(x_dim);
    break;
  }
  return area;
}
```

Note that code can instantiate the required objects anywhere, as long as their scope includes the block in which they are referenced. An alternative solution, which may be valid in some cases, is to instantiate the objects globally, thus making them visible to all program elements. The **WinArea()** procedure would then be coded as follows:

```
// Object are declared globally
  Rectangle    obj_rect;    // Objects instantiated
  Triangle     obj_tria;
  Square       obj_sqr;
// Implementation of method to calculate window area
int Window :: WinArea() {
  int area;
// Contingency code to select an area calculation object
switch (win_form) {
  case (1):
    area = obj_rect.RecArea(x_dim, y_dim);
    break;
  case (2):
    area =obj_tria.TriArea(x_dim, y_dim);
    break;
  case (3):
    area = obj_sqr.SqrArea(x_dim);
    break;
  }
  return area;
}
```

11.2.3 Acquaintance by Class Pointers

The class acquaintance relationship can also be implemented by means of pointers to classes. Although the term "pointer to class" is commonly used in this context, classes have no existence as a memory entity. A class pointer actually refers to a pointer to an object of a class. This clarified, we will continue to use the term *pointer to class* since it is the more conventional designation in this case. Figure 11.8 shows a class diagram representing acquaintance by class pointers.

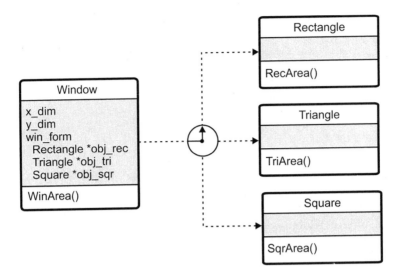

Figure 11.8 *Acquaintance by Pointers to Classes*

In the following program we demonstrate how to achieve acquaintance by means of pointers to classes:

```
//*********************************************************************
// C++ program to illustrate acquaintance by means of pointers
// to classes
// Filename: SAM11-06.CPP
//*********************************************************************
#include <iostream.h>
//***************************
//        classes
//***************************
class Rectangle {
public:
    int RectArea(int height, int width) {
    return height * width;
    }
};
class Triangle {
public:
    int TriaArea(int height, int width) {
    return ((height * width) /2);
    }
};
class Square {
public:
    int SqrArea(int side) {
    return side * side;
    }
```

```
   };
   class Window {
   private:
      int x_dim;                    // Window dimensions
      int y_dim;
      int win_form;                 // Window form code:
                      // 1 = rectangle, 2 = triangle
                      // 3 = circle
      Rectangle   *obj_rec;         // Pointers to classes
      Triangle    *obj_tri;
      Square      *obj_sqr;
   public:
      Window (int, int, int);       // Constructor declaration
      int WinArea();                // Area method declaration
   };

   // Implementation of parameterized constructor
   Window :: Window (int dim1, int dim2, int form ) {
      x_dim = dim1; y_dim = dim2, win_form = form;
      }

   // Implementation of method to calculate window area
   int Window :: WinArea() {
      int area;
   // Contingency code to select an area calculation object
   switch (win_form) {
     case (1):
       area = obj_rec->RectArea(x_dim, y_dim);
       break;
     case (2):
       area = obj_tri->TriaArea(x_dim, y_dim);
       break;
     case (3):
       area = obj_sqr->SqrArea(x_dim);
       break;
     }
     return area;
   }

   //****************************
   //           main()
   //****************************
   main() {
      Window obj1(2, 4, 1);         // A rectangular window
      Window obj2(3, 5, 2);         // A triangular window
      Window obj3(4, 0, 3);         // A square window
   //                 -  -  -
   //                 |  |  |_____ window form code:
   //                 |  |          1 = rectangular, 2 = triangular
   //                 |  |          3 = circular
   //                 |  |_____ second window dimension
   //                 |_____ first window dimension
```

```
// Calculating and displaying area of Window-type objects

    cout << "\n\nArea of obj1: ";
    cout << obj1.WinArea();
    cout << "\nArea of obj2: ";
    cout << obj2.WinArea();
    cout << "\nArea of obj3: ";
    cout << obj3.WinArea();

    return 0;
}
```

There is some debate regarding when to use instantiation and when to use class pointers in implementing object composition. Instantiation, by definition, produces an object of the target class. Creating a pointer, on the other hand, does not commit to instantiating an object. Thus, when an object is a data member of the containing class, it is automatically instantiated when an object of the class is created. However, when the data member is a class pointer, then all that is created is a pointer variable.

It is important to know *where* in the code is the class pointer referenced, and whether the constructor of the containing class participates in creating an object of the contained class. Three general cases:

1. The class pointer is defined as a data member of the containing class. Consequently, every time an object is instantiated, a corresponding class pointer is created for that object. Sometimes the pointer is filled by the class constructor; other times it is filled by class methods, by a method of another class, or even by client code. Since the scope and visibility of the pointer depend on its definition as a private, public, or protected data member of the containing class, there are some restrictions on accessibility.

2. The class pointer is defined inside a method. In this case the pointer is created when the method executes. The scope of this pointer is the scope of the method that contains it and its visibility is restricted to the method.

3. The class pointer is defined globally. In this case it is visible to all methods, to functions, and to client code.

The following are general guidelines on when to use object instantiation and when to use a class pointer.

1. If the contained class has a default constructor then use instantiation.

2. When the contained class has no default constructor or when the constructor of the containing class creates the objects, then use a class pointer.

Note that C++ does not provide a mechanism for implementing run-time pointer selection when object composition is equivalent to dynamic polymorphism in class inheritance. Although some class diagrams (such as Figure 11.8) seem to suggest that a generic pointer is resolved to one of the three target classes at run time, this is not really the case. The only way of implementing the object association shown in Figure 11.7, or the pointer to classes in Figure 11.8, is to have a pointer to each one of the participating classes and contingency code that selects the corresponding one. In Section 11.4 we investigate the possibility of combining inheritance and object composition to dynamically bind contained methods and classes.

11.3 Preserving Encapsulation

The program SAM11-02.CPP has an interesting feature: the selection of the corresponding method is made transparently to the client. Figure 11.9 presents the client's view of the acquaintance association in Figure 11.6.

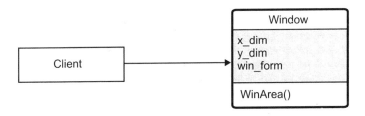

Figure 11.9 *Client's View of Class Acquaintance Association*

Referring to Figure 11.6, we note that the client's view (in Figure 11.9) does not see the classes that are used in object composition. In this case the class named **Window** provides the interface and hides all implementation details. In inheritance this is often not the case. If we use run-time polymorphism, the polymorphic class structure can be hidden from the client, but all other methods must be made visible. For example, in Figure 10.11 the client must see at least one of the derived classes in order to access the nonvirtual functions of the library. If the nonvirtual functions are moved to a concrete class, then that class must be visible to the client. In the program SAM10-06.CPP we see that it is the client's responsibility to provide contingency code to operate the selection mechanism, as reproduced in the following code fragment:

```
// Set pointer to selected mode
  current_mode = obj_112H.GetVesaMode();
  switch (current_mode)
{
  case 0x112:
    base_ptr = &obj_112H;
    break;
  case 0x115:
    base_ptr = &obj_115H;
    break;
  case 0x118:
    base_ptr = &obj_118H;
    break;
  case 0x11b:
    base_ptr = &obj_11bH;
    break;
}
```

Elements of the class structure are revealed to the client, who must have knowledge of at least some derived classes in order to create the corresponding objects and set the pointer variable as required. This fact has led some authors (Gamma et al.) to state that reuse by subclassing (inheritance) breaks encapsulation, and that the subclasses become so tightly linked to the parent class that changes in either element propagate over the entire class structure. Object composition, on the other hand, preserves encapsulation and hides implementation details from the client, who only sees a functionality black box that hides most implementation specifics.

The preferred approach, object composition or class inheritance, depends on the problem to be solved. Composition is a good choice when one class is-a-part-of, has, or uses another class. Inheritance models a relationship in which one class is a-kind-of another class. Nevertheless, some problems can be modeled using either approach. For example, we can consider that a stack *is a special kind* of list, or that a stack *contains* a list. Either visualization is viable and can be satisfactorily used as a model.

How we wish to implement the necessary functionality is often the deciding factor of whether to model a problem in terms of object composition or in terms of class inheritance. For run-time polymorphism use inheritance, since there is no mechanism in C++ to dynamically implement object composition. However, inheritance often requires uncovering some elements of the underlying class structure to the client. Composition hides more implementation details and helps keep classes focused on a single task. Class hierarchies remain manageable, although there are usually more objects to handle.

Object composition has no provision for creating generic pointers resolved at run time. Some forms of polymorphic inheritance allow method selection at run time by means of a pointer to the base class. The inheritance mechanism adds great flexibility to the model. One specific advantage is that the program can respond to events that take place during its execution without having to provide a great amount of contingency code.

A subtle distinction is that in dynamic polymorphic inheritance, method selection takes place at run time, but the actual inheritance structure is defined at compile time. Object composition, on the other hand, is defined when the objects are created, which always must be at run time; although, in object composition, method selection takes place at compile time. In other words, in inheritance, class associations are early-bound, and methods are late-bound. In object composition the class structure is late-bound, but method selection is early-bound.

11.4 Combining Inheritance and Composition

Combining inheritance and object composition is the best solution to many programming problems. Object composition is used to hide implementation details and to create code in which processing decisions take place at run time; polymorphic inheritance allows dynamic method selection without a great amount of contingency code.

Reconsidering the problem depicted in Figure 11.3 and its implementation in the program SAM11-02.CPP, we note that its principal drawback is that the selection mechanism, although neatly shown in the diagram, must be implemented by means of contingency code, and that this code executes on every iteration of the method that calculates the area. However, we can redefine the classes and redesign the class structure so that dynamic, polymorphic inheritance is used to set a pointer variable that selects the area calculation method appropriate for each object. Figure 11.10 shows one possible approach.

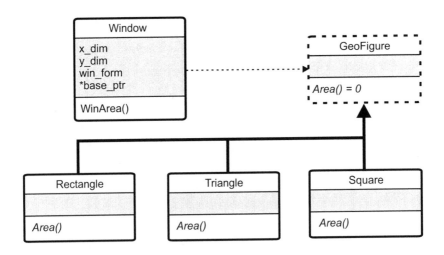

Figure 11.10 *Combining Inheritance and Object Composition*

The following program shows the combined use of inheritance and object composition:

```
//*****************************************************************
// C++ program to illustrate combining object composition and
// class inheritance
// Filename: SAM11-07.CPP
//*****************************************************************
 #include <iostream.h>

//***************************
//        classes
//***************************
// Base class
class GeoFigure {
public:
    virtual int Area(int dim1, int dim2) = 0;
};

// Classes derived from GeoFigure
class Rectangle : public GeoFigure {
public:
    virtual int Area(int height, int width) {
    cout << "\nUsing Rectangle::Area() = ";
```

```
      return height * width;
      }
};

class Triangle : public GeoFigure{
public:
    virtual int Area(int height, int width) {
    cout << "\nUsing Triangle::Area() = ";
    return ((height * width) /2);
    }
};

class Square : public GeoFigure{
public:
    virtual int Area(int side, int dummy) {
    cout << "\nUsing Square::Area() = ";
    return side * side;
    }
};

// Classes outside of the inheritance path
class Window {
private:
    int x_dim;                    // Window dimensions
    int y_dim;
    int win_form;                 // Window form code:
                      // 1 = rectangle, 2 = triangle
                      // 3 = circle
    Rectangle rec_obj;            // Member objects
    Triangle  tri_obj;
    Square    sqr_obj;
    GeoFigure *base_ptr;          // Pointer to base class
public:
    Window (int, int, int);       // Constructor declaration
    int WinArea();                // Area method declaration
};
 // Implementation of parameterized constructor
Window :: Window (int dim1, int dim2, int form ) {
    x_dim = dim1; y_dim = dim2, win_form = form;
// Selection of class::method is performed by the constructor
// and stored in the base_ptr attribute
  switch (win_form) {
    case (1):
      base_ptr = &rec_obj;
      break;
    case (2):
      base_ptr = &tri_obj;
      break;
    case (3):
      base_ptr = &sqr_obj;
      break;
  }
};
```

```
// WinArea method finds the correct method using the pointer
// contained in each object
int Window :: WinArea() {
   return (base_ptr-> Area(x_dim, y_dim));
};


//****************************
//           main()
//****************************
main() {
// Three objects of type Window
   Window obj1(2, 4, 1);      // A rectangular window
   Window obj2(3, 5, 2);      // A triangular window
   Window obj3(4, 0, 3);      // A square window
//                -  -  -
//                |  |  |_____ window form code:
//                |  |        1 = rectangular, 2 = triangular
//                |  |        3 = circular
//                |  |_____ second window dimension
//                |_____ first window dimension
// Calculating and displaying the area of Window-type objects
   cout << "\n\nArea of obj1: ";
   cout << obj1.WinArea();
   cout << "\nArea of obj2: ";
   cout << obj2.WinArea();
   cout << "\nArea of obj3: ";
   cout << obj3.WinArea();
   return 0;
}
```

The program SAM11-07.CPP requires some explanations. Note that it is an improvement of SAM11-05.CPP, in which contingency code contained in a switch construct executes on every iteration of the method that calculates the window's area. The new approach attempts to solve this problem by inspecting the object at the time it is constructed, and storing a pointer to the method that is adequate for calculating its area according to the window's type. If the window is rectangular, then a pointer to the **Area()** method of the **Rectangle** class is stored; if it is triangular, then a pointer to the **Area()** method of the **Triangle** class is stored, and similarly if the window is square. The pointer then becomes bound to the object, so that each object is constructed *knowing* how to calculate its own area. The constructor performs this selection as follows:

```
// Selection of class::method is performed by the constructor
// and stored in the base_ptr attribute
   switch (win_form) {
     case (1):
       base_ptr = &rec_obj;
       break;
```

```
   case (2):
     base_ptr = &tri_obj;
     break;
   case (3):
     base_ptr = &sqr_obj;
     break;
 }
};
```

To make this work at run time we had to introduce changes in the code and create new variables. The first major modification was to rename the area-calculating methods in the classes **Rectangle**, **Triangle**, and **Square**; now they have a common name, **Area()**. In this process we also had to modify the interface of the area-calculating method in the class **Square** to match the polymorphic methods in the **Rectangle** and **Triangle** classes. Then we had to create an abstract class, which we called **GeoFigure**. The **GeoFigure** class has a pure virtual function named **Area()**. Since the classes **Rectangle**, **Triangle**, and **Square** are derived from **GeoFigure**, we have created an inheritance hierarchy.

In order to implement dynamic binding with the preceding class hierarchy we created a pointer to the base class, as follows:

```
GeoFigure    *base_ptr;
```

The pointer is a private data member of the class **Window**, making it visible to the **Window** method but not outside the class. Also as data members of the **Window** class, we created objects of the three derived classes, as follows:

```
Rectangle rec_obj;           // Member objects
Triangle  tri_obj;
Square    sqr_obj;
```

Note that we need not create an object of the base class **GeoFigure** since there can be no implementation for the **Area()** method in the abstract class. Equipped with these objects and the pointer variables, the constructor for the **Window** class is now able to select a value for the pointer according to the form of the window. Also, the **WinArea()** method is able to calculate the area of each Window-type object by dereferencing the pointer kept for each object. The entire processing is performed in a single code line, as follows:

```
int Window :: WinArea() {
   return (base_ptr-> Area(x_dim, y_dim));
};
```

11.5 Dynamic Object Allocation

A class is a user-defined data type and an object is an instance of a class. Therefore, the object is to the class as a variable is to a built-in data type. This similarity is shown in the respective declaration of variables and objects:

```
int      var_1;          // var_1 is a variable of type int
ClassA   obj_a;          // obj_a is an instance of ClassA
```

However, C++ does not provide a mechanism for creating *named variables* or *named objects* at run time. We cannot request that the user input a character string and then create a variable (or an object) that can be referenced by its name. Data objects can be created by the programmer, but these objects must be accessed by means of their address, which is stored in a pointer variable. Pointer variables can be scalars or vectors.

11.5.1 Allocating Single Objects

Because data objects created dynamically have no name, access to these entities must be through a pointer that holds their address. In C++ the *new* operator is used in dynamically allocating data objects from the free store area. **New** returns the address of the allocated storage, usually stored in a pointer of vector (array) or scalar type. For example:

```
#include <iostream.h>
main() {
    int   *dyn_array;        // Pointer to array of int type
    static int SIZE = 5;     // Constant for array size
    dyn_array = new int[SIZE]; // Array is created in free store
for(int x = 0; x < 5; x++) {
  dyn_array[x] = x;          // Consecutive integers are stored
  }                          // in array
  cout << "\nvalues in array:";
for(x = 0; x < 5; x++) {     // Array is displayed
    cout << dyn_array[x];
    cout << " ";
    }
  delete [] dyn_array;       // Array is deleted
return 0;
}
```

We can create and initialize an object of a class in the same way that we can allocate and initialize a vector or scalar variable at run time. The general format for allocating an object with the new operator is shown in the following fragment:

```
DemoA        *ptr_var;        // Declare pointer to class
ptr_var = new DemoA;          // Pointer initialized to new object
```

Hereafter, the dynamically created object of the class **DemoA** can be accessed by means of the pointer. For example, if there is a method named **MethodA()** in this class, we can code:

```
ptr_var.MethodA();
```

Note again that a dynamically created object is nameless and that access to this object must be by means of a pointer. Also observe that dynamically allocated objects can have constructors and destructors, which can be parameterless or parameterized. With constructors, the object can be initialized at the time it is created. Parameters are enclosed in parenthesis in the conventional manner. The following short program shows dynamic object creation using a parameterized constructor:

```
//********************************************************************
// C++ program to illustrate dynamic allocation of individual
// objects
// Filename: SAM11-08.CPP
//********************************************************************
#include <iostream.h>

//****************************
//         classes
//****************************
class Rectangle {
private:
  int width;
  int height;
public:
// Method ShowArea() is expanded in line
  void ShowArea() {
  cout << "Area is: "
       << width * height;
  }

// Parameterized constructor
  Rectangle (int x, int y) {
  width = x;
  height = y;
  }
};
```

```
//****************************
//            main()
//****************************
main() {
   Rectangle   *ptr_rec;        // Pointer to rectangle
   ptr_rec = new Rectangle(10, 12);  // Object created and
initialized
   ptr_rec->ShowArea();              // Method accessed using object
   return 0;

}
```

11.5.2 Allocating an Object Array

In a manner similar to the one used to create a single object at run time, we can create an array of objects. However, it is impossible to initialize an array allocated at run time; therefore, in the case of an array of objects allocated dynamically, the class can have no parameterized constructors. The following short fragment shows the code elements that participate in the dynamic allocation of an array of objects. Code assumes that there is a class called BaseA.

```
BaseA   *array_ptr;
static int SIZE = 5;
array_ptr = new BaseA[SIZE];    // Array of objects is created
```

At this point an array of five objects of the class **BaseA** has been created and the variable **array_ptr** is a pointer to the address of the first object. Pointer arithmetic is valid for arrays of objects; therefore, code can use all the operations that are legal for conventional arrays. The address of the corresponding object is what is stored in the array. The following program shows the processing operations for allocating, initializing, and accessing an array of objects:

```
//******************************************************************
// C++ program to illustrate dynamic allocation of an array
// of objects
// Filename: SAM11-09.CPP
//******************************************************************
#include <iostream.h>

//****************************
//         classes
//****************************
class Demo1 {
public:
   void ShowMsg() { cout << "Hello there \n"; }
};
```

```
//****************************
//          main()
//****************************
main() {
    Demo1   obj_d;          // An object of class Demo1
    Demo1   *obj_ptr;       // A pointer to objects of class Demo1
    static int SIZE = 5;    // Size of array
    obj_ptr = new Demo1[SIZE];    // Array of objects is created
// Initialize object array to 5 copies of an object of class Demo1
for(int x = 0; x < SIZE; x++)   {
  obj_ptr[x] = obj_d;
  }

// Access method ShowMsg() using stored objects
    cout << "\nExecuting method ShowMsg(): \n";
 for(x = 0; x < SIZE; x++) {
    cout << "object No. " << x << "      ";
    obj_ptr[x].ShowMsg();
    }
    delete [] obj_ptr;          // Array of objects is deallocated
 return 0;
}
```

In the program SAM11-09.CPP, previously listed, the special syntax used with the **delete** operator for deleting dynamically allocated arrays also applies to arrays of objects.

The program SAM11-09.CPP shows one possible manipulation in the dynamic allocation of an array of objects, but many variations of implementation are also legal and occasionally useful. For example, code can define and allocate an object array statically and then dynamically create and store objects in this array. Or both array and objects can be allocated dynamically. The following program shows the static allocation of an object array initialized with dynamically allocated objects.

```
//*********************************************************************
// C++ program to illustrate static allocation of an array
// of objects initialized with dynamically allocated objects
// Filename: SAM11-10.CPP
//*********************************************************************
#include <iostream.h>

//****************************
//          classes
//****************************
class Demo1 {
public:
  void ShowMsg() { cout << "Hello there \n"; }
};
```

```
//****************************
//            main()
//****************************
main() {
   Demo1   *ptr_array[5];    // Static array of objects
   static int SIZE = 5;
// Initialize object array to 5 copies of a dynamically allocated
// object of the class Demo1
for(int x = 0; x < SIZE; x++)   {
  ptr_array[x] = new Demo1;
  }
// Access method ShowMsg() using a pointer to the stored objects
  cout << "\nExecuting method ShowMsg(): \n";
for(x = 0; x < SIZE; x++) {
  cout << "object No. " << x << "     ";
  ptr_array[x]->ShowMsg();
  }
   return 0;
}
```

In Section 12.8 and those following we discuss several applications of pointers to objects and list programs that implement dynamic allocation of object arrays.

11.5.3 Pointers to Pointers to Objects

Occasionally we may need to associate several arrays of objects so that they can be accessed as a unit. Since multiple indirection is also valid with arrays we can implement this association of arrays of objects by means of an array of pointers to pointers to objects. An example program that uses pointers to pointers to objects is listed in Section 12.10 in the context of object factories.

Chapter 12

Class Patterns and Templates

12.0 Introduction to Design Patterns

Engineers and architects have reused design elements for many years; however, the notion of reusing elements of software design dates back only to the beginning of the decade. The work of Coplien, Anderson, and Beck set the background for the book *Design Patterns* by Gamma, Helm, Johnson, and Vlissides, which many considered the first comprehensive work on the subject.

The main justification for reusing program design components is based in the fact that the design stage is one of the most laborious and time-consuming phases of program development. Design reuse is founded in the assumption that once a programmer or programming group has found a class or object structure that solves a particular design problem, this pattern can then be reused in other projects, with considerable savings in the design effort. Anyone who has participated in the development of a substantial software project will appreciate the advantages of reusing program design components.

The present-day approach to design reuse is based on a model of class associations and relationships called a *class pattern* or an *object model*. In this sense, a pattern is a solution to a design problem, therefore, a programming problem is at the origin of every pattern. From this assumption we deduce that a pattern must offer a viable solution: it must represent a class structure that can be readily coded in the language of choice. The fact that a programming problem is at the root of every design pattern, and the assumption that the solution offered by a particular pattern must be readily implementable in code, is the premise on which we base our approach to this topic. In the context of this book we see a design pattern as consisting of two core elements: a class diagram and a coded example or template, fully implemented in C++ code. Every working programmer knows how to take a piece of sample code and tailor it to solve the problem at hand. However, snippets of code that may or may not compile correctly are more a tease than a real aid.

Although we consider that design patterns are a reasonable and practical methodology, we must add that it is the patterns that we ourselves create, refine, or adapt that are most useful. It is difficult to believe that we can design and code a program based on someone else's class diagrams. Program design and coding is a task too elaborate and complicated to be done by imitation or proxy. A programmer must gain intimate familiarity with a particular class and object structure before committing to its adoption in a project. These thoughts lead to the conclusion that it is more important to explain how we can develop our own design patterns than to offer an extensive catalog of someone's class diagrams, which are usually difficult to understand, and even more difficult to apply in practice.

The discussion of design patterns assumes that the reader is already familiar with the class constructs used in inheritance and object composition, topics of Chapters 9, 10, and 11.

12.0.1 Class Templates

Occasionally, a programmer or program designer's need is not for a structure of communicating and interacting classes but for a description of the implementation of a specific functionality within a single class. In this case we can speak of a *class template* rather than of a pattern. The purpose of a class template is also to foster reusability, in this case by providing a specific guide for solving a particular implementation problem. In this chapter we also include several class templates which we think could be useful to the practicing developer.

12.1 A Pattern is Born

We begin our discussion by following through the development of a design pattern, from the original problem, through a possible solution, to its implementation in code, and concluding in a general-purpose class diagram.

One of the most obvious and frequent uses of dynamic polymorphism is in the implementation of class libraries. The simplest usable architecture, discussed in Section 10.2.1, is by means of an abstract class and several modules in the form of derived classes which provide the specific implementations of the library's functionality. Client code accesses a polymorphic method in the base class and the corresponding implementation is selected according to the object referenced. But in the real world a library usually consists of more than one method. Since C++ allows mixing virtual and nonvirtual functions in an abstract class, it is possible to include nonvirtual methods along with virtual and pure virtual ones. The problem in this case is that abstract classes cannot be instantiated; therefore, client code cannot create an object through which it can access the nonvirtual methods in the base class. A possible, but not very effective, solution is to use one of the derived classes to access the nonvirtual methods in the base class. Figure 12.1 depicts this situation.

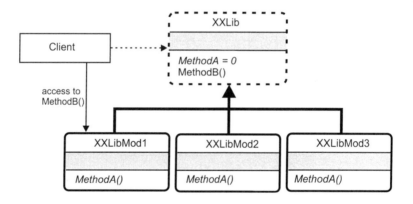

Figure 12.1 *A Class Library Implemented through Dynamic Polymorphism*

The first problem of the class diagram in Figure 12.1 is that client code accesses the nonvirtual **MethodB()** in the base class by means of a pointer to one of the derived classes. A second, and perhaps more important one, is that method selection must take place in the client's code. Both of these characteristics expose the class structure and add a substantial processing burden to the client.

There are several possible solutions to the first problem. We could make the base class a concrete class with **MethodA()** as a simple virtual function, with no real implementation. In this case **MethodB()** becomes immediately accessible. Another solution would be to create a new class to hold the nonvirtual methods originally in the base class and have this new class inherit abstractly from XXLib. However, neither of these solutions addresses the most important problem, which is that client code must perform method selection. It is this characteristic of inheritance that breaks encapsulation.

We can preserve encapsulation by using object composition instead of inheritance. Also, combining object composition and inheritance achieves dynamic binding of polymorphic methods while preserving encapsulation. Figure 12.2 is a possible class diagram for implementing the library by means of object composition and inheritance.

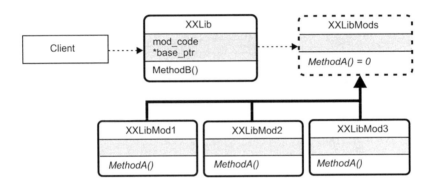

Figure 12.2 *An Alternative Implementation of the Class Library*

12.1.1 Redesign of the VESA True Color Library

In Section 10.2 we considered the design and implementation of a VESA true color graphics library by means of class inheritance. The solution offered in the program SAM10-06.CPP has the shortcomings mentioned in Section 12.1, namely: that the inheritance structure must be made visible to client code, and that the burden of method selection is left to the client. An alternative design for the VESA true color graphics library can be based on combining object composition and class inheritance. The adaptation requires reorganization of the methods and creation of a new class. The minimal functionality of the library was originally stated as follows:

1. A way of setting the desired VESA true color mode

2. A way of obtaining the current VESA mode as well as the vertical and horizontal resolution

3. A way of drawing a screen pixel defined in terms of its x and y screen coordinates and its color attribute

4. A way of reading the color attribute of a screen pixel located at given screen coordinates

Figure 12.3 is a diagram of the redesigned library classes.

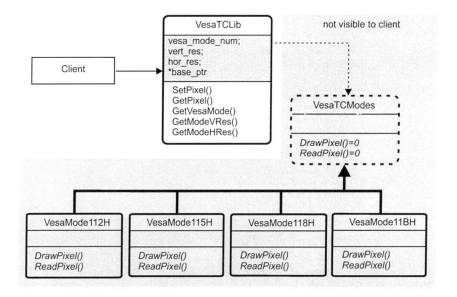

Figure 12.3 *Redesign of the VESA True Color Graphics Library*

Comparing the diagram in Figure 12.3 with the one in 10.11 we detect some changes in the class structure:

1. The nonvirtual methods originally in the class **VesaTCModes** have been moved to a new class called **VesaTCLib**.

2. **VesaTCLib** is a concrete class and can be instantiated by the client.

3. The mode-dependent, polymorphic methods for setting and reading pixels, named **DrawPixel()** and **ReadPixel()** respectively, are located in an inheritance structure.

4. Two new methods named **GetPixel()** and **SetPixel()** in the class **VesaTCLib** provide access by means of a pointer to the polymorphic methods **DrawPixel()** and **ReadPixel()**.

The result of the new design is that most of the implementation is now transparent to the client, as shown by the gray shaded background in Figure 12.3. The following program contains the schematic implementation of the class and inheritance structure in Figure 12.3:

```cpp
//*************************************************************************
// C++ program to illustrate implementation of a VESA true
// color graphics library using object composition and class
// inheritance
// Filename: SAMP12-01.CPP
//*************************************************************************
#include <iostream.h>

//*************************************************************************
//                         classes
//*************************************************************************
// Abstract base class
class VesaTCModes {
public:
// Pure virtual functions
   virtual void DrawPixel(int, int, int) = 0;
   virtual unsigned long ReadPixel(int, int) = 0;
};

//*****************************
//    Polymorphic classes
//*****************************
// Note: methods have stub implementations in this demo
//       program
class VesaMode112H : public VesaTCModes  {
public:
   virtual void DrawPixel(int row, int column, int color) {
   cout << "Setting pixel in Mode 112H\n";
   return;
   }
   virtual unsigned long ReadPixel(int row, int column) {
   cout << "Reading pixel in Mode 112H\n" ;
   return 0;
   }
};
```

```
class VesaMode115H : public VesaTCModes  {
public:
   virtual void DrawPixel(int row, int column, int color) {
   cout << "Setting pixel in Mode 115H\n";
   return;
   }
   virtual unsigned long ReadPixel(int row, int column) {
   cout << "Reading pixel in Mode 115H\n" ;
   return 0;
   }
};

class VesaMode118H : public VesaTCModes  {
public:
   virtual void DrawPixel(int row, int column, int color) {
   cout << "Setting pixel in Mode 118H\n";
   return;
   }
   virtual unsigned long ReadPixel(int row, int column) {
   cout << "Reading pixel in Mode 118H\n";
   return 0;
   }
};

class VesaMode11BH : public VesaTCModes  {
public:
   virtual void DrawPixel(int row, int column, int color) {
   cout << "Setting pixel in Mode 11BH\n";
   return;
   }
   virtual unsigned long ReadPixel(int row, int column) {
   cout << "Reading pixel in Mode 11BH\n";
   return 0;
   }
};

//***********************
//   non-virtual classes
//***********************
class VesaTCLib {
private:
   int vesa_mode_num;          // Object data
   int vert_res;
   int hor_res;
   VesaMode112H  obj_112H;     // Objects of derived classes
   VesaMode115H  obj_115H;     // required for filling pointer
   VesaMode118H  obj_118H;
   VesaMode11BH  obj_11BH;
   VesaTCModes   *base_ptr;    // Base class pointer
public:
   VesaTCLib (int);            // Constructor
// Other methods
   int GetVesaMode();
```

```
    int GetModeVRes();
    int GetModeHRes();
    void SetPixel(int, int, int);
    void GetPixel(int, int);
};


//******************************
// Methods for class VesaTCLib
//******************************
// Constructor
VesaTCLib::VesaTCLib(int vesa_mode) {
/* The constructor is passed a mode code as follows:
      1 = VESA mode 112H
      2 = VESA mode 115H
      3 = VESA mode 118H
      4 = VESA mode 11BH
According to the mode selected, code sets the definition,
VESA mode number, and a pointer to the corresponding
object of the library module.
*/
  switch (vesa_mode) {
  case (1):
      vesa_mode_num = 0x112;
      hor_res = 640;
      vert_res = 480;
      base_ptr = &obj_112H;
      break;
  case (2):
      vesa_mode_num = 0x115;
      hor_res = 800;
      vert_res = 600;
      base_ptr = &obj_115H;
      break;
  case (3):
      vesa_mode_num = 0x118;
      hor_res = 1024;
      vert_res = 768;
      base_ptr = &obj_118H;
      break;
  case (4):
      vesa_mode_num = 0x11b;
      hor_res = 1280;
      vert_res = 1024;
      base_ptr = &obj_11BH;
      break;
  default:
      vesa_mode_num = 0x0;
      hor_res = 0;
      vert_res = 0;
      base_ptr = &obj_112H;
  }
}
// Methods for reading and setting a screen pixel
```

```
void VesaTCLib::SetPixel(int row, int col, int attribute) {
  base_ptr->DrawPixel(row, col, attribute);
};

void VesaTCLib::GetPixel(int row, int col) {
  base_ptr->ReadPixel(row, col);
};

// Methods that return the mode information
int VesaTCLib::GetVesaMode() {
  return vesa_mode_num;
}
int VesaTCLib::GetModeVRes() {
  return vert_res;
}
int VesaTCLib::GetModeHRes() {
  return hor_res;

}
//*****************************************************************
//                        client code
//*****************************************************************

main() {
// Objects of class VesaTCLib
   VesaTCLib obj_1(1);          // Object and mode code
   VesaTCLib obj_2(2);
   VesaTCLib obj_3(3);
   VesaTCLib obj_4(4);

// Operations on obj_1, mode code 1
   cout << "\nVESA mode: " << hex << obj_1.GetVesaMode();
   cout << "\nHorizontal Res: " << dec << obj_1.GetModeHRes();
   cout << "\nVertical Res: " << obj_1.GetModeVRes() << "\n";
   obj_1.SetPixel(12, 18, 0xff00);
   obj_1.GetPixel(122, 133);
   cout << "\n";

// Operations on obj_2, mode code 2
   cout << "VESA mode: " << hex << obj_2.GetVesaMode();
   cout << "\nHorizontal Res: " << dec << obj_2.GetModeHRes();
   cout << "\nVertical Res: " << obj_2.GetModeVRes() << "\n";
   obj_2.SetPixel(12, 18, 0xff00);
   obj_2.GetPixel(122, 133);
   cout << "\n";

// Operations on obj_3, mode code 3
   cout << "VESA mode: " << hex << obj_3.GetVesaMode();
   cout << "\nHorizontal Res: " << dec << obj_3.GetModeHRes();
   cout << "\nVertical Res: " << obj_3.GetModeVRes() << "\n";
   obj_3.SetPixel(12, 18, 0xff00);
   obj_3.GetPixel(122, 133);
   cout << "\n";
```

```
// Operations on obj_4, mode code 4
   cout << "VESA mode: " << hex << obj_4.GetVesaMode();
   cout << "\nHorizontal Res: " << dec << obj_4.GetModeHRes();
   cout << "\nVertical Res: " << obj_4.GetModeVRes() << "\n";
   obj_4.SetPixel(12, 18, 0xff00);
   obj_4.GetPixel(122, 133);
   cout << "\n";
   return 0;
}
```

The code in SAM12-01.CPP is very similar to the one in SAM11-03.CPP; therefore, only a few comments are necessary at this time. The constructor of SAM12-01.CPP receives a code that defines the VESA true color mode requested by the caller. A switch construct stores the VESA mode number, vertical and horizontal resolution, and the address of the library methods used in setting and reading a pixel in this mode. Therefore, the contingency code executes only once, when the object is created. Thereafter, each object of the class **VesaTCLib** is associated with a particular mode and keeps the address of the method to be used in its own pixel setting and reading operations. The methods **GetPixel()** and **ReadPixel()** of the class **VesaTCLib** are the client's interface to the pixel-level primitives in the library. The actual setting and reading of a screen pixel is performed as follows:

```
void VesaTCLib::SetPixel(int row, int col, int atts) {
  base_ptr->DrawPixel(row, col, attribute);
};

void VesaTCLib::GetPixel(int row, int col) {
  base_ptr->ReadPixel(row, col);
};
```

The processing in this case is done with a smaller processing overhead. The principal advantage of the new class design and implementation can be summarized as follows:

1. Contingency code to select the corresponding mode-dependent, pixel-level primitives is now located in the constructor. Therefore, it executes only when the object is created.

2. Client code need not perform the mode selection operations, which have been transferred to the library classes.

3. Client code does not see or access the class inheritance structure since the pixel-level operations are handled transparently.

12.1.2 Developing the Pattern

In the previous sections we addressed a programming problem and found one possible solution that could be implemented in code. We also constructed a class diagram that reflects the relationships and associations of this solution in object-oriented terms. In order to make this solution easier to reuse we can eliminate all the case-specific elements from both the pattern and the coded example. Furthermore, the resulting abstraction can be given a name that provides an easy reference to the particular case.

In selecting a name for a design pattern we must carefully consider its purpose and applicability. Observe that the class structure for constructing the VESA true color library is probably applicable to many programming problems that are not related to computer graphics, or even to libraries. Its fundamental purpose is to provide an interface to an inheritance structure so that its operational details are hidden from client code. Since *interface* is too general a term, we could think of the word *concealer* in this context. For the lack of a better term we call this pattern a concealer, since its purpose is to conceal an inheritance structure so that its existence and operation are made transparent to the client. Figure 12.4 shows the concealer pattern in a more abstract form.

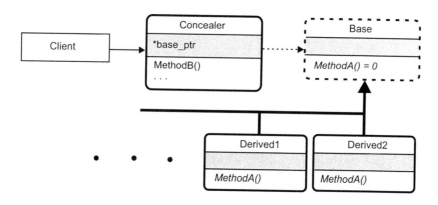

Figure 12.4 *A Concealer Pattern*

The program named SAM11-07.CPP serves as a code sample for the concealer pattern.

12.2 Unifying Dissimilar Interfaces

A simple but frequent design problem is to present a unified and friendly interface to a set of classes that perform different operations; for example, a set of classes that calculates the area of different geometrical figures, such as a parallelogram, a circle, a rectangle, and a square. The formula for the area of a parallelogram requires three parameters: the base, the side, and the included angle. The area of the circle and the square requires a single parameter, in one case the radius and in the other one the side. The area of a rectangle requires two: the length and the width. Our task is to provide the client with a single interface to the calculation of the area at any one of these four geometrical figures.

In this case the implementation could be based on the client passing four parameters. The first one is a code indicating the geometrical figure; the other three parameters hold the pertinent dimensional information. By convention, we agree that unnecessary parameters are set to NULL. The class diagram in Figure 12.5 represents one possible solution.

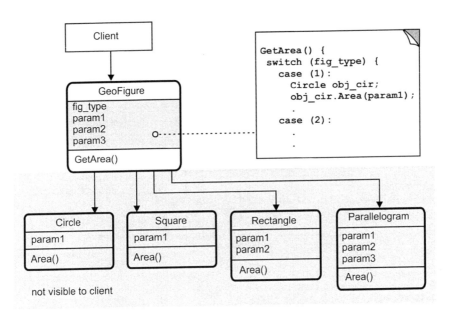

Figure 12.5 *Implementing an Interface Class*

In the case of Figure 12.5 the method selection is based on an object of the corresponding class; therefore, it is a case of object composition. An alternative implementation could easily be based on pointers instead of object instances. Program SAM12-02.CPP shows the necessary processing in the first case:

```cpp
//*****************************************************************
// C++ program to illustrate implementation of an interface
// class
// Filename: SAM12-02.CPP
//*****************************************************************
#include <iostream.h>
#include <math.h>
#define PI 3.1415

//***************************
//         classes
//***************************
//
class Circle {
public:
    float Area(float radius) {
      return (radius * radius * PI);
    }
};

class Rectangle {
public:
    float Area(float height, float width) {
      return (height * width);
    }
};

class Parallelogram {
public:
     float Area(float base, float side, float angle) {
       return (base * side * sin (angle) );
     }
};

 class Square {
public:
     float Area(float side) {
       return (side * side);
     }
};

// Interface class
class GeoFigure {
private:
  int fig_type;
  float param1;
```

```
      float param2;
      float param3;
  public:
      GeoFigure(int, float, float, float);
      void GetArea();
  };

  // Constructor
  GeoFigure::GeoFigure(int type, float data1, float data2,
                  float data3) {
      param1 = data1;
      param2 = data2;
      param3 = data3;
      fig_type = type;
  };

  // Implementation of GetArea() method
  void GeoFigure::GetArea() {
  float area;
      switch (fig_type) {
        case (1):                    // Circle
          Circle  obj_cir;
          area = obj_cir.Area(param1);
          break;
        case (2):                    // Rectangle
          Rectangle obj_rec;
          area = obj_rec.Area(param1, param2);
          break;
        case (3):                    // Parallelogram
          Parallelogram obj_par;
          area = obj_par.Area(param1, param2, param3);
          break;
        case (4):                    // Square
          Square obj_sqr;
          area = obj_sqr.Area(param1);
          break;
      }
        cout << "The area of this object is: "
          << area << "\n";
  };

  //****************************
  //          main()
  //****************************
  main() {
      GeoFigure    obj1(1, 3, NULL, NULL);     // A circle object
      GeoFigurè    obj2(2, 12, 4, NULL);       // A rectangle object
      GeoFigure    obj3(3, 12, 4, 0.7);        // A parallelogram object
      GeoFigure    obj4(4, 3, NULL, NULL);     // A square object
      cout << "\nCalculating areas of objects...\n";
  // Calculate areas
      obj1.GetArea();            // Area of circle object
      obj2.GetArea();            // Area of rectangle object
```

```
    obj3.GetArea();          // Area of parallelogram object
    obj4.GetArea();          // Area of square
    return 0;
}
```

Note that in program SAM12-02.CPP the objects are instantiated inside the switch construct in the **GetArea()** method. This ensures that only the necessary object is created in each iteration of **GetArea()**. Since the objects have local scope their lifetime expires when **GetArea()** returns. Therefore, only the necessary memory is used.

12.2.1 An Interface Pattern

By generalizing the class diagram in Figure 12.5 we can develop an interface pattern in which a class provides access to other classes that implement a certain functionality. Figure 12.6 shows this generalization.

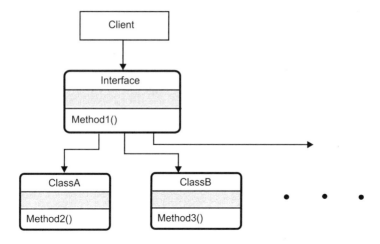

Figure 12.6 *An Interface Pattern*

12.3 Aggregated Class Hierarchies

On occasions we may need to implement a set of classes related hierarchically. For example, a program can draw geometrical figures, such as circles, squares, and triangles, where each of the figures is contained in an invisible, rectangular frame. Also assume that in this case the figure and its containing frame are so related that the creating of a figure (circle, rectangle, or triangle) mandates the creation of its container frame.

A library of figure-drawing primitives could be provided by means of four classes: three to create the circle, square, and triangle figures, and one to generate the containing frame. The client would create an object of the corresponding figure and then one of the frame. Alternatively, figure-drawing classes could be linked to the frame generation class so that for each figure a corresponding frame object would be automatically created. With this approach, the frame generation operation is transparent to the client and programming is simplified.

We can add complications to the preceding example without altering its validity. For instance, we can assume that each frame implies the creation of another element called a border, and that the border must be contained in still another one called a window. Therefore, the resulting hierarchy is a geometrical figure, contained in a frame, requiring a border, which, in turn, must exist inside a window. In this example the object structure is mandated by the problem description since all the classes in the hierarchy are obligatory.

A class hierarchy can be implemented in C++ by inheritance, because the creation of an object of a derived class forces the creation of one of its parent class. If the inheritance hierarchy consists of more than one class, then the constructor of the classes higher in the hierarchy are called in order of derivation. Destructors are called in reverse order. The program SAM12-03.CPP demonstrates constructors and destructors in an inheritance hierarchy:

```
//*****************************************************************
// C++ program to illustrate constructors and destructors in
// a class inheritance hierarchy
// Filename: SAM12-03.CPP
//*****************************************************************
#include <iostream.h>

//***************************
//        classes
//***************************
class BaseA {
public:
  BaseA() {
    cout << "Constructing a BaseA object\n";
  }
  <BaseA() {
    cout << "Destroying a BaseA object\n";
```

```
  }
};
class Derived1 : public BaseA {
public:
  Derived1() {
   cout << "Constructing a Derived1 object\n";
  }
  <Derived1() {
   cout << "Destroying a Derived1 object\n";
  }
};

class Derived2 : public Derived1 {
public:
  Derived2() {
   cout << "Constructing a Derived2 object\n";
  }
  <Derived2() {
   cout << "Destroying a Derived2 object\n";
  }
};

//****************************
//          main()
//****************************
main() {
// Program creates a single object of the lower class in the
// hierarchy. Constructors and destructors of the class higher
// in the hierarchy are automatically executed.
   Derived2 obj_d;
   return 0;
}
```

When program SAM12-03.CPP executes, the following messages are displayed:

```
Constructing a BaseA object
Constructing a Derived1 object
Constructing a Derived2 object
Destroying a Derived2 object
Destroying a Derived1 object
Destroying a BaseA object
```

12.3.1 A Class Hierarchy by Object Composition

One way of solving the problem described at the beginning of this section is to use inheritance. For example, we could implement a class hierarchy in which **Circle**, **Square**, and **Rectangle** were derived from a base class called **Figure**. The **Figure** class could contain polymorphic methods for calculating and drawing the geometrical object, as well as methods for creating the frame, the border, and the window. In this case the client would have the responsibility of calling all of the required methods. Incidentally, this is an example of how inheritance often constrains programming and exposes the underlying class structure.

Although in some cases a solution based on class inheritance may be acceptable, it often happens that the hierarchy of super classes is related to a particular method of a derived class, or to several related methods, but not to all of them. Consider the case of several types of geometrical figures, all of which must be part of a window, contain a border, and be enclosed in a frame as described in Section 12.3. In this case the figure-drawing methods could be made part of an inheritance structure; however, the methods that produce the window, border, and frame need not be part of the inheritance construct since these elements are required for any of the geometrical figures. One possible solution is to implement a class structure in which some methods form part of an inheritance association while others are implemented by means of object composition. Figure 12.7 shows a possible class diagram for this case.

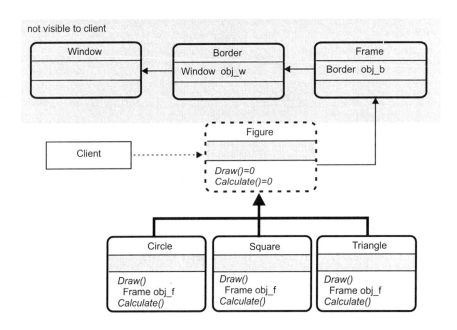

Figure 12.7 *Class Hierarchy by Object Composition*

In Figure 12.7 there are two mechanisms collaborating within the class structure. An inheritance element provides polymorphic methods that can be selected at run time in the conventional manner. Simultaneously, another class hierarchy is based on object composition. Note that the method **Draw()** of the classes **Circle**, **Square**, and **Triangle** contains an object of the class **Frame**. Also that the class **Frame** contains an object of **Border**, which contains an object of **Window**. Therefore, we can say that a circle, a square, and a triangle are *a-kind-of* figure and that all of them *have a* frame, a border, and a window. The program SAM12-04.CPP is an implementation of the class diagram in Figure 12.7:

```cpp
//****************************************************************
// C++ program to illustrate a class hierarchy by object
// composition
// Filename: SAM12-04.CPP
//****************************************************************
#include <iostream.h>
//***************************
//         classes
//***************************
class Window {
public:
Window() {
  cout << "Creating a window\n";
  }
};
class Border {
private:
  Window obj_w;              // Border class contains Window object
public:
  Border() {
    cout << "Drawing a border\n";
  }
};
class Frame {
private:
  Border obj_b;              // Frame class contains Border object
public:
  Frame() {
    cout << "Drawing a frame\n";
  }
  virtual void Draw() { return; };
};
// Abstract class
class Figure {
public:
  virtual void Draw() = 0;
  virtual void Calculate() = 0;
};
// Circle, Triangle and Square are at the bottom of the class
```

```
// hierarchy
class Circle : public Figure {
public:
   virtual void Draw() {
   Frame obj_f;
   cout << "Drawing a circle\n";
   }
   virtual void Calculate() {
   cout << "Calculating a circle\n";
   }
};
class Square : public Figure {
public:
   virtual void Draw() {
   Frame  obj_f;
   cout << "Drawing a square\n";
   }
   virtual void Calculate() {
   cout << "Calculating a square\n";
   }
};
class Triangle : public Figure {
public:
   virtual void Draw() {
   Frame  obj_f;
   cout << "Drawing a triangle\n";
   }
   virtual void Calculate() {
   cout << "Calculating a triangle\n";
   }
};
//***************************
//          main()
//***************************
main() {
    Figure *base_ptr;      // Pointer to base class
    Circle    obj_c;       // Circle, Square, and Triangle
    Square    obj_s;       // objects
    Triangle  obj_t;
    cout << "\n\n";
    base_ptr = &obj_c;     // Draw a circle and its hierarchical
    base_ptr->Draw();      // super classes
    cout << "\n";
    base_ptr = &obj_s;     // Draw a square and its hierarchical
    base_ptr->Draw();      // super classes
    cout << "\n";
    base_ptr = &obj_t;     // Draw a triangle and its hierarchical
    base_ptr->Draw();      // super classes
    cout << "\n";
    base_ptr->Calculate(); // Calculate() method does not generate
                  // an object hierarchy
    return 0;
}
```

Note in the program SAM12-04.CPP, as well as in Figure 12.7, that it is the method named **Draw()** in the concrete classes of the inheritance structure that instantiates the object of the class higher in the hierarchy, in this case the class named **Frame**. Once this object is referenced, the remainder of the hierarchy is produced automatically by means of the member object mechanism. The purpose of this construct is that the object hierarchy is generated when the method named **Draw()** executes, not when an object of the lower classes is instantiated. We can certify this operation when the program executes.

There may be cases in which we prefer that the hierarchy of super classes be instantiated at the time that the object of the lower class is created. In the example in Figure 12.7 this could be achieved by having a member object of the **Frame** class in the base class named **Figure**.

12.3.2 A Chain Reaction Pattern

In the class diagram of Figure 12.7 we note that when the lower classes (Circle, Square, and Triangle) instantiate an object of the class higher in the hierarchy, they start a chain reaction that produces objects of the entire hierarchy. We can abstract this operation by means of a class diagram that focuses exclusively on the chain reaction element, as is the case in Figure 12.8.

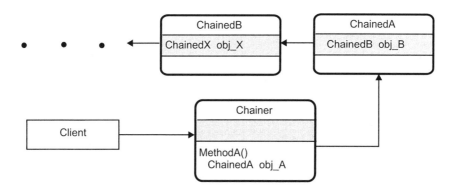

Figure 12.8 *A Chain Reaction Pattern*

In Figure 12.8 we have implemented chaining by referencing the first chained object within a method of the **Chainer** class, and then by member objects of the chained classes. There are many other ways of implementing a chain reaction effect.

12.4 Object Chaining

A programming problem often encountered consists of determining which, if any, among a possible set of actions has taken place. For example, an error handling routine posts the corresponding messages and directs execution according to the value of an error code. A common way of performing the method selection is by contingency code that examines the error code and determines the corresponding action. In C++ this type of selection is usually based on a *switch construct* or on a series of *nested if* statements. Alternatively, we can use object composition to create a chain in which each object examines a code operand passed to it. If it corresponds to the one mapped to its own action, then the object performs the corresponding operation; if not, it passes along the request to the next object in a chain. The last object in the chain returns a special value if no valid handler is found.

One of the advantages of using an object chain is that it can be expanded simply by inserting new object handlers anywhere along its members. To expand a selection mechanism based on contingency code we usually have to modify the selecting method by recoding the **switch** or nested **if** statements.

12.4.1 An Object Chain Example

A slightly more complicated case is one in which the selected object must return a value back to the original caller. For example, we define a series of classes that perform arithmetic operations which take two operands. The classes are called **Addition**, **Subtraction**, **Multiplication**, and **Division**. An operation code is furnished as a third parameter to a class called **Operation**, containing a method called **SelectOp()** that calls the **Add** method in the first object in the chain. In this case the object is of the **Addition** class. **Add()** examines the opcode operand; if it corresponds to the **add** operation, **add** executes and returns the sum to the caller. If not, it passes the object to **Subtract**, which proceeds in a similar fashion. Figure 12.9 shows the class structure for this example.

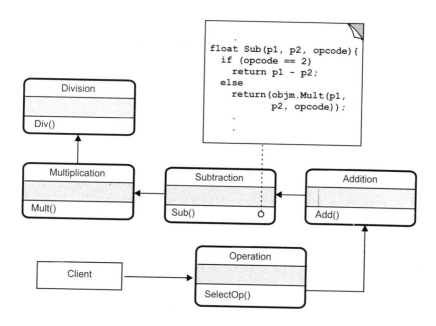

Figure 12.9 *Class Diagram for an Object Chain*

The program SAM12-05.CPP shows the processing details for implementing an object chain:

```
//*****************************************************************
// C++ program to illustrate an object chain
// Filename: SAM12-05.CPP
//*****************************************************************
#include <iostream.h>

//***************************
//        classes
//***************************
class Division {
public:
  float Div(float param1, float param2, int opcode) {
  if (opcode == 4)
     return (param1 / param2);
  else
      return 0;
  }
};

class Multiplication {
private:
  Division obj_div;
```

```
public:
  float Mult(float param1, float param2, int opcode) {
  if (opcode == 3)
     return (param1 * param2);
  else
     return (obj_div.Div(param1, param2, opcode));
  }
};

class Subtraction {
private:
  Multiplication obj_mult;
public:
  float Sub(float param1, float param2, int opcode) {
  if (opcode == 2)
     return (param1 - param2);
  else
     return (obj_mult.Mult(param1, param2, opcode));
  }
};

class Addition {
private:
Subtraction obj_sub;
public:
  float Add(float param1, float param2, int opcode) {
  if (opcode == 1)
     return (param1 + param2);
  else
     return (obj_sub.Sub(param1, param2, opcode));
  }
};

class Operation{
private:
  float param1;
  float param2;
  int   opcode;
  Addition obj_add;
public:
  Operation(float val1, float val2, int op) {
    param1 = val1;
    param2 = val2;
    opcode = op;
  }
  float SelectOp() {
  return (obj_add.Add(param1, param2, opcode));
  }
};

//***************************
//          main()
//***************************
```

```
main() {
    Operation obj_1(12, 6, 1);    // Declaring objects of the
    Operation obj_2(12, 6, 2);    // four established opcodes
    Operation obj_3(12, 6, 3);
    Operation obj_4(12, 6, 4);
    cout << "\n";
// Performing operation on objects
    cout << "Operation on obj_1: " << obj_1.SelectOp() << "\n";
    cout << "Operation on obj_2: " << obj_2.SelectOp() << "\n";
    cout << "Operation on obj_3: " << obj_3.SelectOp() << "\n";
    cout << "Operation on obj_4: " << obj_4.SelectOp() << "\n";
    return 0;
}
```

12.4.2 An Object Chain Pattern

We can generalize the example of an object chain in Figure 12.9 and abstract its basic components. In this case the fundamental characteristic of the class structure is a series of related methods, each one of which inspects a program condition that determines whether the method is to respond with a processing action or pass the request along to the next object in the chain. Figure 12.10 is a class diagram for an object chain pattern.

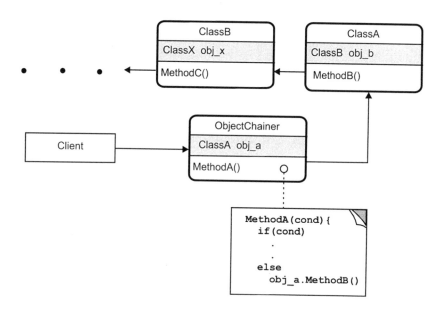

Figure 12.10 *Object Chain Pattern*

12.5 String Handling Class Template

The solution of some program development problems is based on patterns of interacting classes and objects, while others simply require a description of the internal structure of a single class. In this case we speak of a *class template*. For example, programs that deal with strings or that perform substantial string manipulations could profit from a particular class design that is optimized for string handling.

12.5.1 String Operations

When a string is defined at run time it is sometimes difficult to store as an array since its length may not be known beforehand. The C++ **new** and **delete** operators can be used to allocate memory in the free store area, but it is easier to implement a class that performs all string-handling operations consistently and efficiently, rather than to create and delete each string individually. Implementing a string-handling class is possible because the **new** and **delete** operators can be used from within member functions, and pointers are valid class members.

String operations often require knowing the string's length. The **strlen()** function defined in the **string.h** header file returns this value. Alternatively, we can implement a string as an object that contains a pointer to a buffer that holds the string itself and a variable that represents its length. A parameterized constructor can take care of initializing the string object storage using the new operator as well as its length parameter. The contents of the string passed by the caller are then copied into its allocated storage. This operation determines that the two data members associated with each string object are stored independently; however, they remain associated to the object and can be readily accessed as a pair.

In addition to the parameterized constructor, the proposed class could have a default constructor that initializes both data members to zero whenever it is necessary. An explicit destructor method is also required in this case. The fact that the **new** operator is used to allocate space for the string buffer implies that the **delete** operator must be used to free the allocated memory. Other useful methods would be to get the length of the string and to insert a character in a string, to read a string character by specifying its index, and to append a new string to an existing one. Additional functionalities can be added by editing the class or by inheriting its methods. The following class diagram can serve as a template in this case:

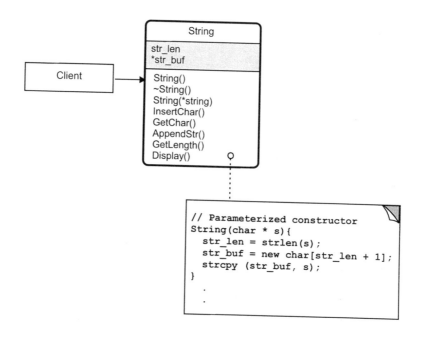

Figure 12.11 *String Handler Class Template*

The following program implements the string operations in the class template of Figure 12.11:

```
//********************************************************************
// C++ program template for string operations
// Filename: SAM12-06.CPP
//********************************************************************
#include <iostream.h>
#include <string.h>
//***************************
//         classes
//***************************
// String-handling class template
class String {
private:
  int str_length;           // Length of string
  char *str_buf;            // Pointer to string buffer
```

```
public:
// Declared constructors
  String();                              // Default constructor
  String(const char *str);               // Parameterized constructor
// String processing methods
  void InsertChar(int index, char new_char);
  char GetChar(int index) const;
  void AppendStr( const char *sub_str);
  <String();                   // Explicit destructor
// Methods expanded in line
  int GetLength() const { return str_length; }
  void Display() const { cout << str_buf; }
};
// Implementation of the default constructor
String :: String() {
  str_buf = 0;
  str_length = 0;
}
// Implementation of the parameterized constructor
String :: String (const char *s) {
  str_length = strlen(s);
  str_buf = new char[str_length + 1];
  strcpy( str_buf, s);
}
// Implementation of operational methods
void String :: InsertChar(int index, char new_char) {
  if ((index > 0) && (index <= str_length))
      str_buf[index - 1] = new_char;
}
char String :: GetChar(int index) const {
  if ((index >= 0) && (index <= str_length))
    return str_buf[index];
  else
    return 0;
}
void String :: AppendStr( const char *sub_str) {
   char *temp_str;
   str_length = str_length + strlen( sub_str);
   temp_str = new char[str_length + 1];   // Allocate buffer
   strcpy (temp_str, str_buf);            // Copy old buffer
   strcat(temp_str, sub_str);             // Concatenate both
strings
   delete [] str_buf;
   str_buf = temp_str;
}
// Implementation of destructor
String :: <String() {
  delete [] str_buf;
}
//***************************
//          main()
//***************************
main() {
// Object of type String
```

```
        String string1( "Montana State University" );
    // Operations using String class
        cout << "\nstring is: ";
        string1.Display();
        cout << "\nlength of string: " << string1.GetLength();
        cout << "\nfirst string character: "
            << string1.GetChar(0)  << "\n";
    // Appending a substring
        cout << "appending the substring: - Northern\n"
            << "string now is: ";
        string1.AppendStr( " - Northern\n\n");
        string1.Display();
        return 0;
    }
```

12.6 Combining Functionalities

In the implementation of libraries, toolkits, and application frameworks we often come across a situation in which a given functionality is scattered among several classes. Rather than giving a client access to each one of these individual classes it is often a reasonable alternative to combine several methods into a single class which can then be presented and documented as standard interface.

12.6.1 A Mixer Pattern

One of the practical uses of multiple inheritance is in combining functionalities by creating a class that inherits from two or more classes. The inheriting class serves to mix and unify the methods of the participating base classes. The class in Figure 12.12 shows a pattern based on multiple inheritance into a mixer class.

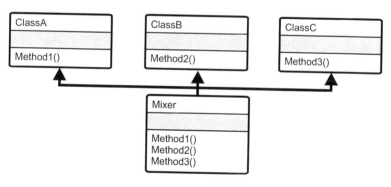

Figure 12.12 *Mixer Pattern for Combining Disperse Functionalities*

The coding of a mixer class was explained in Section 7.4.4. The following code fragment shows how to implement multiple inheritance in the case of the mixer class in Figure 12.12.

```
// Multiple inheritance
class Mixer : public ClassA, public ClassB, public ClassC {
  // Implementation
};
```

When implementing multiple inheritance we must be careful to avoid situations which could lead to resolution conflicts; for example, inheriting a method that has the same name and interface in the parent classes, or inheriting multiple copies of the same method. These cases were discussed in Chapter 7.

12.7 An Object-classifier Template

The objects in a class need not have identical signatures. A class can contain several parameterized constructors that create objects with different numbers or types of parameters. In this sense the constructors serve as object classifiers since each constructor executes according to the object's signature. The constructor can also store the object's type in a variable so that the object can be declassified during processing. For example, we wish to provide a class that calculates the area of various types of geometrical figures. Some figures such as the square require a single parameter; other figures such as the rectangle have two parameters, and still others like the parallelogram have three parameters. If there is a parameterized constructor for each object signature, then the processing is automatically directed to the corresponding constructor, which can also preserve the object's type by storing an associated code. This action of the constructor is consistent with the notion of function overloading. Processing routines can dereference the object type and proceed accordingly.

12.7.1 Implementing the Object Classifier

The following program shows the processing for implementing a class named **GeoFigure** with four constructors: a default constructor that zeroes all the variables, and three parameterized constructors, one for each object signature. The constructors of the **GeoFigure** class perform object classification as the objects are created.

```
//*******************************************************************
// C++ class template for an object classifier class
// Filename: SAM12-07.CPP
//*******************************************************************
#include <iostream.h>
#include <math.h>

//****************************
//          classes
//****************************
class GeoFigure {
private:
  float dim1;
  float dim2;
  float dim3;
  int fig_type;
public:

// Declaration of four constructors for GeoFigure class
  GeoFigure();
  GeoFigure(float);
  GeoFigure(float, float);
  GeoFigure(float, float, float);
// Area() method uses object signature
  float Area();
};

// Parameterless constructor
GeoFigure::GeoFigure() {
  dim1 = 0;
  dim2 = 0;
  dim3 = 0;
  fig_type = 0;
}

// Constructor with a single parameter
GeoFigure :: GeoFigure(float x) {
  dim1 = x;
  fig_type = 1;
}

// Constructor with two parameters
GeoFigure :: GeoFigure(float x, float y) {
  dim1 = x;
  dim2 = y;
  fig_type = 2;
}
// Constructor with three parameters
GeoFigure :: GeoFigure(float x, float y, float z) {
  dim1 = x;
  dim2 = y;
  dim3 = z;
  fig_type = 3;
```

```
}
float GeoFigure::Area() {
  switch (fig_type) {
    case (0):
      return 0;
    case (1):
      return dim1 * dim1;
    case (2):
      return dim1 * dim2;
    case (3):
      return dim1 * (dim2 * sin(dim3));
    }
    return 0;
  }


//****************************
//          main()
//****************************
main() {
  GeoFigure fig0;              // Objects with different
signatures
  GeoFigure fig1(12);
  GeoFigure fig2(12, 6);
  GeoFigure fig3(12, 6, 0.6);
// Calculating areas according to object signatures
  cout << "\nArea of fig1: " << fig1.Area();
  cout << "\nArea of fig2: " << fig2.Area();
  cout << "\nArea of fig3: " << fig3.Area();
  cout << "\nArea of fig0: " << fig0.Area() << "\n";

  return 0;
}
```

Observe in the program SAM12-07.CPP that processing operations that are often the client's burden are now handled by the class. The classifier class encapsulates knowledge about each object type, which is encoded and preserved with its signature. Thereafter, client code need not classify objects into squares, rectangles, or parallelograms, since this information is held in the class and handled transparently by its methods. The objects created by the classifier class know not only their dimensions but also their geometrical type, which in turn defines the processing operations necessary for performing calculations such as the area.

A classifier class is appropriate whenever there are objects with different signatures and their signatures determine the applicable processing operations or methods. Figure 12.13 is a generalized diagram for a classifier class; it can serve as a template for implementing this type of processing.

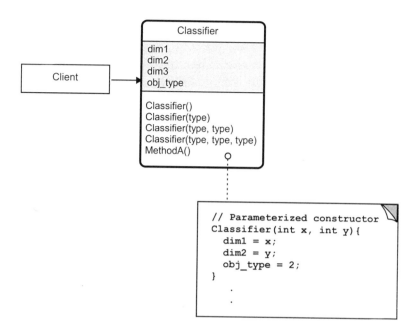

Figure 12.13 *Object Classifier Class Template*

12.8 Composing Mixed Objects

Libraries, toolkits, and frameworks often provide two types of services to a client. A first-level service performs the more elementary operations. A second-level service, called an *aggregate* or *composite*, allows combining several primitives to achieve a joint result.

12.8.1 A Graphics Toolkit

For example, a drawing program provides primitives for drawing geometrical figures such as lines, rectangles, and ellipses, for displaying bitmaps, and for showing text messages. A second-level function (the composite) allows combining the primitive elements into a single unit that is handled as an individual program component. In the context of graphics programming, the term *descriptor* is often used to represent a drawing primitive and the term *segment* to represent a composite that contains one or more primitives.

Often a toolkit designer gives access to both the primitive and composite functions. In other words, the programmer using the drawing toolkit mentioned in the preceding paragraph would be able to create drawings that contained any combination of primitive and composite objects using a single, uniform interface. In this example it may be useful to think of a composite as a list of instructions that includes the methods of one or more primitives. Figure 12.14 shows an image that contains both primitive and composite objects. The composite objects consist of a rectangle, a bitmap, an ellipse, and a text message. The primitive objects are text, a rectangle, and an ellipse.

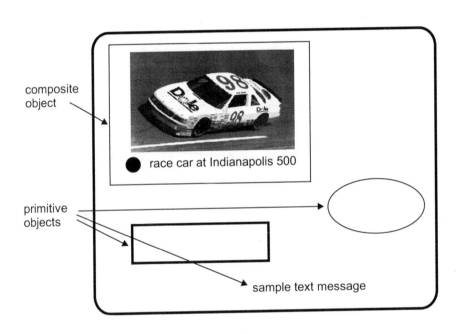

Figure 12.14 *Primitive and Composite Objects in a Graphics Toolkit*

The class structure for the sample toolkit could consist of a class for every one of the primitive operations and a composite class for combining several primitives into a drawing segment. An abstract class at the top of the hierarchy can serve to define an interface. Figure 12.15 shows the class structure for the graphics toolkit.

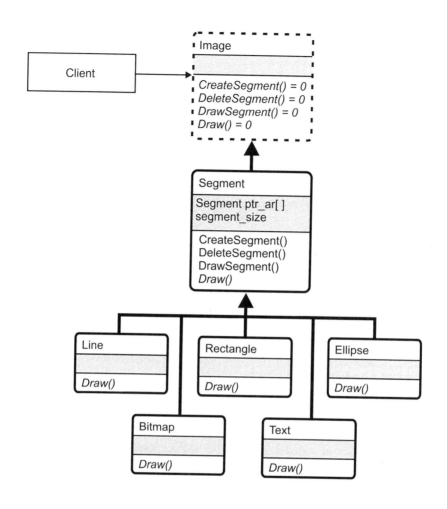

Figure 12.15 *Tree Structure for Creating Simple and Composite Objects*

Note in Figure 12.15 that the abstract class **Image** provides a general interface to the toolkit. The class **Segment** contains the implementation of the segment-level operations, the methods **CreateSegment()**, **DeleteSegment()**, and **DrawSegment()**. The drawing primitives are the leaves of the tree structure. Program SAM12-08.CPP is a partial implementation of the class diagram in Figure 12.15. Note that the classes **Bitmap** and **Text** were omitted in the sample code.

```cpp
//*****************************************************************
// C++ program to illustrate the creation of simple and
// composite objects
// Filename: SAM12-08.CPP
//*****************************************************************
#include <iostream.h>
#include <stdlib.h>
#include <conio.h>

//***************************
//         classes
//***************************
// Image class provides a general interface
class Image {
public:
  void virtual CreateSegment() = 0;
  void virtual DrawSegment() = 0;
  void virtual Draw() = 0;
};

class Segment : public Image {
private:
  Segment *ptr_ar[100];                // Array of pointers
  int seg_size;                        // Entries in array
public:
  void CreateSegment();
  void DrawSegment();
  void DeleteSegment();
  void virtual Draw() { return; };
};

class Rectangle : public Segment {
public:
  void Draw() { cout << "\ndrawing a rectangle"; }
};

class Ellipse : public Segment {
public:
  void Draw() { cout << "\ndrawing an ellipse"; }
};
class Line : public Segment {
public:
  void Draw() { cout << "\ndrawing a line"; }
};

// Implementation of methods in Segment class
void Segment::CreateSegment() {
  char select;
  int n = 0;                          // Entries in the array
// Objects and pointers
  Segment    obj_ss;
  Segment    *ptr_ss;
  Line       obj_ll;
```

```
        Rectangle obj_rr;
        Ellipse    obj_ee;
        cout << "\n  opening a segment...\n";
          cout << "Select primitive or end segment: "
            << "\n   l = line"
            << "\n   r = rectangle"
            << "\n   e = ellipse"
            << "\n   x = end segment"
            << "\n   SELECT: ";
      do {
        select = getche();
        switch(select) {
        case ('l'):
          ptr_ss = &obj_ll;
          ptr_ar[n] = ptr_ss;
          n++;
          break;
        case ('r'):
          ptr_ss = &obj_rr;
          ptr_ar[n] = ptr_ss;
          n++;
          break;
        case ('e'):
          ptr_ss = &obj_ee;
          ptr_ar[n] = ptr_ss;
          n++;
          break;
        case ('x'):
          break;
        default:
          cout << "\nInvalid selection - program terminated\n";
          exit(0);
      }
  }
  while( select != 'x');
      seg_size = n;
      cout << "\n  closing a segment...";
}
void Segment::DrawSegment() {

cout << "\n      displaying a segment...";
  for(int x = 0; x < seg_size; x++)
    ptr_ar[x]->Draw();
  cout << "\n      end of segment display ...";
  return;
}

//***************************
//        main()
//***************************
main() {
    Segment    obj_s;
    Line       obj_l;
```

```
    Rectangle   obj_r;
    Ellipse     obj_e;

// Creating and drawing a segment
    cout << "\n\nCalling CreateSegment() method";
    obj_s.CreateSegment();
    obj_s.DrawSegment();

// Drawing individual objects
    obj_l.Draw();
    obj_r.Draw();
    obj_e.Draw();
    return 0;
}
```

In the program SAM12-08.CPP the segment operation is based on an array of pointers. For this mechanism to work we need to implement run-time polymorphism since the composite (each instance of the **Segment** class) is created during program execution. In C++ run-time polymorphism can be achieved by inheritance and virtual functions. In this case the function **Draw()** is a pure virtual function in the abstract class **Image**, a virtual function in the class **Segment**, and is implemented in the leaf elements of the tree, which are the classes **Line**, **Rectangle**, and **Ellipse**. By making **Draw()** a simple virtual function we avoid making **Segment** into an abstract class. Therefore we can instantiate objects of **Segment** and still access the polymorphic methods in the leaf classes.

The actual code for implementing an array of pointers to objects has several interesting points. The array is defined in the private group of the **Segment** class, as follows:

```
Segment *ptr_ar[100];
```

This creates an array of pointers to the class **Segment**, and assigns up to 100 possible entries for each instantiation. The actual pointers are inserted in the array when the user selects one of the menu options offered during the execution of **CreateSegment()**. At this time a pointer to the **Segment** base class is reset to one of the derived classes, one of the **Draw()** methods at the leaves of the inheritance structure. The selected method is then placed in the pointer array named **ptr_ar[]**. For example, if the user selected the **r** (rectangle) menu option the following lines would instantiate and insert the pointer:

```
case ('r'):
      ptr_ss = &obj_rr;        // Base pointer set to derived object
```

```
ptr_ar[n] = ptr_ss;     // Pointer placed in array
n++;                    // Array index is bumped
break;
```

Although it may appear that the same effect could be achieved by using a pointer to the method in the derived class this is not the case. In this application a pointer to a derived class will be unstable and unreliable.

At the conclusion of the **CreateSegment()** method it is necessary to preserve with each object a count of the number of points that it contains. The **seg_size** variable is initialized to the number of pointers in the array in the statement:

```
seg_size = n;
```

At the conclusion of the **CreateSegment()** method, the array of pointers has been created and initialized for each object of the **Segment** class, and the number of pointers is preserved in the variable **seg_size**. Executing the segment is a matter of recovering each of the pointers in a loop and executing the corresponding methods in the conventional manner. The following loop shows the implementation:

```
for(int x = 0; x < seg_size; x++)
    ptr_ar[x]->Draw();
```

12.8.2 Pattern for a Composite Class

By eliminating all the unnecessary elements in Figure 12.15 we can construct a general class pattern for creating simple and composite objects. The **Composite** class can be considered as a simple object factory which uses an array to store one or more pointers to objects. In addition, each object of the composite class keeps count of the number of pointers in the array. This count is used in dereferencing the pointer array.

Alternatively, the pointer array can be implemented without keeping a pointer counter by inserting a NULL pointer to mark the end of the array. This NULL pointer then serves as a marker during dereferencing. In either case, the corresponding methods in the leaf classes are accessed by means of the pointers in the array. Method selection must be implemented by dynamic binding. In C++ the polymorphic method must be virtual in the composite class. The pattern is shown in Figure 12.16.

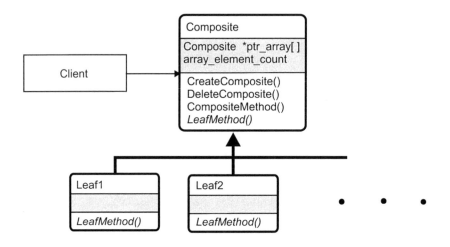

Figure 12.16 *Pattern for a Composite Class*

12.8.3 A Simplified Implementation

We can simplify the concept of primitive and composite objects, as well as its implementation in code, by allowing a composite that consists of a single primitive object. For example, if in Figure 12.15 we permit a segment that consists of a single primitive, then the client needs never access the primitives directly. This makes the interface less complicated. In many cases this option should be examined at design time.

12.9 Recursive Composition

In Section 12.8 we considered the case of a composite class that contains simple or composite objects. We also looked at the alternative of a composite object that consists of a single primitive as a way of simplifying the interface. However, we have not yet considered the possibility of a composite object containing another composite. Based on the class structure shown in Figure 12.15 we can construct an object diagram in which a **Segment** can contain another **Segment** as shown in Figure 12.17. Note that in this case we have preserved the distinction between primitives and composites.

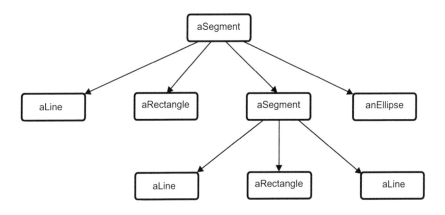

Figure 12.17 *Object Diagram for Recursive Composition*

12.9.1 Implementation Considerations

In the example of Section 12.8, recursive composition is based on a nested reference to the **CreateSegment()** method of the **Segment** class. However, recursion is often accompanied by a new set of problems; this case is no exception. The first consideration is to access the **CreateSegment()** method. Three possibilities are immediately evident:

1. Since **CreateSegment()** is called from within the class, it can be referenced without instantiating a specific object.

2. We can access the **CreateSegment()** method by means of a *this* pointer. In fact, this is a different syntax but has the same result as the previous case. In both instances the current object is used.

3. We can create a new object and use it to access the **CreateSegment()** method.

Which method is suitable depends on the problem to be solved. Figure 12.18 shows a class diagram for recursively accessing the **CreateSegment()** method using the original object.

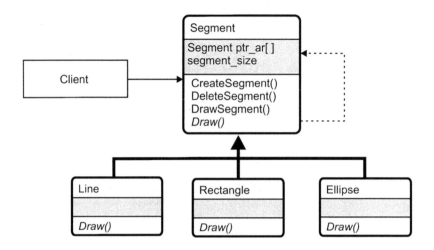

Figure 12.18 *Class Diagram for Recursive Composition*

The program SAM12-09.CPP shows the implementation of the class diagram in Figure 12.18.

```cpp
//********************************************************************
// C++ program to illustrate recursive composition
// Filename: SAM12-09.CPP
//********************************************************************
#include <iostream.h>
#include <stdlib.h>
#include <conio.h>

//***************************
//        classes
//***************************
class Segment {
private:
  Segment *ptr_ar[100];
  int seg_size;                    // Entries in array
public:
  void CreateSegment();
  void DrawSegment();
  void DeleteSegment();
  void virtual Draw() { return; };
};

class Rectangle : public Segment {
public:
  void Draw() { cout << "\ndrawing a rectangle"; }
};
class Ellipse : public Segment {
```

```
public:
  void Draw() { cout << "\ndrawing an ellipse"; }
};
class Line : public Segment {
Public:
  void Draw() { cout << "\ndrawing a line"; }
};

// Global variable for controlling recursive implementation
// of the CreateSegment() method
  int n;
  int instance = 0;

// Implementation of methods in Segment class
void Segment::CreateSegment() {
  char select;

// Entries in the array
// Objects and pointers
  Segment    obj_ss;              // An object
  Segment    *ptr_ss;             // Pointer to object
  Line       obj_ll;              // Object list
  Rectangle  obj_rr;
  Ellipse    obj_ee;
  if(instance == 0)
    n = 0;
    cout << "\n  opening a segment...\n";
    cout << "Select primitive or end segment: "
      << "\n   l = line"
      << "\n   r = rectangle"
      << "\n   e = ellipse"
      << "\n   n = nested segment"
      << "\n   x = end segment"
      << "\n   SELECT: ";

  do {
    select = getche();
    switch(select) {
    case ('l'):
      ptr_ss = &obj_ll;           // Pointer to object initialized
      ptr_ar[n] = ptr_ss;         // and stored in array
      n++;
      break;
    case ('r'):
      ptr_ss = &obj_rr;
      ptr_ar[n] = ptr_ss;
      n++;
      break;
    case ('e'):
      ptr_ss = &obj_ee;
      ptr_ar[n] = ptr_ss;
      n++;
      break;
```

```
      case ('n'):
        cout << "\n        nested segment...";
        instance = 1;
        this->CreateSegment();
        cout << "\n        nested segment closed ...";
        cout << "\n  SELECT: ";
        continue;
      case ('x'):
        break;
      default:
        cout << "\nInvalid selection - program terminated\n";
        exit(0);
    }
  }
 while( select != 'x');
    seg_size = n;
    cout << "\n  closing a segment...";
    instance = 0;                       // Reset instance control
 }

void Segment::DrawSegment() {
  cout << "\n       displaying a segment...";
  for(int x = 0; x < seg_size; x++)
    ptr_ar[x]->Draw();
  cout << "\n       end of segment display ...";
  return;
}


//****************************
//          main()
//****************************
main() {
   Segment      obj_s;
// Creating and drawing a segment with possible nested
// segments
   cout << "\n\nCalling CreateSegment() method";
   obj_s.CreateSegment();
   obj_s.DrawSegment();
   return 0;
}
```

Several points in the code merit comments. In the case of the program SAM12-09.CPP recursion occurs on the same object originally referenced at call time. This is accomplished by means of the C++ **this** pointer, in the following statement:

```
this->CreateSegment();
```

The **CreateSegment()** method could have been accessed without the **this** pointer since it is allowed, within the same class, to access methods directly. When **CreateSegment()** is accessed recursively, all the local variables are automatically reinitialized. Since the program requires a count of the number of pointers in the pointer array, we made the iteration counter (variable **n**) a global variable and created a switch variable named **instance**. This variable is set to 1 when **CreateSegment()** is called recursively, determining that counter variable **n** is not cleared on entry to the method. The result is that **n** holds the number of pointers inserted in the pointer array, whether they were entered directly or recursively.

12.9.3 A Recursion Pattern

The pattern for recursive composition is similar to the one in Figure 12.16, except that in recursion there is an arrow pointing to the same composite class. This is shown in Figure 12.19.

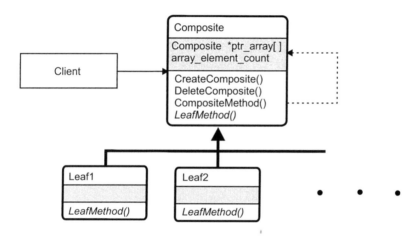

Figure 12.19 *Pattern for Recursive Composition*

12.10 Object Factories

In SAM12-09.CPP the **CreateSegment()** method uses the object created by the client to contain an array of pointers. In this case the array is actually an array of pointers to objects. For example, when we select the line drawing menu option the following statements execute:

```
case ('1'):              // If option selected
  ptr_ss = &obj_11;      // Pointer to object initialized
  ptr_ar[n] = ptr_ss;    // and stored in array
  n++;                   // Array index bumped
  break;
```

The result is that a pointer to an object (**ptr_ss**) is initialized to the object's address and stored in the array of pointers to objects. What has actually happened is that code has selected a particular object, which was defined at compile time, and stored its address so it can be accessed later. Array **ptr_ar[]** can be considered an array of objects; however, all the objects contained in the array were previously defined in the code.

12.10.1 Object Factory Implementation

We speak of an object factory when a class is able to create its own objects independently of the client. Since C++ does not allow creating objects by *name mangling* (see Section 11.5) we must use the object's address as its reference. Program SAM12-09.CPP contains no class that can be truly considered as an object factory. The **CreateSegment()** method of the **Segment** class simply takes the address of objects defined at compile time and places these addresses in an array of objects, but no objects are generated by the code. In this sense we can say that the Segment class is an *object assembler* but not an object factory.

In order to implement a true object factory example we start by modifying the **CreateSegment()** method of the **Segment** class. In the program SAM12-09.CPP **CreateSegment()** keeps a pointer array where the selected objects are stored. We now modify the **CreateSegment()** method so that it returns a pointer to this pointer array. A new class, called **Image**, calls the method **CreateSegment()** and stores the returned pointers-to-pointers in an array defined for this purpose. Since the entries in this array are objects of the **Segment** class, the class **Image** operates as a true object factory. Figure 12.20 is a visualization of the object factory concept.

Program SAM12-10.CPP shows the implementation of the object factory in Figure 12.20.

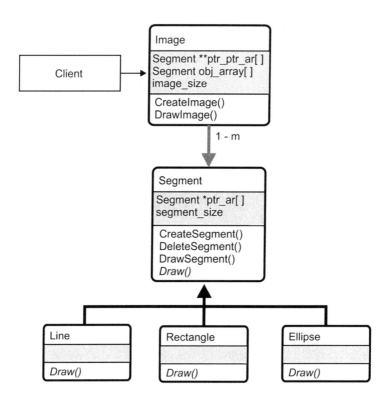

Figure 12.20 *Class Diagram for an Object Factory*

```
//********************************************************************
// C++ program to illustrate an object factory
// Filename: SAM12-10.CPP
//********************************************************************
#include <iostream.h>
#include <stdlib.h>
#include <conio.h>

//***************************
//        classes
//***************************
class Segment {
private:
  Segment *ptr_ar[100];
public:
  Segment** CreateSegment();
  void DrawSegment();
  void DeleteSegment();
  void virtual Draw() { return; };
};
```

```
class Image {
private:
   Segment     **image_array[10];      // Array of pointers to
pointers
   Segment     obj_array[10];          // Array of objects
// Scalar variables
   Segment     **ptr_ptr;              // Pointer to pointer variable
   int         image_size;             // Entries in image array
public:
   void CreateImage();
   void DrawImage();
};

class Rectangle : public Segment {
public:
  void Draw() { cout << "\ndrawing a rectangle"; }
};

class Ellipse : public Segment {
public:
  void Draw() { cout << "\ndrawing an ellipse"; }
};

class Line : public Segment {
public:
  void Draw() { cout << "\ndrawing a line"; }
};

//********************************************************************
// Implementation of methods in Segment class
//********************************************************************
// In this program the method CreateSegment() returns a
// pointer to pointer
Segment** Segment::CreateSegment() {
  char select;               // Storage for user input
  int n = 0;                 // Counter for entries in segment
// Objects and pointers
  Segment   obj_ss;          // Necessary to avoid null pointer
  Segment   *ptr_ss;         // Used in referencing objects
  Segment   **ptr_ptr_ss;    // Used in referencing pointers
  Line      obj_ll;          // Objects of derived classes
  Rectangle obj_rr;
  Ellipse   obj_ee;
    cout << "\n  opening a segment...\n";
    cout << "Select primitive or end segment: "
      << "\n   l = line"
      << "\n   r = rectangle"
      << "\n   e = ellipse"
      << "\n   x = end segment"
      << "\n   SELECT: ";
  do {
    select = getche();
    switch(select) {
    case ('l'):
```

```
           ptr_ss = &obj_ll;      // Object address to pointer variable
           ptr_ar[n] = ptr_ss;    // Object address store in array
           n++;                   // Array index bumped
           break;
         case ('r'):
           ptr_ss = &obj_rr;
           ptr_ar[n] = ptr_ss;
           n++;
           break;
         case ('e'):
           ptr_ss = &obj_ee;
           ptr_ar[n] = ptr_ss;
           n++;
           break;
         case ('x'):
           break;
         default:
           cout << "\nInvalid selection - program terminated\n";
           exit(0);
      }
   }
  while( select != 'x');
     ptr_ar[n] = 0;                        // Set NULL terminator
     ptr_ptr_ss = ptr_ar;
     cout << "\n  closing a segment...";
  return ptr_ptr_ss;
}
void Segment::DrawSegment() {
  cout << "\n     displaying a segment...";
int x = 0;
  while(ptr_ar[x] != 0) {
    ptr_ar[x]->Draw();
    x++;
  }
  cout << "\n     end of segment display ...";
  return;
}

//******************************************************************
// Implementation of methods in Image class
//******************************************************************
void Image::CreateImage() {
   int        i = 0;                      // Iteration counter
   char       user;                       // Storage for user input
// Creating an image that may contain multiple segments
  cout << "\n\nOpening the image\n";
  do {
    cout << "Select: "
      << "\n   e = enter segment into image"
      << "\n   z = end image"
      << "\n    SELECT: ";
    user = getche();
    switch(user) {
```

```
  case ('e'):
    image_array[i] = obj_array[i].CreateSegment();
    i++;
    break;
  case ('z'):
    break;
  default:
    cout << "\nInvalid selection - program terminated\n";
    exit(0);
  }
}
while( user != 'z');
   image_size = i;
   cout << "\n  closing the image...";
}
void Image::DrawImage() {
for(int y = 0; y < image_size; y++) {
  ptr_ptr = image_array[y];
  int x = 0;
    while(ptr_ptr[x] != 0) {
    ptr_ptr[x]->Draw();
    x++;
   }
  }
}


//******************************************************************
//                          main()
//******************************************************************
main() {
  Image          obj_ii;          // Object of type Image
// Access methods in Image class
  obj_ii.CreateImage();
  obj_ii.DrawImage();
  return 0;
}
```

Chapter 13

Multifile Programs

13.0 Partitioning a Program

There are many reasons for dividing a program into several files, the most obvious one is that the source code has grown to such size that it has become unmanageable. In this case partitioning into files is based on physical reasons or a storage and handling convenience. The resulting files are simple physical divisions of the program with no other logical or organizational base. However, even when the fundamental reason for dividing a program into files is a simple matter of size, a programmer or designer usually attempts to find some other more reasonable criteria by which to perform the actual division. For example, one option may be to place all functions and support routines into a separate file, while the main function and other central program components are stored in another one. Although this partitioning rationale is far from ideal, it is better than just arbitrarily slicing the code into two or more parts as if it were a loaf of bread.

In most cases the partitioning of a program's source code into several files is motivated by reasons other than its physical size, for instance, to facilitate development by several programmers or programmer groups. In this case program partitioning is usually done according to the modules defined during the analysis and design stages. The topic of modularization and division of labor was discussed starting in Section 5.5.

The fact that dividing into modules facilitates project organization, as well as the distribution of tasks in the coding phase, does not imply that modularization is nothing more than a project management tool. Modules are logical divisions of a program, and, in themselves, have a legitimate reason for being. The fundamental notion of a program module should be related to the program's conceptual design and not to an administrative convenience. Once the modules are established, placing each one of them in separate program files (or in a group of related files if the module's size so requires) is usually a good idea in itself since it promotes the preservation of the program's logical structure.

The linker programs are furnished with all current versions of C++ for the PC support multiple source files. How C++ multifile programs are actually produced is discussed in Section 13.1.

13.0.1 Class Libraries

Object code libraries are supported by most procedural languages. The fundamental notion is to provide a mechanism for code reuse that does not require scavenging or cut-and-paste operations. Utility programs, sometimes called *library managers*, allow the creation of program files that can be referenced at link time. The implementation of libraries is usually operating-system dependent. In the PC world, DOS libraries are in different format than Windows libraries and library code cannot be easily ported across the two environments. The library is usually organized into files or modules according to its logical design. Libraries for implementing GUI functions, graphics, and to provide special mathematical support such as statistics or vector analysis have been available for many years.

The structure of a conventional DOS library for a non-object-oriented language usually consists of a collection of functions and associated data structures. Class libraries became possible after the advent of object-oriented programming languages. Since classes provide a mechanism for encapsulating data and operations, and because object orientation facilitates modeling the problems of the real world, class libraries are an effective way of providing a specific functionality. In this case the interface between the client code and the library itself is both flexible and clean. The one disadvantage of class libraries is that the client must be relatively fluent in object-oriented programming in order to access its services. This explains why, for many years, developers of Windows libraries have stayed away from object orientation. It is only recently that object-oriented development tools for Windows programming have gained prevalence.

13.0.2 Public and Private Components

The components of class libraries are usually divided into two groups: public and private. The public elements of a class library are files and declarations necessary to document its interface requirements. In C++ the public components are typically furnished in header files that use the **.h** extension. Client code can then use the **#include** directive to physically incorporate the header file into its own source. In object-oriented programs the header files usually contain class declarations. These declarations make it possible for the client to instantiate the corresponding objects in order to access the class' methods, or to inherit from these classes. An interesting possibility is to use abstract classes to define the library's interface and then collect all the abstract classes in a header file.

The private elements of the declared classes usually contain program variables and constants, data structures, and member functions that need not be made visible to client code. Making these program elements private ensures two practical objectives:

1. The client does not have to deal with information that is not necessary for using the class library.

2. The confidentiality of the source code is protected.

According to this division into public and private elements, class libraries for the PC usually contain the following file types.

1. Header files. These are used to encode the public class elements that describe and document the interface and provide the necessary access hooks. These files can be collections of simple predeclarations or prototypes. They can contain actual implementation of the class that provides the library's interface, or they can contain a combination of both declarations and implementations. In C and C++ the header files have the extension **.h**. Assembly language header files for the PC are usually called *include files*, and have the extension .INC.

2. Object files. These contain executable code for the private elements of the library. These object files are usually referenced in the header files previously mentioned. Object files are in binary format; therefore, the source code is not accessible by the client.

3. Library files. These are a collection of object files organized and formatted by a library management utility.

One advantage of libraries over individual object files is that the client can deal with a single program element, instead of several individual components which often interact. Another one is that the library manager checks for consistency in all the component modules and detects any duplicate names or structural errors.

Whenever it is practical and logical to equate files and modules no other partition rationale could be preferable. However, practical considerations often force the designers to include several modules in the same file, or to distribute a single module into several files.

13.0.3 Object-Oriented Class Libraries

Inheritance is a powerful mechanism for code reuse. Its core notion is that a useful type is often a variant of another type. Instead of producing the same code for each variant, a derived class inherits the functionality of a base class. The derived class can then be modified by adding new members, by modifying existing functions, or by changing access privileges. The idea that a taxonomic classification can be used to summarize a large body of knowledge is central to all science.

Both types of polymorphism (compile-time and run-time) promote code reuse. Compile time polymorphism, either by classification or by overloading of functions and operators, allows extending functionality without replacing exiting code. The name-mangling machinery in the compiler generates different internal names for functions that appear with the same external desgination, as long as the passed parameters are different. Run-time polymorphism requires a pointer to a base class which is redirected to a derived object that contains a virtual function. In this case the type of object determines the version of the function that is called. In the case of run-time polymorphism no variations in the parameter list are necessary; in fact, any variation in the parameter list generates an overloaded function and its virtual nature is lost.

In a programming language such as C++, a class library can take advantage of all the mechanisms and constructs of object orientation to create a product that is powerful and easy to access. By allowing class inheritance the library permits the client to modify or extend its functionalities without changing what has already been tested and tried. Furthermore, a library may use object composition to free the client from having to perform many elaborate or complicated tasks, and to hide other details of implementation, as shown in some of the patterns described in Chapter 12.

13.1 Multifile Support in C++

In the reality of commercial programming all but the simplest applications require multiple files. All commercial C++ compilers and development platforms provide support for multifile projects. Some environments (such as the project managers in Borland C++ and Microsoft Visual C++) include development tools that automate the creation and maintenance of multifile projects. In these environments the programmer defines a list of sources and object files, as well as other structural constraints, and the project manager handles the compiling and linking operations that are necessary to produce executable code.

Alternatively, each source file can be compiled separately, then a linker can be called from the command line with a list of the object files and libraries that must be used to produce the executable. Or the files can be listed in a special text file that is read by the linker. In either case the result is a program that is composed of more than one source file. Figure 13.1 shows the various components of a C++ multifile program.

Multifile program architecture promotes reusability by locating the potentially reusable components in easily referenced individual program elements. Such is the case with header files, class, and object file libraries.

13.2 Multilanguage Programming

So far we have considered a multifile program as one composed of several files coded in the same programming language. However, the use of more than one language in the creation of a program is a powerful development technique. When we refer to multilanguage programming we mean the mixing of two or more high- or low-level languages. Mixing high-level languages can be a way of reusing code developed in another programming environment. For example, we may have avail-

able a powerful mathematical library developed in FORTRAN that we
wish to use in an application coded in C++.

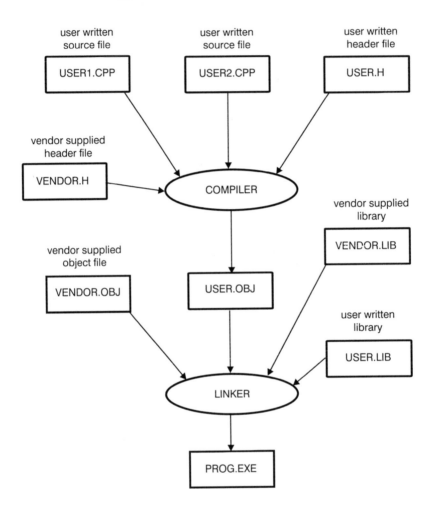

Figure 13. 1 *Components of a C++ Multifile Program*

In many language implementations it is possible to access a procedure, function, or subroutine coded in another high level language.
Thus, we may be able to create C++ code that calls the functions in a
FORTRAN mathematical library. In most development environments
the interface is implemented at the object file level, not at the source
code level. Three issues must be considered in multilanguage programming: naming, calling, and parameter-passing conventions.

13.2.1 Naming Conventions

This refers to how a compiler or assembler alters names as they are read from the source file into the object file, as well as to the number of upper- or lowercase characters and symbols that are recognized. For example, a much used FORTRAN compiler sold by Microsoft translates all lowercase characters to uppercase and admits at most six characters per name, while a recent C++ compiler recognizes thirty-two characters, which can be in upper- or lowercase, and appends an underscore symbol in front of the name.

Not taking into account the naming conventions of each language may lead to the linker reporting an unresolved external symbol. For example, the routine named *Add* in FORTRAN source code will appear as ADD in the object file. The same routine is labeled _Add in C++. Since ADD and _Add are not the same name, a link-time error takes place. Therefore, the multilanguage programmer often has to consider the calling convention of the participating languages and make the necessary adjustments. For example, an assembly language routine that is to be referenced as ADD in C++ code must be coded as _ADD in the assembly source, since the C++ compiler automatically appends the underscore to the name. Specific adjustments depend on the particular languages and implementations being interfaced.

13.2.2 Calling Conventions

Calling conventions refer to the specific protocol used by a language in implementing a function, procedure, or subroutine call. In this sense we may often speak of the C, BASIC, or Pascal calling conventions.

The Microsoft languages BASIC, FORTRAN, and Pascal use the same calling convention. When a call is made in any of these languages, the parameters are pushed onto the stack in the order in which they appear in the source. On the other hand, the C and C++ calling convention is that the parameters are pushed onto the stack in reverse order of appearance in the source. The result is that in a **BASIC CALL** statement to a subroutine named **Add(A, B)** the parameter **A** is pushed on the stack first, and **B** is pushed second. However, in a C function **Add(A, B)** the reverse is true.

A language's calling convention determines how and when the

stack is cleaned up. In the BASIC, FORTRAN, and Pascal calling conventions, the stack is restored by the called routine, which has the responsibility of removing all parameters before returning to the caller. The C calling convention, on the other hand, is that the calling routine performs the stack clean-up after the call returns.

An advantage of the BASIC, FORTRAN, and Pascal calling convention is that the generated code is more efficient. The C and C++ calling convention has the advantage that the parameters show the same relative position in the stack. Since, in the C convention, the first parameter is the last one pushed, it always appears at the top of the stack, the second one appears immediately after the first one, and so on. This allows the creation of calls with a variable number of parameters since the frame pointer register always holds the same relative address independently of the number of parameters stored in the stack.

Some programming languages allow changing the default calling convention to that of another language. For example, most C and C++ compilers allow using the Pascal calling convention whenever the programmer desires. In this case, the C compiler imitates the behavior of Pascal by pushing the parameters onto the stack in the same order in which they are declared and by performing a stack clean-up before the call returns. In C and C++ the calling convention keyword can be included in the function declaration.

13.2.3 Parameter-Passing Conventions

In C and C++, parameters can be passed to a function by reference or by value. When a parameter is passed by reference, use the address of a scalar variable or a pointer variable. When passed by value, a copy of the variable's value is stored in the stack so that it can be removed by the called function. In passing by reference, it is the variable's address that is placed in the stack.

In the segmented memory architecture of systems based on the Intel x86 processors (such as the PC) we have two possible representations of the memory address of a parameter. If the parameter is located in the same segment, then its address is a word offset from the start of the segment. However, if it is located in a different segment, then the address must contain two elements: one identifies the segmentwithin the machine's address space and the other one the offset within the segment. When a parameter is in the same segment we sometimes speak of a *near reference*. When in another segment then we say that it is a *far reference*. A third option is when the architecture is based on a flat memory space, in which case the address is a linear, 32-bit value which locates the element within a 4 gigabyte memory area.

For these reasons the calling and the called routines must agree on whether parameters are passed by reference or by value as well as on the memory model. If a parameter is passed by value, the called routine removes the parameter directly from the stack. If it is passed by reference, then the called routine obtains the address of the parameter from the stack and uses this address to dereference its value. Additionally, when making a call by reference in an environment with segmented memory architecture, such as a PC under DOS, the called routine must know if the address stored in the stack is a near or far reference and proceed accordingly.

Programming languages sometimes allow selecting the parameter passing convention. In C and C++, the memory model selected at compile time determines the default address type for functions and pointers. The language also allows the use of the **near** and **far** keywords as address type modifiers to force pointers and addresses to be of a type different from the default.

13.2.4 Difficulties and Complications

One of the difficulties of mixed-language programming is that the interface between language components changes in the different language combinations and in products from different software vendors. Furthermore, different implementations or versions of the same language combinations may interface differently. Such is the case in the languages developed by Borland and Microsoft.

In an effort to facilitate mixed-language programming Borland and Microsoft have both published directives and conventions that attempt to simplify the interface requirements. The main difficulty is that these directives and conventions are not identical. Therefore, multilanguage code is often not portable between development environments from different vendors.

Another difficulty related to mixed-language programming is insufficient technical information. Although software manuals sometimes include a few paragraphs on how to interface program elements in different languages, the discussion often does not contain all the necessary data. For example, consider the rather simple problem of passing an array from Borland C++ to x86 assembly language. Borland documentation states that in C++, array variables are passed by reference. What the manual does not say is that if the array is declared public in the C++ code, then it is assigned space in the program's data area. Otherwise, the array is allocated dynamically in the stack. In both cases the calling routine passes the array by reference, as mentioned in the manual, but in one case the called code finds the segment base of the address in the SS segment register and in another case in DS.

From these observations we must conclude that multilanguage programming, although a powerful and versatile technique, usually compromises the portability of the code, even to other versions of the languages or development environment. A decision to use several languages in the development process should always consider this possible loss of portability.

13.3 Mixing Low- and High-Level Languages

Although many mixtures of programming languages are possible, by far the most likely and useful one is that of a low- and a high-level language. For a C++ programmer working in the PC environment this means mixing x86 assembly language with the C++ code.

Objections to assembly language programming are usually related to difficulties in learning the language and with lower programmer productivity. Both points are debatable, but even if we were to grant their validity, there are still many other valid reasons for using assembly language in PC programming. The following list covers some of the more important ones:

1. Power. Assembly language allows access to all machine functions. The language itself places no limitations on the functionalities that can be achieved. In other words, every operation which the machine is capable of performing can be achieved in assembly language. It is valid to state that if it cannot be done in assembly language code, then it cannot be done at all.

2. Compactness. Programs coded in assembly language are more com-

pact than those coded in any high-level language since the code is customized to contain only those instructions that are necessary for performing the task at hand. Compilers, on the other hand, must generate substantial amounts of additional code in order to accommodate the multiple alternatives and options offered by the language.

3. Speed. Programs coded in assembly language can be optimized to execute at the fastest possible speed allowed by the processor and the hardware. Here again, code generated by high-level languages has to be more complicated and intricate, which determines its slower speed of execution.

4. Control. In order to locate program defects, or to discover processing bottlenecks, assembly language code can be traced or single-stepped one machine instruction at a time. The fact that there is no software layer between the program and the hardware determines that all defects can be found and corrected. The only exception are those bugs caused by defects in the hardware or in the microcode. Defects in high-level language programs are sometimes caused by the compiler generating incorrect code. These bugs are very difficult to locate and impossible to fix.

These advantages of assembly language code are summarized in four words: power, speed, compactness, and control. Whenever one of these four elements is at a premium, then the possible use of assembly language should be investigated.

13.3.1 C++ to Assembly Interface

Of all high-level languages, C and C++ provide the easiest interface with assembly language routines. The reason is that C (and its descendant C++) call an assembly language procedure in the same manner as they would a C or C++ function.

C++ passes variables, parameters, and addresses to the assembly language routine on the stack. As previously mentioned, these values appear in opposite order as they are listed in the C++ code. A unique feature of the C++ language interface is that it automatically restores stack integrity. For this reason the assembly language routine can return with a simple RET or RETF instruction, without keeping count of the parameters that were pushed on the stack by the call. One consequence of this mode of operation is that assembly language routines can be designed to operate independently of the number of parameters passed by the C++ code, as long as the stack offset of those that are necessary to the routine can be determined.

Not all implementations and versions of C++ follow identical interface conventions. In the Microsoft versions of C and C++, the memory model adapted by the C program determines the segment structure of the assembly language source file. Table 13.1 shows the segment structure of the various memory models used by the Microsoft C and C++ *compilers.*

To the programmer, Table 13.1 means that if the C++ source file was compiled using the small or compact model, then the assembly language procedure should be defined using the NEAR directive. On the other hand, if the C++ source was compiled using the medium or large models, then the assembly language procedure should be defined with the FAR directive.

13.4 Sample Interface Programs

In this section we provide two examples of interfacing C++ and assembly language code. The first one is based on the use of C or C++ compilers by Microsoft or IBM, and the second one on Borland compilers. In the first example a parameter is passed by value to a routine coded in assembly language. In this case the assembly language code also changes a variable declared in the C++ source file. In the second example we use a Borland C or C++ compiler to pass the address of a structure to assembly language code. The assembly code modifies the structure variables in the C++ source.

In either case it is our intention to furnish the reader with a general example that illustrates the interface, but by no means are these examples to be taken as universally valid. When interfacing C++ and assembler language each implementation must be carefully analyzed for its interface requirements. The elements of naming, calling, and parameter-passing conventions must all be taken into account. Even different versions of the same language often differ from each other. In general, it is safer to use language development tools from the same vendor since it is reasonable to expect that these tools have been designed to interact with each other. In this sense when using a Microsoft C++ compiler, use a Microsoft assembler, such as MASM. The same applies to products from Borland or any other vendor.

Table 13.1 *Segment Structures in Microsoft C++ Memory Models*

MEMORY MODEL	SEGMENT TYPE	NAME	ALIGN TYPE	COMBINE TYPE	CLASS NAME	GROUP
Small	CODE	_TEXT	word	PUBLIC	'CODE'	
	DATA	_DATA	word	PUBLIC	'DATA'	DGROUP
	CONST		word	PUBLIC	'CONST'	DGROUP
		_BSS	word	PUBLIC	'BSS'	DGROUP
	STACK	STACK	para	STACK	'STACK'	DGROUP
Compact	CODE	_TEXT	word	PUBLIC	'CODE'	
	DATA	_DATA	word	PUBLIC	'DATA'	DGROUP
		CONST	word	PUBLIC	'CONST'	DGROUP
		_BSS	word	PUBLIC	'BSS'	DGROUP
		FAR_DATA	para	private	'FAR_DATA'	
		FAR_BSS	para	private	'FAR_BSS'	
	STACK	STACK	para	STACK	'STACK'	DGROUP
Medium	CODE	xx_TEXT	word	PUBLIC	'CODE'	
	DATA	_DATA	word	PUBLIC	'DATA'	DGROUP
		CONST	word	PUBLIC	'CONST'	DGROUP
		_BSS	word	PUBLIC	'BSS'	DGROUP
	STACK	STACK	para	STACK	'STACK'	DGROUP
Large	CODE	xx_TEXT	word	PUBLIC	'CODE'	
	DATA	_DATA	word	PUBLIC	'DATA'	DGROUP
		CONST	word	PUBLIC	'CONST'	DGROUP
		_BSS	word	PUBLIC	'BSS'	DGROUP
		FAR_DATA	para	private	'FAR_DATA'	
		FAR_BSS	para	private	'FAR_BSS'	
	STACK	STACK	para	STACK	'STACK'	DGROUP

Both the Microsoft and the Borland versions of C and C++ have an additional interface constraint: the SI and DI machine registers are used to store the values of variables defined with the "register" keyword. Therefore, the assembly language procedure should always preserve these registers. The Microsoft implementations also assume that the processor's direction flag (DF) is clear when C regains control. Therefore, if there is any possibility of this flag being changed during processing, the assembly language code should contain a CLD instruction before returning. Although the Borland manuals do not document this requirement, it is probably a good idea to clear the direction flag in any case even though it may not be strictly necessary. Even if a compiler does not use the direction flag, as appears to be the case with those from Borland, the CLD instruction produces no undesirable effects.

C and C++ compilers automatically add an underscore character in front of every public name. This is true for both the Microsoft and the Borland C and C++ compilers. For this reason, a C++ language reference to a function named **RSHIFT** is compiled so that it refers to one named **_RSHIFT**. In coding the assembly language program element it is necessary to take this into account and add the required underscore character in front of the name.

This convention applies not only to functions but also to data items that are globally visible in C++ code. For example, if the C++ source contains a variable named **ODDNUM** this variable is visible to an assembly language source under the name **_ODDNUM**. The assembly language code can gain access to the variable by using the **EXTRN** statement. Note the spelling in this case, which is different from the **extern** keyword of C and C++.

13.4.1 Microsoft C-to-Assembly Interface

The first interface example uses code generated by a Microsoft C or C++ compiler and the MASM assembler. The example consists of a C++ program that calls an assembly language routine. The caller passes an integer variable to assembly language code and the assembly language returns the value with all bits shifted right by one position. In addition, the assembly language routine modifies the value of a C++ variable named **NUMB2**, which is defined globally.

The example is implemented in two source files. The C++ file (TESTC.CPP) was created using a standard editor and compiled using a Microsoft C++ compiler. The assembly language source was created with an ASCII text editor and assembled with a DOS MASM assembler. The assembled file is named CCALLS.OBJ. Note that the examples work with all the Microsoft full-featured C and C++ compilers, but not with the Microsoft QuickC programming environment.

The following is a listing for the C++ source file in this interface example.

```
/* File name: TESTC.CPP                                        */
/* C++ source to show interfacing with assembly language
   code. This sample assumes the use of Microsoft C or C++
   compilers, excluding QuickC */
#include <iostream.h>
extern int RSHIFT(int);
/* Variables visible to the assembly source must be declared
   globally in the C++ source */
int numb1, NUMB2;
main() {
      cout << "Enter the variable numb1: ";
      cin >> numb1;
      cout << "The shifted number is: %d\n"
           << RSHIFT(numb1));
      cout << "The variable NUMB2 has the value: %u\n"
           << NUMB2;
}
```

Note the following points in the C++ source file:

1. The assembly language source is declared external to the C code with the **extern** keyword. The name in this declaration is not preceded with an underscore character, since it is automatically appended by the compiler.

2. Once declared external, the **RSHIFT** routine is called as if it were a C++ function.

3. The variables **numb1** and **NUMB2** are declared to be of **int** type. Both are global in scope. The value of **numb1** is transferred by the C++ code to the assembly language source file in the statement **RSHIFT(numb1)**. The assembler code recovers the value of the variable **numb1** from the stack. During execution the assembly language code accesses the variable **NUMB2** directly, using its name. Note that the variable to be accessed by name is declared using capital letters. This is for compatibility with assembler programs that automatically convert all names to uppercase.

The assembly language code is as follows:

```
;*****************************************************************
;                        CCALLS.ASM
;*****************************************************************
; Example of C++ to assembly language interface for Microsoft
; C and C++ compilers, excluding QuickC
;
PUBLIC    _RSHIFT
EXTRN     _NUMB2: WORD
```

```
_TEXT     SEGMENT word    PUBLIC  'CODE'
          ASSUME  CS:_TEXT
;*******************************|
;  C language interface routine |
;*******************************|

_RSHIFT       PROC     NEAR
; Function to right-shift the bits in an integer passed by
; right-shifted value returned to caller
        PUSH      BP            ; Save caller's BP
        MOV       BP,SP         ; Set pointer to stack frame
        MOV       AX,[BP+4]     ; Value passed by value
                                ; which is C language default mode
        CALL      INTERNAL_P    ; Procedure to perform shift and
                                ; to access C variable NUMB2
        CLD                     ; Clear direction flag
        POP       BP            ; Restore caller's BP
        RET                     ; Simple return. C repairs stack
_RSHIFT       ENDP
;

INTERNAL_P      PROC      NEAR
; value of arbitrary new value assigned to C variable
        SHR       AX,1          ; Shift right AX 1 bit
                                ; Return value is left in AX
        MOV       CX,12345      ; Arbitrary value to CX
        MOV       _NUMB2,CX     ; and to C variable NUMB2
        RET
INTERNAL_P      ENDP
_TEXT       ENDS
        END
```

Note the following points of the assembly language source file:

1. The procedure _RSHIFT is declared PUBLIC to make it visible at link time. An underscore character is affixed at the start of the procedure's name so that it matches the name used by the C++ compiler.

2. The segment structure is compatible with the Microsoft small memory model as shown in Table 13.1. The memory model of the C program is determined at link time by the library selected. Also note that the code segment is defined with the statement:

```
_TEXT         SEGMENT word    PUBLIC  'CODE'
```

which is the same as that listed for the C and C++ small and compact models in Table 13.1.

3. Procedures to be linked with C++ programs of the small or compact model must be declared with the NEAR operator, as follows:

```
_RSHIFT        PROC    NEAR
```

If the C++ program used the medium, large, or huge models then the assembly language procedure would have been declared using the FAR operator.

4. The _RSHIFT procedure in the assembly language code can serve as a general interface template for Microsoft C++/assembly programming. However, note that this template requires modifications in order to adapt it to C++ programs that use other memory models or that pass or return parameters of other data types.

5. The structure of the stack frame at call time also depends on the adopted memory model. In this case, since the chosen model is small, the parameter passed is located at BP+4 and the return address consists of only the offset component.

6. The variable declared as **NUMB2** and initialized as **int** in the C source is declared as **EXTRN _NUMB2: WORD** in the assembly language code. The underscore character is added in the assembly source file because C++ appends this character at the beginning of the variable name. The variable is assigned an arbitrary value in the **INTERNAL_P** procedure.

7. Upon exiting, the assembly language routine clears the direction flag (CLD), restores the BP register (POP BP), and returns with a simple RET instruction. Note that the processing routine in this example does not use the SI or DI registers; hence they were not preserved. However, if SI or DI is used in processing, the entry value must be saved and restored by the assembler code.

The actual configuration of the stack frame at call-time varies with the different memory models. One of the determining factors is that the return address requires two bytes in the small and compact models and four bytes in the other ones. Also, each parameter passed by value will occupy a storage space equivalent to its type. Therefore, a **char** variable takes up one byte, an **int** takes up two bytes, and so forth. When parameters are passed by reference, the amount of space taken up by each parameter depends exclusively on whether it is of **NEAR** or **FAR** type. In the PC environment, **FAR** addresses require four bytes and **NEAR** addresses two bytes. Figure 13.2 shows a stack frame in which two parameters of **int** type were passed using the small or compact memory models (**NEAR** reference).

high addresses

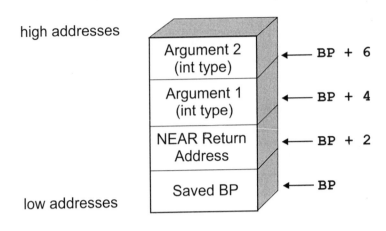

low addresses

Figure 13.2 *C++ Stack Frame Example*

Return Values in Microsoft C++ Compilers

In the Microsoft implementations of C++ for the PC, parameters are returned to the calling routine in the AX register, or in the AX and the DX registers. Table 13.2 shows the Microsoft language conventions for returning values.

Table 13.2 *Microsoft C++ Returned Values*

DATA TYPE OR POINTER	REGISTER OR REGISTER PAIR
char	AX
short	
int	
unsigned char	
unsigned short	
unsigned int	
long	DX = high-order word
unsigned long	AX = low-order word
struc or union	AX = address value
float or double	
near pointer	AX = offset value of address
far pointer	DX = segment value of address
	AX = offset value of address

Another way of interchanging values between the C++ and assembly language code is to access the C++ variables by name (as demonstrated in the previous example). This method requires that the assembly code use the same storage format as the C++ source. Since variable storage formats change in different implementations of C++, this access technique must be adapted to each particular implementation of the language.

13.4.2 Borland C++ to Assembly Interface

The following example, coded in Borland C++ and in x86 assembly language, also implements a C++ to assembly language interface. The C++ code can be compiled using Borland C++ Version 3.1 and later. The assembler code is created using either Borland's TASM or Microsoft MASM. The example consists of passing a structure to an assembly language source. The call is made using the **FAR** access type and the address of the structure is a **FAR** reference.

```
/* Program name: TEST1.CPP
   Other files:
       Project: ASMTEST.PRJ (in C:\BORLANDC)
       Assembly Source File: CCALLS.OBJ (in C:\BORLANDC)
*/
#include <iostream.h>
#include <string.h>
extern "C" {
        int SETSTR(struct pix_params *t);  /* Passing a structure by
        |     |              |                             reference
        |     |              |_____ structure tag name
        |     |_____ Procedure name (_SETSTR in
        |                             assembler source file)
        |_____ Return type
                        Procedure SETSTR sets new values in the
                        pix_params structure variable passed to
                        it by reference */
}

// STRUCTURE
struct pix_params
{
  int x_coord;                  // point coordinate on x axis
  int y_coord;                  // point coordinate on y axis
  unsigned char blue;           // color components
  unsigned char green;
  unsigned char red;
  char text_string[80];
};
```

```
main() {
      struct pix_params point1;      // Declare one structure
variable
      point1.x_coord = 0x20;         // Initialize structure
variables
      point1.y_coord = 0x40;
      point1.blue = 0x30;
      point1.green = 0x31;
      point1.red = 0x32;
      strcpy ( point1.text_string, "This is a test message" );
      SETSTR[&point1];
   return (0);
}
```

The following points should be observed regarding the C++ program:

1. Which sources are linked is determined by the files referenced in the project.

2. The names of the assembly procedures to be called from C++ are defined with the extern "C" directive.

3. Assembly procedures must take into account the memory model when accessing parameters in the stack. If the procedure is accessed with a **NEAR** call then the stack frame holds a 2-byte return address and the first parameter is located at BP+4. If the procedure is accessed with a FAR call, then the stack frame holds a 4-byte return address and the first parameter is located at BP+6. In the Borland compilers, the C++ model is determined by the setting of the Options/Compiler menu item. In this case the memory model is **LARGE** and the call is **FAR**.

4. C language code prefixes the function name with a leading underscore character (_) at call time. The assembler code must take this into account by inserting the corresponding _ symbol in front of the public name.

The following is the assembly language source that receives the C++ call:

```
;********************************************************************
;                        CCALLS.ASM
;********************************************************************
; Example C++ to assembly language interface routine for Borland
; compilers
;
```

```
        PUBLIC  _SETSTR
;**********************************************************************
;                           local code
;**********************************************************************
_TEXT    SEGMENT word    PUBLIC  'CODE'
         ASSUME  CS:_TEXT
;*******************************|
;  C language interface routine |
;*******************************|
_SETSTR          PROC    FAR
; Function to access a structure located in the C++ code and change
; the value of some of its variables
; On entry:
;          structure address passed by reference
         PUSH    BP              ; Save caller's BP
         MOV     BP,SP           ; Set pointer to stack frame
; The C++ register operator uses SI and DI for temporary storage
; therefore, it is usually a good idea to save these registers
         PUSH    SI              ; Saved in stack
         PUSH    DI
; The FAR model locates the first word-size parameter at +6
         MOV     BX,[BP+6]       ; Offset of address
         MOV     ES,[BP+8]       ; Segment of address
; At this point ES:BX holds address of structure in C++ source
; The following code accesses the variables within the C++ structure
; and modifies them
         MOV     WORD PTR ES:[BX],80      ; change x_coord
         MOV     WORD PTR ES:[BX+2],90    ; change y_coord
         MOV     BYTE PTR ES:[BX+4],0A0H  ; change red
         MOV     BYTE PTR ES:[BX+5],0B0H  ; change blue
         MOV     BYTE PTR ES:[BX+6],0C0H  ; change green
; C exit code
         POP     DI              ; Restore DI and SI from stack
         POP     SI
         CLD                     ; Clear direction flag
         POP     BP              ; Restore caller's BP
         MOV     AX,0            ; Return 0
         RET                     ; Simple return. C repairs stack
_SETSTR          ENDP
_TEXT    ENDS

         END
```

13.4.3 Using Interface Headers

Note in the above examples that the assembly language code is designed to accommodate C++ calling conventions. Therefore, the procedure **_SETSTR** does not work with another high-level language. Furthermore, the C++ memory model determines where in the stack the passed parameters are placed. If the calling routine is compiled with a different memory model, the interface fails.

One way to accommodate varying calling conventions between languages or between implementations of the same language is by means of *interface headers*. These are usually short routines that receive the parameters passed by one language and locate them in the machine registers or data structures expected by the other language. This scheme allows portability while maintaining maximum coding efficiency in both languages. It also allows reusing code that is not designed to interface with a particular language. For example, an assembly language library of graphics primitives can be used from C++ by means of interface headers, even though the assembly source was not originally designed to be called from a high-level language. The one drawback of using interface header routines is some loss of performance, since each call has the added load of traversing the header code.

In C++ programming, interface header routines can be coded in line and placed in include files that are selected by means of preprocessor conditional directives. This simple technique allows choosing a different header routine according to the memory model of the C++ program, thus solving a major interface limitation of the language.

Bibliography

Boehm, B.W. *Software Risk Management*, IEEE Computer Society Press, 1989.

Booch, Grady. *Object Solutions: Managing the Object-Oriented Software Project*. Addison-Wesley, 1996.

Capron, H. L. *Systems Analysis and Design*. Benjamin/Cummings, 1986.

Carroll, Martin D. and Margaret A. Ellis. *Designing and Coding Reusable C++*. Addison-Wesley, 1995.

Charette, R. N. *Software Engineering Risk Analysis and Management*. McGraw-Hill, 1989.

Coad, Peter. *Object Models: Strategies, Patterns, & Applications*. Yourdon Press, Prentice-Hall, 1995.

Coad, Peter and Edward Yourdon. *Object Oriented Analysis*. Prentice-Hall, 1991.

Coad, Peter and Edward Yourdon. *Object Oriented Design*. Prentice-Hall, 1991.

Cohen, Edward. *Programming in the 1990's*. Springer-Verlag, 1990.

DeMarco, Tom. *Structured Analysis and System Specification*. Prentice-Hall, 1979.

Dewhurst, Stephen C. and Kathy T. Stark. *Programming in C++*. Prentice-Hall, 1989.

Dijkstra, E. W. *A Discipline of Programming*. Prentice-Hall, 1976.

419

Elmasri, Ramez and S. B. Navathe, *Fundamentals of Database Systems - Second Edition*. Benjamin/Cummings, 1994.

Entsminger, Gary. *The Tao of Objects*. M & T Books, 1995.

Gamma, Erich, R. Helm, R. Johnson, and J. Vlissides. *Design Patterns: Elements of Reusable Object-Oriented Software*. Addison-Wesley, 1995.

Gane, T. and C. Sarson, *Structured Systems Analysis*. McDonnell Douglas, 1982.

Ghezzi, Carlo, Mehdi Jazayeri, and Dino Mandrioli. *Fundamentals of Software Engineering*. Prentice-Hall, 1991.

Goldberg, Adele and D. Robson. *Smalltalk 80: The Language and Its Implementation*. Addison-Wesley, 1983.

Graham, Ian. *Object Oriented Methods*. Second Edition. Addison-Wesley, 1994.

Gries, D. and Fred B. Schneider. *A Logical Approach to Discrete Math*. Springer-Verlag, 1993.

Gries, David. *The Science of Programming*. Springer-Verlag, 1981.

Harley, D. J. and I. A. Pribhai. *Strategies for Real-Time Systems Specifications*. Dorset House, 1987.

Headington, Mark R. and David D. Riley. *Data Abstractions and Structures Using C++*. D.C. Heath and Company, 1994.

Hoare, C. A. R. *Proof of Correctness of Data Representations*, Acta Informatica, Vol. I, 1972.

Kay, Allan. *The Reactive Engine*. Ph.D. Thesis. University of Utah, 1969.

Kernighan, Brian W. and Dennis M. Ritchie. *The C Programming Language*. Prentice-Hall, 1978.

Knuth, Donald E. *The Art of Computer Programming. Fundamental Algorithms*. Vol. 1, Second Edition. Addison-Wesley, 1973.

Kochan, Stephen G. and Patrick H. Wood. *Topics in C Programming.* Revised Edition. Wiley, 1991.

Lafore, Robert. *Object-Oriented Programming in C++.* Second Edition. Waite Group, 1995.

Martin, J., *Computer Data Base Organization.* Prentice-Hall, 1982.

Martin, Robert C. *Designing Object-Oriented C++ Applications Using the Booch Method.* Prentice-Hall, 1995.

Microsoft Corporation. *Programmer's Guides: C++ Tutorial, Class Library User's Guide, and Programming Techniques.* Microsoft Press, 1993.

Pohl, Ira. *Object-Oriented Programming Using C++.* Benjamin/Cummings, 1993.

Polya, George. *How to Solve It.* Princeton University Press, 1945.

Pree, Wolfgatroustrup B. *The Annotated C++ Reference Manual.* Addison-Wesley, 1990.

Pressman, Roger S. *Software Engineering: A Practitioner's Approach.* McGraw-Hill, 1992.

Ranade, Jay and Saba Zamir. *C++ Primer for C Programmers.* McGraw-Hill, 1992.

Rowe, W.D. *An Anatomy of Risk. Robert E. Krieger Publishing, 1988.*

Rumbaugh, James, Michael Blaha, William Premerlani, Frederick Eddy, and William Lorensen. *Object Oriented Modelling and Design.* Prentice-Hall, 1991.

Savitch, Walter. *Problem Solving with C++: The Object of Programming.* Addison-Wesley, 1996.

Sebesta, Robert W. *Concepts of Programming Languages.* Third Edition. Addison-Wesley, 1996.

Schammas, Amir C. *Object-Oriented Programming for Dummies.* IDG Books, 1996.

Shaw, Mary and David Garlan. *Software Architecture: Perspectives on an Emerging Discipline.* Prentice-Hall, 1996.

Schildt, Herbers. *C++ the Complete Reference.* Second Edition. Osborne McGraw-Hill, 1995.

Swan, Tom. *Borland C++ 4.5.* Second Edition. Sams, 1995.

Tausworthe, Robert C. *Standardized Development of Computer Software. Part I Methods. Part II Standards.* Prentice-Hall, 1977.

Ward, P. T. and S. J. Mellor. *Structured Development for Real-Time Systems.* Yourdon Press, 1985.

Whitten, Jeffrey L., L. D. Bentley, and V. M. Borlow. *Systems Analysis and Design Methods.* Second Edition. Irwin, 1989.

Index